Russia and the Fight Against Globalisation
by
Kerry R Bolton

Copyright © 2018 Black House Publishing Ltd

ISBN-13: 978-1-912759-02-6

Black House Publishing Ltd
Kemp House
152 City Road
London
United Kingdom
EC1V 2NX

www.blackhousepublishing.com
Email: info@blackhousepublishing.com

Russia and the Fight Against Globalisation

by

Kerry R Bolton

Dr. Walter Schubart

In Memory of

Dr. Walter Schubart

1897-1942

Herald of a Russo-European New Dawn

Contents

Foreword

Kerry Bolton's new book is a continuation of his long-term work on the study of Russia. It does not repeat, but complements and deepens his previous publications about the peculiarities of the Orthodox world, the secrets of the Bolshevik revolution, the historical role of Stalin and Putin's modern policy.

The encyclopedic scope of knowledge, the possession of the cultural heritage of the right thinkers, the use of the methods of theology, dialectical philosophy, conspiracy, geopolitics, sociology and psychology transform the author into a knight of the spiritual sword. All together this allows Kerry Bolton to understand the dramatic nature of global change, and in this regard - the world mission of Russia, which makes his work extremely relevant, and the author himself put on a par with such Western thinkers as Walter Schubart, Francis Parker Yockey, Guillaume Faye.

The book will be especially useful to those who share the ideals of the New Right, revolutionary conservatives, supporters of the original Third Way in the name of the revival of our race, consciously opposing the aggressive dictatorship of the New World Order led by the United States of America.

Dr. Pavel Tulaev

12 May 2018.

Dr. Tulaev has taught at the Moscow State Pedagogical Institute, lectured on "Russian Culture and Civilization" at Utica College, Syracuse University, USA; and at Moscow State Linguistic University. He is an art patron and curator, and has been the recipient of numerous awards for cultural and scholarly activities, including honorary diplomas from the Institute of Latin America of the USSR Academy of Sciences, Slavic Parliamentary Union, and All-Slavic Council. He has developed numerous courses and textbooks including: "The Newest History of Foreign Countries", "The Russian World in Historical Development", "History of the Fatherland", and "Fundamentals of Slavic Studies". Dr. Tulaev is presently Professor of History at the International Slavic Institute.

Foreword

Foreword by Aleksandr Mezentsev

One of the most remarkable intellectual achievements of Kerry Bolton is his understanding of Russian History in its continuity. Here he differs from Solzhenitsyn, who saw the USSR as anti-Russia per se and the entire Soviet period as a radical break from normal historical evolution. While Solzhenitsyn insisted that the Soviet Union was a bloody occupation of Russia by the International Communism, Bolton solves the problem in a much more scientifically correct way, invoking the topic of "National Bolshevism" and considering the politics of Iosif Stalin and his faction inside the Soviet regime as a real National Counter-Revolution against the cosmopolitan Bolshevism of Trotsky and the so-called "old Leninists".

A look at the Soviet system as either a healthy alternative to the "decaying West" or, at least, as a reliable partner and even an ally, not the enemy, was and remains surprisingly widespread among both the foreign and Russian "Right". The list would be very long. We may just mention such names as Tsarist General Potapov and famed Libertarian Murray Rothbard, the great Tory Enoch Powell and the Third Reich hero Major General Otto Remer, Cossack Nationalist Pavel Kudinov and Reaganite Paul Craig Roberts, famous "New Rightist" Alain De Benoist and Australian nationalist Dr. Jim Saleam, the Arab Nationalists, and both General Juan Peron and his enemies from the Junta Military of 1976 – 1983, and so on.

Indeed, modern anti-globalists, nationalists and "Rightists" should study the Soviet period in order to learn about its true achievements and not to repeat its real faults, which lead to "the greatest geopolitical catastrophe of the 20th century", as Putin described the collapse of the Soviet Union. In this particular regard Kerry Bolton`s books and essays would serve perfectly well.

Aleksandr Mezentsev

May 2018

Aleksandr Mezentsev, a resident of North Ossetia, undertook his diploma in history under the supervision of the eminent Russian historian Dr. Vladimir Degoev, continued post-graduate studies, and has lectured at universities in Vladikavkaz. He is presently on the staff of the National Library (Vladikavkaz).

Introduction

The USA is the end of something old. It is the product of transplanting rationalism and materialism onto the 'New World', which became the end of something already centuries in decline. While America poses as the 'leader of The West', it is the leader of the dregs of a civilisation whose culture has long since ossified and is on a downward spiral into decadence and decay. The USA animates a corpse whose diseases contaminate all corners of the world in the name of 'globalisation'. What remains of 'Western culture' is no more than a façade hiding the decay. The façade is the glitter of Hollywood, MTV, hip hop, fast food, the narcosis of consumerism. This pathogen is heralded as the epitome of human aspiration. Its historians such as Dr. Francis Fukuyama, proclaim the victory of the American world revolution against all tradition as 'the end of history', beyond which there is nothing more for humanity to achieve. Despite the spiritless character of 'American civilisation' the roots are in its founding religions – Puritanism and Deism. Both provided the USA with a messianic mission to build what is inscribed on their Great Seal since 1782: *Novus ordo seclorum*: 'new order of the ages'. The Puritanism of the USA founding colonies provided a world-view that elevated profit into a beneficence from God, and commerce as the epitome of godly living, in contrast to traditional societies that subordinate economics. Deism made revolution an expression of an undefined but all-seeing godhead that would destroy traditional faiths. The Founding Fathers of the USA were from the start conscious of their messianic world mission, Thomas Paine writing:

> The cause of America is in a great measure the cause of all mankind... 'Tis not the concern of a day, a year, or an age; posterity are virtually involved in the contest, and will be more or less affected, even to the end of time, by the proceedings now.[1]

This doctrine at the USA's founding has not deviated. The Jacobins of 1789 had fed from the same philosophical trough as the American revolutionaries, with interconnections through eminences in both counties, such as Lafayette, Thomas Jefferson, and Benjamin

---

1   Thomas Paine, *Common Sense* (1776).

Introduction

Franklin. The Jacobins declared their revolution to be universal, as did the Americans, and later the Bolsheviks. All these sought to change the world, in the name of 'progress' and 'human rights' and create a universal order. All three plunged the world into a mountain of debris of the shattered remnants of tradition, and pools of blood of the best strata of society in the name of 'equality'. After two world wars the USA emerged triumphant over the ruins of the old European empires of both 'allies' and enemies.

However, Russia, full of promise for U.S. and other oligarchs during the first phases of revolution, soon resorted, even while still under Lenin, to the traditional impress of its own messianic mission, even if now called 'Bolshevism', to redeem mankind spiritually while enduring martyrdom. The wartime alliance with the USSR against Fascism was brief, as Stalin rejected the USA's offer for Russia to become a junior partner in a post-war world order, and a Cold War ensued. However, even after the fall of the Soviet bloc, with Russia again showing such promise under the very brief interregnum of Boris Yeltsin, she reverted to type under Putin, and again became the primary obstacle – the *Katechon* – to the globalist oligarchs.

Russia, while experiencing mini-cycles of rise and fall and rise, and an attempt by Peter the Great, and Leon Trotsky, to impose alien outlooks from the West, as a wide-ranging historical and cultural unit has a people that are still vigorous, that have maintained a youthful vigour and have a consciousness of their own special place in history. Hers is consciousness of Mission that is antithetical to that of the mercantile mission of the USA (having taken that role from Britain), or of Jewish supremacist messianism. Russian messianism is Christian and hence universal; Russia embodies the martyrdom of Christ in perpetuity, self-sacrificing for the redemption of mankind. Russia retained its sense of mission even under years of Bolshevism. The imported Bolshevik ideology, contrived in the reading room of the British Museum by Karl Marx, did not transcend the materialist-mercantile spirit of the age (*zeitgeist*) that was represented by England. Marxism, as Spengler pointed out in *The Decline of The West, Prussianism and Socialism*, and *The Hour of Decision*, did not transcend capitalism; it merely sought to co-opt capitalism. Hence, within a few years of Marxism the Anglo-U.S. agent Trotsky was eliminated, Stalin reversed psychotic Bolshevik doctrines in such areas as family, and education; Holy Mother Russia became the focus of 'Soviet patriotism', and the Orthodox Faith was even resurrected with thousands of Churches reopened.

Russia and the Fight Against Globalisation

While the West, and everyone the West touched, rotted under capitalism, hedonism and democracy, the Soviet peoples retained a toughness that has left them as the only vital *ethnos* in the world today; one comparatively uncontaminated by Western decadence, or at least having the potential to resist and expel U.S. led culture-pathology. That Putin is conscious that there even is a threat of culture-disease from the USA places him head and shoulders above most leaders, who are so decadent themselves they do not have the detachment to realise there even is a problem. The USSR referred to the 'decadent West', and to the 'rootless cosmopolitans' within the Soviet Union acting as agents of culture-pathology in a manner that was more a legacy of Russia's Christian heritage as the *Katechon*, or opponent of the *Antichrist*, than as a Marxist state. This is the legacy under which Putin was educated and served, and it is continued. This is the real meaning of Russia and why she is in perpetual conflict with the USA and any other power factor that represents satanic powers, whether literally or metaphorically.

Many conservatives, especially those in Germany, recognised something in Russia that was enduring, despite the veneer of Marx's and Trotsky's 'dialectical materialism'. Alien imports would go through what Spengler called 'historical pseudomorphosis', where an imported culture does not have the strength to undermine the foundations of a stronger host culture, despite outward forms. Therefore Russia remains *eternal Russia* despite Marxism or liberalism or technocracy. Like the Japanese, for millennia the Chinese, and the Hebrews, accepting anything from the outside is done so on Russian terms alone, and any interference with that is repulsed. After the German defeat in 1918 German Right-nationalists sought out Russia as an ally against Western democratic plutocracy. The most anti-Communist Germans of the 'Right' joined associations to foster Soviet-German friendship. Oswald Spengler wrote and spoke just a few years after the Bolshevik revolution about the prospects for Germany of an alliance with Russia, and how Marxism would soon be replaced by a Russian national-collectivism. The Treaty of Rapallo between post-war Germany and the USSR was in the Bismarckian spirit of *realpolitik*. The Hitler-Stalin pact was in accord with this tradition also, but was ill-fated due to the redundant chauvinism that was still intrinsic to the Third Reich. After World War II, when Stalin repudiated his wartime alliance with the plutocracies, the 'Cold War' was the result. Germans who had fought a horrendous war against Russia were in no mood to do so again in the interests of the USA. 'Neutralism' was a widespread sentiment in Germany, and many veterans such as Major General Otto Remer stated they would prefer Russian domination to American culture-decay. Even then one could see a dichotomy of culture health confronting culture decay, manifested in Stalin's fight against what the USSR called 'rootless cosmopolitanism'. The USA launched what in recent years has been called the 'Cultural Cold War' when, with the support of Trotskyites, whose hatred of Stalinist Russia became an obsession, the CIA established the Congress for Cultural Freedom. Jazz and Abstract Expressionism were carried like spiritual syphilis throughout the world as a blessing of American democracy, just as the U.S. State Department now sponsors Hip Hop overseas, to infect youth with 'American freedom'.

Western Civilisation is being fulfilled to a world-destructive end. Contrary to Spengler's hopes, The West's fulfilment has not been heroic. Two *intra-cultural* world wars exhausted Western Civilisation. These wars enabled the USA to impose its own imperium in the name of the 'West', but representing all that was diseased in the Late West, and nothing of its traditional ethos. There thus remains of the West led by the USA only a disease-ridden corpse animated by money and the zeal of converging Jewish, Masonic and Puritan messianisms.

Walter Schubart, a German scholar in Latvia and convert to the Orthodox faith, now largely forgotten, suggested that Europe might revive in a symbiotic relationship with Russia, resulting in a new culture epoch, that of *messianic man*.[2] He suggested that the West's *Promethean* (Spengler's *Faustian*) outlook, that impels him to dominate nature and impose order, and Russia's sense of spiritual mission, might be synthesised, each supplementing what the other lacks, into another civilisation: the *messianic*. He wrote of this new man and new epoch even then developing under a 'Bolshevism' purged of Marxism:

> In Russia a type of humanity is developing which is neither that of the period prior to 1917 nor prior to 1689[3], but a quite new species with an Eastern soul that has been influenced by Western culture as by a hardening process. This new type, while truly Russia, is yet heir to the eternal values of the West. A man of this type is inspired by his inborn Slav nature, but no less also by the conflicts and contradictions of European civilisation. And it is only he who, as a new type of humanity, will be capable of uttering the word of reconciliation, in the settlement of the problem of East and West. Although the

---

2   Walter Schubart, *Russia and Western Man* (1938] New York: Frederick Ungar Publishing, 1950).

3   Year of the start of Peter the Great's reign.

Russian of today is not as yet the Man of the Millennium, yet it is he – and only he – who will succeed in evolving him; the Russian will purify himself until he has attained the height of development necessary to produce him. Even sworn enemies of Bolshevism, like Solonevitch, speak of the 'strong generation' growing up in the Soviet Republic - a generation no longer characterised by the repellent, proverbial Russian indolent, the degenerated form of primitive trust.

The new generation is full of energy and is with enthusiasm for all efforts made in the direction of reconstruction. The *Stakhanov* movement, the *Udarniki* and the *Olitshniki* (elite workers) are all manifesting a growing interest in their work and developing a sense of duty in every branch of activity, instead of their previous indifference. A consciousness of the dignity of labour has superseded the servile attitude of former times, instead of their previous indifference.[4]

Putin has spoken in similar manner of Russia's associations with Europe, in the manner of those such as Dostoyevsky and Schubart, who foresaw that Russia might redeem the soul of Europe without succumbing to its decay.

Russia is the eternal martyr, self-sacrificing, with a spiritual ethos forged by struggle, a culture of brotherhoods that eschews materialism and hedonism, an ethos that is communal rather than fragmented, which Dostoyevski called 'Russian socialism', that soon replaced the alien elements in Bolshevism. *Messianic man*, embodied in the Russian, sees the modern world, that is, the decayed 'West', as a separation of man from God, and from the divinity animating nature. Between the U.S.-led rotting West, which more accurately should now be called 'Anti-West', Israel and Russia there are three messianic world-views struggling for universal domination, while China, albeit having succumbed to the Western economic model and committed to 'globalisation' in its own image, waits in the wings of the world stage, ready to make its ancient claim as being the 'centre of the world'. Russia, the *Katechon*, stands as ever against powers devoid of spirit.

---

4   Schubart, op. cit.., 296.

Russia and the Rise of a New Era

Amidst the geopolitical confrontation between Vladimir Putin's Russia and the U.S. and its allies, little attention has been paid to the role played by religion either as a shaper of Russian domestic politics or as a means of understanding Putin's international actions. The role of religion has long tended to get short thrift in the study of statecraft (although it has been experiencing a bit of a renaissance of late), yet nowhere has it played a more prominent role – and perhaps nowhere has its importance been more unrecognized – than in its role in supporting the Russian state and Russia's current place in world affairs.[1]

Paul Coyer, research professor at the Institute of World Politics, writing the above for *Forbes* in 2015, while critical of Russia's turn to 'authoritarianism' under Putin, nonetheless has rare insight in understanding the spiritual basis (albeit calling it 'ideological') of the conflict between the USA and Russia. All the hype about 'human rights' and democracy' is a façade of humbug in the offensive against Russia. These catchphrases have long been used to demonise any state targeted for elimination by plutocracy, including for example the fight against 'the Hun' during the First World War, and others before.[2] Same old rhetoric.

Under Putin the Orthodox Church has again become a foundation of the State and of Russian national identity. Professor Coyer laments that the revived special place of Orthodoxy has gone in tandem with authoritarianism; 'the slow death of Russia's fledgling democracy'.[3] That is to say, the State-Church symbiosis that has for centuries

---

1   Paul Coyer, '(Un)Holy Alliance: Vladimir Putin, The Russian Orthodox Church And Russian Exceptionalism', *Forbes,* May 21, 2015, http://www.forbes.com/sites/paulcoyer/2015/05/21/unholy-alliance-vladimir-putin-and-the-russian-orthodox-church/

2   One can think of the way Yankee 'abolitionists' and post-civil war 'Reconstructionists' portrayed the Old South, and how British imperialists portrayed the Boers in denying rights to 'Uitlannders' to justify war and conquest for economic interests; or even hark back to when Roman historians were portraying the Druid priesthood as practitioners of human sacrifice, and a bloody, dark religion.

3   Paul Coyer, op. cit.

formed the Russian character, challenges the globalist designs to plunge Russia into their world abyss of cultural, moral and spiritual syphilis. 'In terms of church-state relations, this privileging of the ROC status in Russian society marked the beginning of a political alliance between the ROC and the Russian state that has grown increasingly close and formalized under Putin and which has been beneficial to both parties', writes Coyer.[4] The extent of the State-sponsored revival of Orthodoxy under Putin was detailed by Coyer, writing:

> Over the past decade and a half, Putin has ordered state-owned energy firms to contribute billions to the rebuilding of thousands of churches destroyed under the Soviets, and many of those rich oligarchs surrounding him are dedicated supporters of the ROC [Russian Orthodox Church] who have contributed to the growing influence of the church in myriad ways. Around 25,000 ROC churches have been built or rebuilt since the early 1990's, the vast majority of which have been built during Putin's rule and largely due to his backing and that of those in his close circle of supporters. Additionally, the ROC has been given rights that have vastly increased its role in public life, including the right to teach religion in Russia's public schools and the right to review any legislation before the Russian Duma.[5]

The significance of this is that Russia is asserting its traditional form of *messianism* in seeing its role as the Biblical *Katechon* in thwarting the 'Antichrist', represented by the USA. Coyer talks about the return of 'Russian exceptionalism'. But there has also been an 'American exceptionalism' since the foundation of the USA by a symbiosis of Puritanism and Deism, both with messianic outlooks. The conflict between the USA and Russia is a conflict between these two antithetical messianic outlooks: the Amercian directed towards conquering mankind in the interests of money; the Russian, ever-willing to undertake martyrdom to restore the connexion between God and man. Unsurprisingly, Professor Coyer does not see developments in those terms but just in regard to how Russia in reverting to type rather than remaking itself in America's image; a perversity expected of all states by the globalists in the name of 'democracy':

> The glue that holds together the alliance between Vladimir Putin and the ROC, and the one that more than any other explains

---

4   Ibid.

5   Ibid.

their mutually-supporting actions, is their shared, sacralized vision of Russian national identity and exceptionalism. Russia, according to this vision, is neither Western nor Asian, but rather a unique society representing a unique set of values which are believed to be divinely inspired. ... The conflict between Russia and the West, therefore, is portrayed by both the ROC and by Vladimir Putin and his cohorts as nothing less than a spiritual/civilizational conflict.[6]

What rankles Western liberals as mouthpieces for plutocracy is the thought that there remains a powerful State and the forming of a geopolitical bloc that is not succumbing to the Late West's swan song. Coyer describes it clearly:

> The West's goal, says the Kremlin, is to spread liberal Western values within Russia and so dilute the Russian national character and keep Russia weak and divided. The Russian nation, therefore, must remain united behind Putin's leadership, and hold fast to its distinctive national identity. Putin has so successfully tied his fate to the fate of the Russian nation that a senior Russian government official stated last year that ''.[7]

It all sounds suspiciously close to Putin becoming another 'Little Father' that the demo-plutocratic cabals and Jewish messianists hated in the Czar. Coyer writes of the parallels:

> The close relationship between the Russian Orthodox Church (ROC) and the Russian state based upon a shared, theologically-informed vision of Russian exceptionalism is not a new phenomenon. During the days of the Czar, the Russian ruler was seen as God's chosen ruler of a Russian nation tasked with representing a unique set of values embodied by Russian Orthodoxy, and was revered as "the Holy Orthodox Czar". Today, a not dissimilar vision of Russian exceptionalism is once again shared by the ROC and the Kremlin, and many Russians are beginning to see Vladimir Putin in a similar vein – a perception encouraged both by Putin and by the Church, each of which sees the other as a valuable political ally and sees their respective missions as being interrelated.[8]

---

6   Ibid.

7   Ibid.

8   Ibid.

If Putin is reminiscent of a latter-day Czar, then the present torrent of propaganda directed against Russia and Putin is also reminiscent of the torrent of propaganda against the Czar that was undertaken over a century ago by George Kennan courtesy of funding from Jacob H. Schiff and other wealthy patrons of the cynically named 'Friends of Russian Freedom'. Today we have in those roles Freedom House, NED, George Soros, and a multitude of others documented in this volume, and the motives are the same. Coyer refers to this Czar-like quality that is being accorded to Putin:

> The Russian Orthodox concept of the spiritual father, which encourages almost complete deference to the Church's hierarchy and clergy, is one that most Russians understand, and a defining aspect of Russian culture. This widely understood theological concept has paved the way for Russians to accept and defend Putin's authoritarianism and to see him as the country's spiritual father. Government officials, as well as religious leaders, have been known to speak of Putin in quasi-religious terms. Vladislav Surkov, who has held various senior positions surrounding Putin, including Deputy Prime Minister, has referred to Putin as 'a man whom fate and the Lord sent to Russia'.[9]

Despite the misgivings of some Russian patriots, Vladimir Putin has emerged as a new Russian strong-man. For one commentator the rise of Putin had mystical implications that could impact on the world in an epochal way: Putin's inauguration as Prime Minister on 9 August 1999 occurred during the week of the solar eclipse and the planetary alignment of the Grand Cross, 'a highly auspicious astrological event... traditionally held to be the end of an epoch'.[10]

Multipolar vs. Unipolar World

Putin had no intention of continuing a process that had begun with Gorbachev: the integration of Russia into a world political and economic system, with its concomitant cultural degradation. Putin's Russia has pursued the building of a 'multipolar' world.

Multipolarity is a doctrine that permeates much of the academic and ruling elite of Russia. Its most well-known proponent is Dr. Alexander Dugin. As for Dugin's influence in Russia, two antagonistic

---

9   Ibid.

10   Viacheslav N. Lutsenko, 'Who are you Mr Putin?', *New Dawn*, September-October 2001, p. 86.

academics lament of him: 'The growing interest among political scientists and other observers in Dugin and his activities is the result of his recent evolution from a little-known marginal radical right-winger to a notable and seemingly influential figure within Russia's mainstream'.[11] Coyer refers to what Western liberals and globalists see as Dugin's Rasputin-like sinister influence in the Kremlin:

> The Kremlin's chief ideologue in this regard is Alexander Dugin. According to this vision of the relationship between church, state, and society, the state dominates, the ROC partnering with the state, and individuals and private organizations supporting both church and state.[12]

Predictably Dugin is called a 'fascist' and a 'right-wing extremist' by the globalist propaganda machine, but he is an 'Old Believer' of the Orthodox Church and entirely within the Russian messianic tradition. He calls his geopolitical concept 'Eurasianism', writing of this:

> In the broad sense the Eurasian Idea and even the Eurasian concept do not strictly correspond to the geopolitical boundaries of the Eurasian continent. The Eurasian Idea is a global-scale strategy that acknowledges the objectivity of globalisation and the termination of nation-states, but at the same time offers a different scenario of globalisation, which entails no unipolar world or united global government. Instead it offers several global zones (poles). The Eurasian Idea is an alternative or multipolar version of globalisation, but globalisation is the currently fundamental world process that is deciding the main vector of modern history.[13]

Vladimir Putin

One of the numerous globalist NGO's directed at Russia, The Jamestown Foundation[14], offered several opinions in regard to the direction of Russia with Putin's re-election in 2011. A major concern

---

11   Anton Shekhovtsov, and Andreas Umland, 'Is Aleksandr Dugin a Traditionalist? 'Neo-Eurasianism' and Perennial Philosophy', *The Russian Review*, October, 2009, 662–78.

12   Paul Coyer op. cit.

13   A Dugin, *The Eurasian Idea*, 2009.

14   The Jamestown Foundation, 'Mission', http://www.jamestown.org/aboutus/

is whether Putin's anti-American expressions during the elections were based on electoral rhetoric in drumming up Russians against an external enemy, or a genuinely held perception of the USA as intrinsically inimical to Russia. The very fact of the existence of The Jamestown Foundation, among a gaggle of other NGOs whose board members often have close connections with U.S. governmental agencies, including the military and intelligence,[15] indicates this.

Citing a report from Chattham House by James Nixey, entitled 'Russia's Geopolitical Compass', Nixey points to four 'geostrategic axes for Russia: the West, Russia's many 'souths' – the Black Sea region and the Islamic world – Russia's Far East and the Arctic North'. Nixey states that Russia no longer views the 'West' as all-powerful, and that President Obama's post-Bush so-called 'Reset' policy for rapprochement with Russia was 'losing direction'. What is particularly interesting is that Nixey agrees with Sinologist Bobo Lo, Senior Research Fellow at the Centre for European Reform in London, who states 'that Russia's relations with China are nothing more than an "alliance of convenience" by which Russia seeks to leverage influence with the West to gain acceptance. In this context, China is only a "geopolitical counterweight to the West."'[16]

There are those both on the 'fringes' of politics and in influential positions who see Russia as an ally rather than as a threat to a united Europe. France having more than the usual number of geopolitical realists, has included a strong Russophile element that looked to Russia, including during its Soviet days, as a counterweight to U.S. hegemony contrary to the propaganda of the Soviet bogeyman poised to ravish the Occident. One probably most immediately recalls the call of President Charles de Gaulle for a united Europe 'from the Atlantic to the Urals'. The Jamestown Foundation's article cites a view offered by Marc Rousset, a French historian and political analyst and author of *La nouvelle Europe: Paris-Berlin-Moscou* ['The New Europe: Paris-Berlin-Moscow'] (2009):

> According to Rousset, Putin would bring 'bravery, foresight and pragmatism' to Russian policy in the interest of creating a geopolitical order from the Atlantic to Vladivostok. Rousset

---

15   See for example The Jamestown Foundation's board members: 'Board Members', http://www.jamestown.org/aboutus/boardmembers/

16   Jacob W. Kipp, 'The Elections are over and Putin won: whither Russia?', 30 March 2012, http://www.jamestown.org/programs/edm/single/?tx_ttnews[tt_news]=39215& cHash=5bc45dc36c8f713aa6f5e393e5eae5b4

emphasized that Putin is a European from St. Petersburg working toward closer ties among Russia, Ukraine and Belarus. His conception of a Eurasian union had the possibility of creating an imperial order to rival that of the American empire and the emerging new orders in China and India (*Rossiiskaia Gazeta*, March 6). Rousset was quoted in November of last year as seeing the emergence of an axis of Paris, Berlin and Moscow being the answer to the present crisis in the Eurozone and the means to restore Europe's position as a major player in the international system (*Rossiiskaia Gazeta*, November 17, 2011). Sergei Karaganov answered that line of thought in December of last year by calling on Russia to turn away from Europe and make its future with a dynamic Asia-Pacific region led by China (*Rossiiskaia Gazeta*, December 28, 2011).[17]

While Sergei Karaganov [18] is in accord with the Dugin conception of 'Eurasianism' vis-à-vis Russia's place with China in Asia, Dugin also sees Russia in alliance with united Europe, and her historical relationship with 'Hindustan'. Historically a Sino-Russian alliance is an aberration, as indicated by other geopolitical analysts such as Bobo Lo. Putin hopes to play the China card, a policy that the USA pursued during the 1970s against the USSR. However, there are more scenarios for geopolitical discord between Russia and China than what there ever have been and possibly ever will be between the much-hyped supposed rivalry between China and the USA. The deployment of the Russian military in the Far East indicates Putin's realism on the issue.[19] Hopefully such manoeuvres are more reflective of Russian aims than Karaganov's ideal of a Sino-Russian partnership, since China will always seek a dominant position, and now sees itself as the new leader of globalisation. Whether globalisation is undertaken by American or Chinese state sponsorship, it is still undertaken in the interests of the same international oligarchy.[20]

---

17   Jacob W. Kipp. op. cit.

18   Interestingly, Sergei Karaganov, founder of the think tank, the Council for Foreign and Defense Policy, has also been a member of the Rockefeller-founded globalist think tank, the Trilateral Commission since 1998, and a member of the International Advisory Board of the Council on Foreign Relations, 1995-2005; http://karaganov.ru/en/pages/biography

19   K. R. Bolton, 'Aircraft Deployment in Russian Far East: Sign of Looming Conflict?', *Foreign Policy Journal*, May 27, 2011; https://www.foreignpolicyjournal.com/2011/05/27/aircraft-deployment-in-russian-far-east-a-sign-of-looming-conflict/2/

20   K. R. Bolton, 'Will China Assume the Leadership of Globalisation?', *Foreign Policy*

Dugin's Analysis

Indicating the seriousness with which Alexander Dugin is taken by Russia's friends and enemies alike, Kipp comments of Dugin's reaction to the re-election of Putin:

> In the aftermath of Putin's election, Aleksandr Dugin, the chief ideologue of anti-Western Eurasianism, stated that Putin stood at a moment of strategic choice: embrace the liberalism and Westernism of Russia's bourgeois elite or the nationalism of the Russian common folk – historically the victims of the corruption of Russia's liberal elite, which champions Russia's subservience to the West. Dugin wrote that by promoting a Eurasian Union, Putin had already spoken the word that defined his choice.

This was the path to national revival and to an economy based upon the reconstruction of Russia's defence sector. Dugin states:

> 'Both sides want reforms from Putin but they desire direct opposites. The elites want democratization, modernization, liberalization and growing closer to the West. The people want the national idea, a firm hand, a strengthening of sovereignty, a great power state, paternalism and social justice.' This choice for Putin comes at a particularly critical moment, according to Dugin. The hegemony of the U.S. and its allies is being tested in an emerging multi-polar world. The immediate challengers are Syria and Iran. But once those two states have been defeated by military intervention, Russia itself will have to face the threat of such intervention. …after the prepared attacks on Syria and Iran, the logical next target will be Russia. Of course, Russia will not survive such a confrontation with the West alone'.[21]

The Assault on Russia

For those who see Russia and China as natural allies in a bloc that can thwart U.S.-led globalisation, it might be instructive to consider Washington and Wall Street's attitudes towards both over the decades. While some 'neocon' elements in the USA raise their voices

---

Journal, April 7, 2017; https://www.foreignpolicyjournal.com/2017/04/07/will-china-assume-the-leadership-of-globalization/
Bolton, 'The Silk Road to Globalisation', *Geopolitica.ru*; October 26, 2017; https://www.geopolitica.ru/en/article/silk-road-globalisation

21   Jacob W. Kipp, op. cit.

against China's aims, Rockefeller, Soros and others of the globalist elite have maintained a pro-China attitude. Globalist foreign policy luminaries such as Henry Kissinger and Zbigniew Brzezinski have seen Russia as the USA's perennial obstacle to world hegemony while their attitudes towards China have been more generous, Rockefeller Trilateralism and Soros globalism seeing China as an essential partner in a 'new world order'.[22] One might also consider the immense efforts of the USA to 'contain' Russia from the days of Stalin to the present, and a comparative lack of action regarding China's ambitions. The Rockefeller dynasty has led the pro-China policy for decades. The 'Pacific Asian Group' of David Rockefeller's Trilateral Commission includes representatives from China. However, Rockefeller interests in China go back well prior to the Trilateral Commission, to the Asia Society. The Asia Center New York office states that John D. Rockefeller III founded the Society in 1956.[23]

U.S. actions against Putin's Russia remain as determined as those against the USSR during the Cold War. Dr. Paul Craig Roberts, U.S. Assistant Secretary of the Treasury under the Reagan Administration, has written of the subversion against Russia:

> The Russian government has finally caught on that its political opposition is being financed by the US taxpayer-funded National Endowment for Democracy and other CIA/State Department fronts in an attempt to subvert the Russian government and install an American puppet state in the geographically largest country on earth, the one country with a nuclear arsenal sufficient to deter Washington's aggression.[24]

Roberts was referring to an Act passed by the Duma requiring the registration of NGOs receiving foreign funds, similar to the requirements of U.S. laws that have long been in place. Roberts continued:

> The Washington-funded Russian political opposition masquerades behind 'human rights' and says it works to 'open Russia.' What the disloyal and treasonous Washington-funded

---

22 Paul Joseph Watson, 'Billionaire globalist warns Americans against resisting new global financial system, Soros: China Will Lead New World Order', *Prison Planet.com*, October 28, 2009.

23 Bolton, 'Aircraft deployment in Russian Far East'…, op. cit.

24 Paul Craig Roberts, 'War on all fronts', *Foreign Policy Journal*, 19 July 2012, http://www.foreignpolicyjournal.com/2012/07/19/war-on-all-fronts/

Russian 'political opposition' means by 'open Russia' is to open Russia for brainwashing by Western propaganda, to open Russia to economic plunder by the West, and to open Russia to having its domestic and foreign policies determined by Washington.[25]

The globalist think tanks are blatant in their intentions. The Council on Foreign Relations (CFR), opines that 'Russia is heading in the wrong direction'.[26] One of the CFR recommendations is to interfere with the Russian political process, urging U.S. Congress to fund opposition movements by increased funding for the *Freedom Support Act*, in this instance referring specifically to the 2007-2008 presidential elections.[27] Authors of the CFR report include Mark F. Brzezinski, who served on the National Security Council as an adviser on Russian and Eurasian affairs under President Clinton, as his father Zbigniew served in the Carter Administration; Antonia W. Bouis, founding executive director of the Soros Foundations; James A. Harmon, senior advisor to the Rothschild Group, et al. The role of the think tanks and NGOs, a vast globalist network, in trying to subvert Russia, will be considered later.

Russia and the New World Order

Putin has embraced 'Eurasianism' as the alternative to a 'new world order' based around U.S. hegemony. In a major foreign policy article in 2012 Putin outlined the main premises: Putin stated that Russia would be guided by her own interests first, based on Russia's strength, and would not be dictated to by outsiders. While Putin uses the term 'new world order', it is one that is antithetical to the globalist version. He questioned the U.S. missiles being placed on Russia's borders, and the continuing belligerence of NATO, stating that 'The Americans have become obsessed with the idea of becoming absolutely invulnerable'.[28] Importantly, Putin is fully aware that globalist agendas are being imposed behind the facade of 'human rights', and criticises the selectivity by which this morality is applied:

The recent series of armed conflicts started under the pretext

---

25 Ibid.

26 Jack Kemp, et al, *Russia's Wrong Direction: What the United States Can and Should Do*, Independent Task Force Report no. 57 (New York: Council on Foreign Relations, 2006) xi. The publication can be downloaded at: http://www.cfr.org/publication/9997/

27 Ibid.

28 Vladimir Putin, 'Russia and the changing world', RiaNovosti, 27 February 2012, http://en.rian.ru/world/20120227/171547818.html

of humanitarian aims is undermining the time-honoured principle of state sovereignty, creating a moral and legal void in the practice of international relations.[29]

Putin referred to the 'Arab Spring', noting outside inference in a 'domestic conflict'. 'The revolting slaughter of Muammar Gaddafi… was primeval', Putin stated, and the Libyan scenario should not be permitted in Syria.

It appears that with the Arab Spring countries, as with Iraq, Russian companies are losing their decades-long positions in local commercial markets and are being deprived of large commercial contracts. The niches thus vacated are being filled by the economic operatives of the states that had a hand in the change of the ruling regime'. One could reasonably conclude that tragic events have been encouraged to a certain extent by someone's interest in a re-division of the commercial market rather than a concern for human rights.[30]

Putin sees Russia developing her historic relations with the Arab states, despite the 'regime changes'. He also pointed out the political uses that are being made of social media which played such a significant role in mobilising and agitating masses during the 'Arab Spring', and indeed in the 'colour revolutions' on Russia's doorstep.[31] Putin also acknowledges the subversive role of the NGO's not least of whose actions are being directed against Russia, stating: '…the activities of "pseudo-NGOs" and other agencies that try to destabilise other countries with outside support are unacceptable'. He remarked on the failure of U.S. and NATO intervention in Afghanistan and mentioned Russia's historic relationship there.[32]

While Russia is seen as having an important role in the Asia-Pacific region, and Putin puts stress on alignment with a strong China he also declared:

> Russia is an inalienable and organic part of Greater Europe and European civilisation. Our citizens think of themselves as

---

29 Ibid.

30 Ibid.

31 K. R. Bolton, 'Twitters of the World Revolution: The Digital New-New Left', *Foreign Policy Journal*, 28 February 2011, http://www.foreignpolicyjournal.com/2011/02/28/twitterers-of-the-world-revolution-the-digital-new-new-left/
K. R. Bolton, *Revolution from Above*, op. cit., pp. 235-240.

32 V Putin, op. cit.

Europeans. We are by no means indifferent to developments in united Europe. That is why Russia proposes moving toward the creation of a common economic and human space from the Atlantic to the Pacific Ocean - a community referred by Russian experts to as 'the Union of Europe,' which will strengthen Russia's potential and position in its economic pivot toward the 'new Asia'.[33]

Putin refers to a vision of a bloc expanding from 'Lisbon to Vladivostok'. He sees Russia's acceptance to membership of the World Trade Organisation as 'symbolic', while having defended Russian's interests. With Russia looking at the Asia-Pacific region, will she be a nexus between this region and Europe, or will she enter the region as a junior partner with China? Some geopolitical analysts are referring to a new geopolitical bloc, challenging both the USA and China, as Eurosiberia[34] rather than Eurasia.

Syria: Pivotal Roadblock in the Globalist Agenda

Now the world looks on again in confusion and fear as the USA extends its dialectical strategy of 'controlled crises' over one of the few remaining redoubts of independence: Syria. Again the lines of opposition are drawn between Russia and the USA in a geopolitical struggle for world conquest. Syria in fact has long been viewed as the major obstacle to globalist ambitions: moreso even than Libya, Iraq or Iran. In 1996 the Study Group for a New Israeli Strategy Toward 2000, established by the Institute for Advanced Strategic Studies, Jerusalem, issued a paper titled *A Clean Break*. The think tank included people who would become influential in the Bush Administration, such as Richard Perle, Douglas Feith and David Wurmser. The major obstacle was Syria, and the major aim was to 'roll back Syria', and to 'foil Syria's regional ambitions'. Even the recommendation of removing Saddam – 'an important Israeli strategic objective in its own right' – was seen as a step towards Syria.[35]

The 1996 paper recommends a propaganda offensive against Syria,

---

33   Ibid.

34   Guillaume Faye, *'The New Concept of "Eurosiberia"'*, Counter-Currents Publishing,http://www.counter-currents.com/2010/08/faye-on-eurosiberia/

35   A Clean Break, Study Group for a New Israeli Strategy Toward 2000, 1996, http://www.informationclearinghouse.info/article1438.htm

along the lines of that employed against Saddam, and indeed against everyone who is an obstacle to the 'new world order' and/or Israel, suggesting that the 'move to contain Syria' be justified by 'drawing attention to its weapons of mass destruction'.[36] The report suggests 'securing tribal alliances with Arab tribes that cross into Syrian territory and are hostile to the Syrian ruling elite'. They suggest the weaning of Shia rebels against Syria.[37]

The plan of attack against Syria has been long in the making. Arab regimes have recently fallen like dominoes as a prelude to the elimination of Syria and Iran. *The Clean Break* recommends the use of Cold War type rhetoric in smearing Syria. We can see the plan unfolding before our eyes. The 'weapons of mass destruction' charade used to justify the U.S. bombing of Iraq takes the form of alleged chemical attacks on Syrian 'civilians', with a compliant media showing lurid pictures of suffering children, but usually with the comment that the reports are 'unconfirmed'. The U.S. assurances of 'proof' sound as unconvincing to the critical observer as the 'evidence' against Saddam. Sure enough, reports have come out that U.S.-backed rebels have committed the chemical attacks as a means of securing a U.S. assault on the Bashar al-Assad government. Two Western veteran journalists, while captives of the Free Syria Army, overheard their captors – including a FSA general - discussing the chemical weapons attack rebels had launched in Damascus as a means of provoking Western intervention.[38]

Since the above was written, the scenario proceeds under Trump with increasing gusto. The USA, with French and British backing, responded to another unproven allegation of a chemical attack as justification for launching an air strike on supposed Syrian government chemical weapons manufacturing plants in April 2018. Relations with Russia have again been strained. Trump stated that Russia would 'pay a big price' for supporting Syria. Prior to the U.S. bombing Trump in cowboy style tweeted: 'Russia vows to shoot down any and all missiles fired at Syria. Get ready Russia, because they will be coming, nice and new and "smart!" You shouldn't be partners with a Gas Killing Animal who kills his people and enjoys it!' This is the

---

36   Ibid., 'Securing the Northern Border'.

37   Ibid., 'Moving to a Traditional Balance of Power Strategy'.

38   'Journalist and writer held hostage for five months in Syria "overheard captors conversation blaming rebels for chemical attacks"', *Mail Online*, 12 September 2013, http://www.dailymail.co.uk/news/article-2418378/Syrian-hostage-Domenico-Quirico-overheard-rebels-blame-Damascus-chemical-attacks.html

president that has recognised Jerusalem as the capital of a gangster-state, a state that kills Palestinians as part of ethnic cleaning that has been ongoing since 1948, and has a stock-pile of nuclear weapons. Putin called the bombing raid an 'act of aggression' that could 'have a destructive effect on the entire system of international relations'.[39]

Putin sees the offensive against Syria in world historical terms in determining what type of world is being moulded. While Russian ships face U.S. and some French and British ships, he rebuked Obama's statements – like those of U.S. presidents before him – that the USA has 'an exceptional role'. In his appeal to the American people published in *The New York Times*, Putin questioned the USA's strategy stating that, 'It is alarming that military intervention in internal conflicts in foreign countries has become commonplace for the United States'. Condemning the basis of the 'new world order' that is being imposed with U.S. weaponry, Putin wrote that having studied Obama's recent address:

> ...I would rather disagree with a case he made on American exceptionalism, stating that the United States' policy is 'what makes America different. It's what makes us exceptional'. It is extremely dangerous to encourage people to see themselves as exceptional, whatever the motivation. There are big countries and small countries, rich and poor, those with long democratic traditions and those still finding their way to democracy. Their policies differ, too. We are all different, but when we ask for the Lord's blessings, we must not forget that God created us equal.[40]

Putin Steers a Straight Course

Putin has maintained his ideological position, and reiterated Russia's determination to maintain her sovereignty and identity in the face of globalisation. Putin's course for Russia was unequivocally stated in a September 2013 speech at a Government-backed plenary session of the Valdai Club, which included foreign dignitaries and Russian luminaries from politics, academia and media. Putin has declared

---

39   'The US has bombed Syria to punish it for a chemical attack', Vox, 16 April 2018; https://www.vox.com/2018/4/13/17221420/trump-syria-attack-strike-assad-russia-response-chemical-weapon

40   Vladimir V Putin, 'A Plea for Caution from Russia', *New York Times*, 11 September 2013, http://www.nytimes.com/2013/09/12/opinion/putin-plea-for-caution-from-russia-on-syria.html?_r=0

himself a traditionalist and a nationalist who will not countenance interference in Russia's interests.

To Putin, tradition and Christianity are the foundations of Russia's independence, while the globalists seek to impose over the world a nihilistic creed where the fluctuating needs of the market place are the cultural basis of a 'new world order'. Putin stated: 'Without the values at the core of Christianity and other world religions, without moral norms that have been shaped over millennia, people will inevitably lose their human dignity'.[41] This indicates a Perennial Traditionalist approach whereby Putin refers to the core values shared by 'Christianity and other world religions', of the 'Euro-Atlantic countries [where] any traditional identity, including sexual identity, is rejected'.

Putin stated that while every nation needs its technical strength, at the basis of all is 'spiritual, cultural and national self-determination' without which 'it is impossible to move forward'. '[T]he main thing that will determine success is the quality of citizens, the quality of society: their intellectual, spiritual and moral strength'. Putin rejects the economic determinism of the modern era, stating:

> After all, in the end economic growth, prosperity and geopolitical influence are all derived from societal conditions. They depend on whether the citizens of a given country consider themselves a nation, to what extent they identify with their own history, values and traditions, and whether they are united by common goals and responsibilities. In this sense, the question of finding and strengthening national identity really is fundamental for Russia.[42]

Putin pointed to the threat posed to Russian identity by 'objective pressures stemming from globalisation', as well as the blows to Russia inflicted by the attempts to erect a market economy, which it might be added, was sought by internal oligarchs and outside plutocrats; attempts that are ongoing. Putin moreover points to the lack of national identity serving these interests:

---

41 Putin at Valdai conference, Valdai Club, 19 September 2013, http://valdaiclub.com/
    valdai_club/62642.html
    A significant proportion of the speech can be read at: http://therearenosunglasses.
    wordpress.com/2013/09/22/putins-address-at-valdai-international-discussion-club-
    eng-transcript/

42 Putin at Valdai conference, op. cit.

In addition, the lack of a national idea stemming from a national identity profited the quasi-colonial element of the elite – those determined to steal and remove capital, and who did not link their future to that of the country, the place where they earned their money.[43]

What the globalists and oligarchs wish to impose on Russia from the outside cannot form an identity, which must arise from Russian roots, and not as a foreign import in the interests of commerce:

Practice has shown that a new national idea does not simply appear, nor does it develop according to market rules. A spontaneously constructed state and society does not work, and neither does mechanically copying other countries' experiences. Such primitive borrowing and attempts to civilize Russia from abroad were not accepted by an absolute majority of our people. This is because the desire for independence and sovereignty in spiritual, ideological and foreign policy spheres is an integral part of our national character. Incidentally, such approaches have often failed in other nations too. The time when ready-made lifestyle models could be installed in foreign states like computer programmes has passed.[44]

'Russia's sovereignty, independence and territorial integrity are unconditional', states Putin. He has called for unity among all factions, above ethnic separatism and urges an ideological dialogue among political factions.

Putin also recognises that what is today called the 'West', with the USA as the 'leader of the Western world', as the media and U.S. State Department constantly remind us, shows little evidence of any vestige of its traditional foundations:

Another serious challenge to Russia's identity is linked to events taking place in the world. Here there are both foreign policy and moral aspects. We can see how many of the Euro-Atlantic countries are actually rejecting their roots, including the Christian values that constitute the basis of Western civilisation. They are denying moral principles and all traditional identities: national, cultural, religious and even sexual.[45]

---

43   Ibid.

44   Ibid.

45   Ibid.

In this demise of Western values, Putin attacks 'political correctness', where religion has become an embarrassment, and Christian holidays are, for example, changed or eliminated in case a minority takes offence. This nihilism is being exported over the world and will result in a 'profound demographic and moral crisis', resulting the in 'degradation' of humanity. While multiculturalism is problematic for many states in Europe, Russia has always been multiethnic and this diversity should be encouraged in forging local identities, but within the context of a Russian state-civilisation. As will be apparent to the Russian leadership, the agitation of ethnic and religious separatism is a significant means by which the globalists undermine target nations, while paradoxically their own societies fall to pieces around them.[46]

Simultaneous with the moral and religious decline is the attempt to impose a 'standardised, unipolar world' where nations become defunct, rejecting the 'God-given diversity' of the world in favour of 'vassals'. Above this, Putin is promoting a 'Eurasian Union', a geopolitical bloc that will enable the states of the region to withstand globalisation.

Putin's Valdai speech shows that he has a fully developed world-view on which to base Russia's course. It also indicates that Putin has established Russia as the most likely axis of a new Civilisation and a new era. As history shows, once a civilisation succumbs to internal decay and often thereafter outside invasion, another civilisation assumes its place on the world stage, created by a people who have retained their vigour and have not succumbed to moral rot. Western Civilisation began its cycle of decay several centuries ago.

---

46   See K. R. Bolton, *Babel Inc.* (Black House Publishing, 2013).

Russia's World Mission

It would be easy to regard the eminent German conservative historian-philosopher Oswald Spengler, author of the epochal *Decline of The West* in the aftermath of World War I, as a Russophobe. In so doing the role of Russia in the unfolding of history from this era onward could be easily dismissed, opposed or ridiculed by proponents of Spengler, while in Russia his insights into culture-morphology would be understandably unwelcome as being from a Slavophobic German nationalist. However, while Spengler, like many others of the time in the aftermath of the Bolshevik Revolution, regarded Russia in a role as the Asianised leader of a 'coloured revolution' against the white world, he also considered other possibilities. Spengler, defining the morphology of history for this epoch and for Westerners, has much to teach Westerners about the life-course of Western Civilisation, and the possibilities of a new Civilisation arising from Russia in the shadow of the West's decline.

Russia's 'Soul'

Spengler regarded Russians as formed by the vastness of the land-plain, as innately antagonistic to the Machine, as rooted in the soil, irrepressibly peasant, religious, and 'primitive'. Without a wider understanding of Spengler's philosophy it appears that he was a Slavophobe. However, when Spengler wrote of these Russian characteristics he was referencing the Russians as a still youthful people in contrast to the senile West. Hence the 'primitive' Russian is not synonymous with 'primitivity' as popularly understood at that time in regard to 'primitive' tribal peoples. Nor was it to be confounded with the Hitlerite perception of the 'primitive Slav' incapable of building his own State. To Spengler, the 'primitive peasant' is the well-spring from which a race draws its healthiest elements during its epochs of cultural vigour. Agriculture is the foundation of a High Culture, enabling stable communities to diversify labour into specialisation from which Civilisation proceeds.

However, according to Spengler, each people has its own soul, a German conception derived from the German Idealism of Herder, Fichte et al.

A High culture reflects that soul, whether in its mathematics, music, architecture; both in the arts and the physical sciences. The Russian soul is not the same as the Western *Faustian*, as Spengler called it, the 'Magian' of the Arabian civilisation, or the Classical of the Hellenes and Romans. The Western Culture that was imposed on Russia by Peter the Great, what Spengler called *Petrinism*, is a veneer.

The basis of the Russian soul is not *infinite space* – as in the West's *Faustian*[1] imperative, but is *'the plain without limit'*.[2] The Russian soul expresses its own type of infinity, albeit not that of the Western which becomes even *enslaved* by its own technics at the end of its life-cycle.[3] (Although it could be argued that Sovietism enslaved man to machine, a Spenglerian would cite this as an example of *Petrinism*). However, Civilisations follow their life's course, and one cannot see Spengler's descriptions as moral judgements but as observations. The finale for Western Civilisation according to Spengler cannot be to create further great forms of art and music, which belong to the youthful or 'spring' epoch of a civilisation, but to dominate the world under a technocratic-military dispensation, before declining into oblivion like prior world civilisations. It is after this Western decline that Spengler alluded to the next world civilisation being that of Russia.

According to Spengler, Russian Orthodox architecture does not represent the infinity towards space that is symbolised by the Western high culture's Gothic Cathedral spire, nor the enclosed space of the Mosque of the Magian Culture,[4] but the impression of sitting upon a horizon. Spengler considered that this Russian architecture is 'not yet a style, only the promise of a style that will awaken when the real Russian religion awakens'.[5] Spengler was writing of the Russian culture as an outsider, and by his own reckoning must have realised the limitations of that. It is therefore useful to compare his thoughts on Russia with those of Russians of note.

Nikolai Berdyaev in *The Russian Idea* affirms what Spengler describes:

> There is that in the Russian soul which corresponds to the immensity, the vagueness, the infinitude of the Russian land,

---

1   Spengler, *The Decline of The West*, (London: George Allen & Unwin, 1971), Vol. I, 183.

2   Ibid., I, 201.

3   Ibid., II, 502.

4   Ibid., I, 183-216.

5   Ibid., I, 201.

spiritual geography corresponds with physical. In the Russian soul there is a sort of immensity, a vagueness, a predilection for the infinite, such as is suggested by the great plain of Russia.[6]

The connections between family, nation, birth, unity and motherland are reflected in the Russian language:

род [rod]: family, kind, sort, genus
родина [ródina]: homeland, motherland
родители [rodíteli]: parents
родить [rodít']: to give birth
роднить [rodnít']: to unite, bring together
родовой [rodovói]: ancestral, tribal
родство [rodstvó]: kinship

Western-liberalism, rationalism, even the most strenuous efforts of Bolshevik dialectal materialism, have so far not been able to permanently destroy, but at most repress, these conceptions – conscious or unconscious – of what it is to be 'Russian'. Spengler, as will be seen, even during the early period of Russian Bolshevism, already predicted that even this would take on a different, even antithetical form, to the *Petrine* import of Marxism.

'Russian Socialism'

Of the Russian soul, the ego/vanity of the Western culture-man is missing; the persona seeks impersonal growth in service, 'in the brother-world of the plain'. Orthodox Christianity condemns the 'I' as 'sin'.[7]

The Russian concept of 'we' rather than 'I', and of impersonal service to the expanse of one's land implies another form socialism to that of Marxism. It is perhaps in this sense that Stalinism proceeded along lines often antithetical to the Bolshevism envisaged by Trotsky et al.[8]

A recent comment by an American visitor to Russia, Barbara J. Brothers, as part of a scientific delegation, states something akin to Spengler's observation:

6   Nikolai Berdyaev, *The Russian Idea* (MacMillan Co., New York, 1948), 1.

7   Spengler, 1971, op. cit., I, 309.

8   Leon Trotsky, *The Revolution Betrayed*: what is the Soviet Union and where is it going? (1936).

The Russians have a sense of connectedness to themselves and to other human beings that is just not a part of American reality. It isn't that competitiveness does not exist; it is just that there always seems to be more consideration and respect for others in any given situation.[9]

Of the Russian traditional ethos, intrinsically antithetical to Western individualism, including that of property relations, Berdyaev wrote:

Of all peoples in the world the Russians have the community spirit; in the highest degree the Russian way of life and Russian manners, are of that kind. Russian hospitality is an indication of this sense of community.[10]

Taras Bulba

Russian National Literature starting from the 1840s began to consciously express the Russian soul. Firstly Nikolai Vasilievich Gogol's *Taras Bulba*, which along with the poetry of Pushkin, founded a Russian literary tradition; that is to say, truly Russian, and distinct from the previous literature based on German, French and English. John Cournos states of this in his introduction to *Taras Bulba*:

The spoken word, born of the people, gave soul and wing to literature; only by coming to earth, the native earth, was it enabled to soar. Coming up from Little Russia, the Ukraine, with Cossack blood in his veins, Gogol injected his own healthy virus into an effete body, blew his own virile spirit, the spirit of his race, into its nostrils, and gave the Russian novel its direction to this very day.

Taras Bulba is a tale on the formation of the Cossack folk. In this folk-formation the outer enemy plays a crucial role. The Russian has been formed largely as the result of battling over centuries with Tartars, Muslims and Mongols.[11]

Their society and nationality were defined by religiosity, as was the West's by Gothic Christianity during its 'Spring' epoch, in Spenglerian

---

9   Barbara J. Brothers, 'From Russia with Soul', *Psychology Today*, January 1, 1993; https://www.psychologytoday.com/us/articles/199301/russia-soul

10   Berdyaev, op. cit., 97-98.

11   H. Cournos, 'Introduction', N. V .Gogol, *Taras Bulba & Other Tales* (1842), http://www.gutenberg.org/files/1197/1197-h/1197-h.htm

terms. The newcomer to a *Setch*, or permanent village, was greeted by the Chief as a Christian and as a warrior: 'Welcome! Do you believe in Christ?' —'I do', replied the new-comer. 'And do you believe in the Holy Trinity?'— 'I do'.—'And do you go to church?'—'I do.' 'Now cross yourself'.[12]

Gogol depicts the scorn in which trade is held, and when commerce has entered among Russians, rather than being confined to non-Russians associated with trade, it is regarded as a symptom of decadence:

> I know that baseness has now made its way into our land. Men care only to have their ricks of grain and hay, and their droves of horses, and that their mead may be safe in their cellars; they adopt, the devil only knows what Mussulman customs. They speak scornfully with their tongues. They care not to speak their real thoughts with their own countrymen. They sell their own things to their own comrades, like soulless creatures in the market-place..... Let them know what brotherhood means on Russian soil! [13]

Here we might see a Russian socialism that is, so far form being the dialectical materialism offered by Marx, the mystic we-feeling forged by the vastness of the plains and the imperative for brotherhood above economics, imposed by that landscape. Russia's feeling of world-mission has its own form of messianism whether expressed through Christian Orthodoxy or the non-Marxian form of 'world revolution' under Stalin, or both in combination, as suggested by the later rapport between Stalinism and the Church from 1943 with the creation of the Council for Russian Orthodox Church Affairs [14] In both senses, and even in the embryonic forms taking place under Putin, Russia is conscious of a world-mission, expressed today as Russia's role in forging a multipolar world, with Russia as being pivotal in resisting unipolarism.

Commerce is the concern of foreigners, and the intrusions bring with them the corruption of the Russian soul and culture in general: in speech, social interaction, servility, undermining Russian 'brotherhood', the Russian 'we' feeling that Spengler described.[15]

---

12   N. V. Gogol, ibid., III.

13   Spengler, 1971, op. cit., II, 113.

14   T. A. Chumachenko, *Church and State in Soviet Russia* (New York: M. E. Sharpe Inc., 2002). See chapter herein: 'Saint Joseph': Was Stalin Defender of the Church?'

15   Spengler 1971, op. cit., I, 309.

The Cossack brotherhood is portrayed by Gogol as the formative process in the building up of the Russian people. This process is not one of biology but of spirit, even transcending the family bond. Spengler treated the matter of race as that of soul rather than of zoology.[16] To Spengler landscape was crucial in determining what becomes 'race', and the duration of families grouped in a particular landscape – including nomads who have a defined range of wandering – form *a character of duration*, which was Spengler's definition of 'race'.[17] Gogol describes this 'race' forming process among the Russians. So far from being an aggressive race nationalism it is an expanding mystic brotherhood under God:

> The father loves his children, the mother loves her children, the children love their father and mother; but this is not like that, brothers. The wild beast also loves its young. But a man can be related only by similarity of mind and not of blood. There have been brotherhoods in other lands, but never any such brotherhoods as on our Russian soil.[18]

The Russian soul is born in suffering. The Russian accepts the fate of life in service to God and to his Motherland. Russia and Faith are inseparable. When the elderly warrior Bovdug is mortally struck by a Turkish bullet his final words are exhortations on the nobility of suffering, after which his spirit soars to join his ancestors.[19] The mystique of death and suffering for the Motherland is described in the death of Tarus Bulba when he is captured and executed, his final words being ones of resurrection:

> Wait, the time will come when ye shall learn what the orthodox Russian faith is! Already the people scent it far and near. A czar shall arise from Russian soil, and there shall not be a power in the world which shall not submit to him![20]

Pseudomorphosis

A significant element of Spengler's culture morphology is 'Historic Pseudomorphosis'. Spengler drew an analogy from geology, when

---

16 Spengler, ibid., II, 113-155.

17 Spengler, ibid., II, 113.

18 Gogol, op. cit., IX.

19 Ibid.

20 Gogol, ibid., XII.

crystals of a mineral are embedded in a rock-stratum: where 'clefts and cracks occur, water filters in, and the crystals are gradually washed out so that in due course only their hollow mould remains'.[21]

> By the term 'historical pseudomorphosis' I propose to designate those cases in which an older alien Culture lies so massively over the land that a young Culture, born in this land, cannot get its breath and fails not only to achieve pure and specific expression-forms, but even to develop its own fully self-consciousness. All that wells up from the depths of the young soul is cast in the old moulds, young feelings stiffen in senile works, and instead of rearing itself up in its own creative power, it can only hate the distant power with a hate that grows to be monstrous.[22]

A dichotomy has existed for centuries, starting with Peter the Great, of attempts to impose a Western veneer over Russia. This is called *Petrinism*. The resistance of those attempts is what Spengler called 'Old Russia'.[23] Nikolai Berdyaev wrote in terms similar to Spengler's:

> 'Russia is a complete section of the world, a colossal East-West. It unites two worlds, and within the Russian soul two principles are always engaged in strife - the Eastern and the Western.[24]

With the orientation of Russian policy towards the West, 'Old Russia' was 'forced into a false and artificial history'.[25] Spengler wrote that Russia had become dominated by Late Western culture:

> Late-period arts and sciences, enlightenment, social ethics, the materialism of world-cities, were introduced, although in this pre-cultural time religion was the only language in which man understood himself and the world.[26]

'The first condition of emancipation for the Russian soul', wrote Ivan Sergyeyevich Aksakov, founder of the anti-Petrinist 'Slavophil' group, in 1863 to Dostoyevski, 'is that it should hate Petersburg with all its might and all its soul'. Moscow is holy, Petersburg Satanic. A widespread popular legend presents Peter the Great as Antichrist.

---

21   Spengler, op. cit., II, 89.

22   Ibid.

23   Ibid., II, 192.

24   Berdyaev, op. cit., 1.

25   Spengler, II, 193

26   Spengler, op. cit., II, 193.

The hatred of the 'West' and of 'Europe' is the hatred for a Civilisation that had already reached an advanced state of decay into materialism and sought to impose its primacy by cultural subversion rather than by combat, with its City-based and money-based outlook, 'poisoning the unborn culture in the womb of the land'.[27] Russia was still a land where there were no bourgeoisie and no true class system but only lord and peasant, a view confirmed by Berdyaev, writing: 'The various lines of social demarcation did not exist in Russia; there were no pronounced classes. Russia was never an aristocratic country in the Western sense, and equally there was no bourgeoisie'.[28]

The cities that emerged threw up an intelligentsia, copying the intelligentsia of Late Westerndom, 'bent on discovering problems and conflicts, and below, an uprooted peasantry, with all the metaphysical gloom, anxiety, and misery of their own Dostoyevski, perpetually homesick for the open land and bitterly hating the stone-grey world into which the Antichrist had tempted them. Moscow had no proper soul'.[29] Berdyaev likewise states of the *Petrinism* of the upper class that 'Russian history was a struggle between East and West within the Russian soul'.[30]

Russia the *Katechon*

Berdyaev states that while *Petrinism* introduced an epoch of cultural dynamism, it also placed a heavy burden upon Russia, and a disunity of spirit.[31] However, Russia has her own religious sense of Mission, which is as universal as the Vatican's. Spengler quotes Dostoyevski as writing in 1878: 'all men must become Russian, first and foremost Russian. If general humanity is the Russian ideal, then everyone must first of all become a Russian'.[32] The Russian Messianic idea found a forceful expression in Dostoyevski's *The Possessed*, where, in a conversation with Stavrogin, Shatov states:

> Reduce God to the attribute of nationality?...On the contrary, I elevate the nation to God...The people is the body of God.

---

27   Spengler, 1971, II, 194

28   Berdyaev, op. cit., 1.

29   Spengler, 1971, II, 194

30   Berdyaev, 15

31   Ibid.

32   Spengler, 1963, 63n

Every nation is a nation only so long as it has its own particular God, excluding all other gods on earth without any possible reconciliation, so long as it believes that by its own God it will conquer and drive all other gods off the face of the earth. ...The sole 'God bearing' nation is the Russian nation...[33]

This is Russia as the *Katechon*, as the 'nation' whose world-historical mission is to resist the son of perdition, a literal Anti-Christ, according go the Revelation of St. John, or as the birthplace of a great Czar serving the traditional role of nexus between the terrestrial and the divine around which Russia is united in this mission. This mission as the *Katechon* defines Russia as something more than merely an ethno-nation-state, as Dostoyevsky expressed it.[34] Even the USSR, supposedly purged of all such notions, merely re-expressed them with Marxist rhetoric, which was no less apocalyptic and messianic, and which saw the 'decadent West' in terms analogous to elements of Islam regarding the USA as the 'Great Satan'. It is not surprising that the pundits of secularised, liberal Western academia, politics and media could not understand, and indeed were outraged, when Solzhenitsyn seemed so ungrateful when in his Western exile he unequivocally condemned the liberalism and materialism of the a 'decadent West'. A figure who was for so long held up as a martyr by Western liberalism transpired to be a traditional Russian and not someone who was willing to remake himself in the image of a Western liberal for the sake of continued plaudits. He attacked the modern West's conceptions of 'rights', 'freedom', 'happiness', 'wealth', the irresponsibility of the 'free press', 'television stupor', and referred to a 'Western decline' in courage. He emphasised that this was a spiritual matter:

But should I be asked, instead, whether I would propose the West, such as it is today, as a model to my country, I would frankly have to answer negatively. No, I could not recommend your society as an ideal for the transformation of ours. Through deep suffering, people in our own country have now achieved a spiritual development of such intensity that the Western system in its present state of spiritual exhaustion does not look attractive. Even those characteristics of your life which I have just enumerated are extremely saddening.[35]

---

33   Dostoyevski The Possessed, ([1872] Oxford University Press, 1992), Part II: I: 7, 265-266

34   Ibid.

35   Alexander Solzhenitsyn, A World Split Apart — Commencement Address Delivered At Harvard University, June 8, 1978.

These are all matters that have been addressed by Spengler, and by traditional Russians, whether calling themselves Czarists Orthodox Christians or even 'Bolsheviks' or followers of Putin.

Spengler's thesis that Western Civilisation is in decay is analogous to the more mystical evaluations of the West by the Slavophils, both reaching similar conclusions. Solzhenitsyn was in that tradition, and Putin is influenced by it in his condemnation of Western liberalism. Putin recently pointed out the differences between the West and Russia as at root being 'moral' and religious:

> Another serious challenge to Russia's identity is linked to events taking place in the world. Here there are both foreign policy and moral aspects. We can see how many of the Euro-Atlantic countries are actually rejecting their roots, including the Christian values that constitute the basis of Western civilisation. They are denying moral principles and all traditional identities: national, cultural, religious and even sexual.[36]

Spengler saw Russia as outside of Europe, and even as 'Asian'. He even saw a Western rebirth vis-à-vis opposition to Russia, which he regarded as leading the 'coloured world' against the whites, under the mantle of Bolshevism. Yet there were also other destinies that Spengler saw over the horizon, which had been predicted by Dostoyevski.

Once Russia had overthrown its alien intrusions, it could look with another perspective upon the world, and reconsider Europe not with hatred and vengeance but in kinship. Spengler wrote that while Tolstoi, the *Petrinist*, whose doctrine was the precursor of Bolshevism, was 'the former Russia', Dostoyevski was 'the coming Russia'. Dostoyevski as the representative of the 'coming Russia' 'does not know' the hatred of Russia for the West. Dostoyevski and the old Russia are transcendent. 'His passionate power of living is comprehensive enough to embrace all things Western as well'. Spengler quotes Dostoyevski: 'I have two fatherlands, Russia and Europe'. Dostoyevski as the harbinger of a Russian high culture 'has passed beyond both Petrinism and revolution, and from his future he looks back over them as from afar. His soul is apocalyptic, yearning, desperate, but of this future he is *certain*'. [37]

To the 'Slavophil', of which Dostoyevski was one, Europe is precious. The Slavophil appreciates the richness of European high culture while

---

36   V. Putin, address to the Valdai Club, 19 September 2013.

37   Spengler, 1971, op. cit., II, 194.

realising that Europe is in a state of decay. Berdyaev discussed what he regarded as an inconsistency in Dostoyevski and the Slavophils towards Europe, yet one that is comprehensible when we consider Spengler's crucial differentiation between *Culture* and *Civilisation*:

> Dostoyevsky calls himself a Slavophil. He thought, as did also a large number of thinkers on the theme of Russia and Europe, that he knew decay was setting in, but that a great past exists in her, and that she has made contributions of great value to the history of mankind.[38]

It is notable that while this differentiation between *Kultur* and *Zivilisation* is ascribed to a particularly *German* philosophical tradition, Berdyaev comments that it was present among the Russians 'long before Spengler', although deriving from German sources:

> It is to be noted that long before Spengler, the Russians drew the distinction between 'culture' and 'civilization', that they attacked 'civilization' even when they remained supporters of 'culture'. This distinction in actual fact, although expressed in a different phraseology, was to be found among the Slavophils.[39]

Dostoyevski was indifferent to the Late West, while Tolstoi was a product of it, the Russian Rousseau. Imbued with ideas from the Late West, the Marxists sought to replace one Petrine ruling class with another. Neither represented the soul of Russia. Spengler states: The real Russian is the disciple of Dostoyevski, even though he might not have read Dostoyevski, or anyone else, nay, perhaps because he cannot read, he is himself Dostoyevski in substance'.[40]

The intelligentsia hates, the peasant does not. He would eventually overthrow Bolshevism and any other form of *Petrinism*. Here we see Spengler unequivocally stating that the post-Western civilisation will be Russian.

> For what this townless people yearns for is its own life-form, its own religion, its own history. Tolstoi's Christianity was a misunderstanding. He spoke of Christ and he meant Marx. But to Dostoyevski's Christianity, the next thousand years will belong.[41]

---

38 Berdyaev, op. cit., 70.

39 Ibid.

40 Spengler op. cit., 196.

41 Ibid.

To the true Russia, as Dostoyevski stated:

> Not a single nation has ever been founded on principles of science or reason ... nations are built up and moved by another force which sways and dominates them, the origin of which is unknown and inexplicable: that force is the force of an insatiable desire to go on to the end, though at the same time it denies that end. It's the spirit of life, as the Scriptures call it. It's the aesthetic principle, as the philosophers call it, the ethical principle with which they identify it, 'the seeking for God', as I call it more simply. The object of every national movement, in every people and at every period of its existence is only the seeking for its god, who must be its own god, and the faith in Him is the only true one. God is the synthetic personality of the whole people, taken from its beginning to its end. ... It's the sign of the decay of nations when they begin to have gods in common. When gods begin to be common to several nations the gods are dying and the faith in them, together with the nations themselves. The stronger a people the more individual their God. ... [42]

The atheism and materialism that Marxists sought to impose on Russia did not last long, as will be shown in a proceeding chapter. Even the Bolshevism soon had to take on messianic forms specific to Russia, in a process that Spengler called *pseudomorphosis*. No amount of repression, propaganda, and blood could alter the inward course of the Russian.

By the time Spengler had published *The Hour of Decision* in 1934 he was stating that Russia had overthrown *Petrinism* and the trappings of the Late West, and while he called the new orientation of Russia 'Asian', he said that it was 'a new *Idea*, and an idea with a future too'.[43] To clarify, Russia looks towards the 'East', but while the Westerner assumes that 'Asia' and East are synonymous with Mongol, the etymology of the word 'Asia' comes from Greek *Aσία*, ca. 440 BC, referring to all regions east of Greece.[44] During his time Spengler saw in Russia that:

> Race, language, popular customs, religion, in their present form... all or any of them can and will be fundamentally transformed. What we see today then is simply the new kind

---

42   Dostoyevski, 1872, op. cit., II: I: VII.

43   Spengler, *The Hour of Decision*, ([1934] New York: Alfred A Knopf, 1963), 60.

44   Ibid., 61.

of life which a vast land has conceived and will presently bring forth. It is not definable in words, nor is its bearer aware of it. Those who attempt to define, establish, lay down a program, are confusing life with a phrase, as does the ruling Bolshevism, which is not sufficiently conscious of its own West-European, Rationalistic and cosmopolitan origin.[45]

Of Russia in 1934 Spengler already saw that 'of genuine Marxism there is very little except in names and programs'. He doubted that the Communist programme is 'really still taken seriously'. He saw the possibility of the vestiges of *Petrine* Bolshevism being overthrown, to be replaced by a 'nationalistic' Eastern type which would reach 'gigantic proportions unchecked'.[46] Spengler also referred to Russia as the country 'least troubled by Bolshevism',[47] and the 'Marxian face [was] only worn for the benefit of the outside world'. [48]A decade after Spengler's death the direction of Russia under Stalin had pursued clearer definitions, and *Petrine* Bolshevism had been transformed in the way Spengler foresaw.[49]

Conclusion

As in Spengler's time, and centuries before, there continues to exist two tendencies in Russia: the Old Russian and the *Petrine*. Neither one nor the other spirit is presently dominant, although under Putin Old Russia struggles for resurgence. U.S. political circles see this Russia as a threat, and expend a great deal on promoting 'regime change' via the National Endowment for Democracy, and many others; these activities recently bringing reaction from the Putin government against such NGOs.[50]

Spengler in a published lecture to the Rheinish-Westphalian Business Convention in 1922 referred to the 'ancient, instinctive, unclear, unconscious, and subliminal drive that is present in every Russian,

---

45 Ibid.

46 Ibid., 63.

47 Ibid.,182.

48 Ibid., 212.

49 D. Brandenberger, *National Bolshevism: Stalinist Culture and the Formation of Modern Russian National Identity 1931-1956* (Massachusetts: Harvard University Press, 2002).

50 Vladimir Putin signs new law against 'undesirable NGOs', Telegraph, May 24, 2015, http://www.telegraph.co.uk/news/worldnews/europe/russia/11626825/Vladimir-Putin-signs-new-law-against-undesirable-NGOs.html

no matter how thoroughly westernised his conscious life may be – a mystical yearning for the South, for Constantinople and Jerusalem, a genuine crusading spirit similar to the spirit our Gothic forebears had in their blood but which we can hardly appreciated today'.[51]

Bolshevism destroyed one form of *Petrinism* with another form, clearing the way 'for a new culture that will some day arise between Europe and East Asia. It is more a beginning than an end'. The peasantry 'will some day become conscious of its own will, which points in a wholly different direction'. 'The peasantry is the true Russian people of the future. It will not allow itself to be perverted or suffocated'.[52]

The arch-Conservative anti-Marxist, Spengler, in keeping with the German tradition of *realpolitik*, considered the possibility of a Russo-German alliance in his 1922 speech, the Treaty of Rapallo being a reflection of that tradition. 'A new type of leader' would be awakened in adversity, to 'new crusades and legendary conquests'. The rest of the world, filled with religious yearning but falling on infertile ground, is 'torn and tired enough to allow it suddenly to take on a new character under the proper circumstances'. Spengler suggested that 'perhaps Bolshevism itself will change in this way under new leaders'. 'But the silent, deeper Russia,' would turn its attention towards the Near and East Asia, as a people of 'great inland expanses'.[53]

While Spengler postulated the organic cycles of a High Culture going through the life-phases of birth, youthful vigour, maturity, old age and death, it should be kept in mind that a life-cycle can be disrupted, aborted, murdered or struck by disease, at any time, and end without fulfilling itself. Each has its analogy in politics, and there are plenty of Russophobes eager to stunt Russia's destiny with political, economic and cultural contagion. The Soviet bloc fell through inner and outer contagion.

Spengler foresaw new possibilities for Russia, yet to fulfil its historic mission, messianic and of world-scope, a traditional mission of which Putin seems conscious, or at least willing to play his part. The invigoration of Orthodoxy is part of this process, as is the leadership style of Putin, as distinct from a Yeltsin for example. Whatever Russia

---

51   Spengler, 'The Two Faces of Russia and Germany's Eastern Problems', *Politische Schriften*, Munich, 14 February, 1922.

52   Ibid.

53   Ibid.

is called outwardly, whether, monarchical, Bolshevik or democratic, there is an inner – eternal – Russia that is unfolding, and whose embryonic character places her on an antithetical course to that of the USA.

The Next Civilization?

Walter Schubart's Messianic Promethean Synthesis

That Western Civilisation has indeed embarked on a prolonged cycle of decay into death, as per Spengler, can only be rejected by the ignorant such as those who overpopulate academia, who are too befuddled by the West's technology and ability to impose democracy over the world with a combination of bombs and moral degeneracy, to see what is unfolding before the eyes of anyone who does not live a mentally and/or physically closeted existence. Like the optimism of the Victorians (or at least the strata that did not live in squalor) during the Industrial Revolution, with their Social Darwinism, the West is supposedly continuing to march forward in progress as the epitome of human ascent, toward which all that has gone before was merely a prelude. In this scenario, we are about to enter a dispensation that will 'end history', as Professor Francis Fukuyama put it,[1] having achieved all that there is to achieve with the universal triumph of liberal-democracy. Those such as Fukuyama and American millenialists such as Colonel Ralph Peters,[2] and fellow 'neocon' ideologues such as Michael Ledeen[3] see for the West life eternal, where detached realists see for Western Civilisation death, and the Western organism as a zombified rotting corpse animated by technology and money, infecting all it touches with a cultural syphilis that those such as Colonel Peters actually applaud as wonderfully 'toxic'[4] to whatever remains in the world of traditional cultures.

---

1   F. Fukuyama, "The End of History?," *The National Interest*, Summer 1989, http://www. wesjones.com/eoh.htm

2   R. Peters, "Constant Conflict," Parameters, U. S. Army War College, Summer 1997, http://ssi.armywarcollege.edu/pubs/parameters/Articles/97summer/peters.htm

3   M. Ledeen, 'Dishonorable Congressman', National Review, 10 September 2003, http://www.nationalreview.com/article/207982/dishonorable-congressman-michael-ledeen

4   R. Peters, op. cit.

Even if the USA is, as the centre of contagion, beyond remedy, must Europe exhaust its possibilities and succumb to *fellaheen* level? Organic relationships can be symbiotic and complementary or amalgamate through synthesis. They need not be parasitic, distorting, or retarding in regard to a culture-organism's life cycle. That is how Russian ethnologist Lev Gumilev, postulated that new ethnic groups (*ethni*) are formed.[5] Whatever one's view of the late Gumilev's theories, he must be taken into account as having become influential in Russia and in Eurasian states;[6] particularly in Kazakhstan, where his name is honoured with the L. N. Gumilyov Eurasian National University.

Like any mixture, inter-ethnicity depends on the qualities and circumstances of what is being mixed as to whether the consequences will be invigorating or pathogenic. A blood transfusion of compatible types might save a life, but will sicken or kill if the blood types are incompatible. A virus can create a vaccine, or it can cause sickness and death, depending on the amount and transformation of the virus.

Dr. Walter Schubart,[7] a Baltic-German convert to Orthodoxy, married to a Russian, widely known as an authority on Russia prior to World War II, reaching a similar cyclical-organic historical-philosophy to Spengler's, proposed the synthesis of the 'Promethean' (what Spengler called 'Faustian') Westerner and the messianic Russian, each complementing the other.

Of the two types, *Promethean* and *Messianic*, Schubart wrote that 'Messianic man' 'longs to bring the discordant external world to harmony with the image that he carries within him'. 'He does not love the world for itself but only so that he can build within it the Kingdom of God'. The world is 'raw material for his mission'. 'Messianic man' seeks reconciliation; unity.[8] The Kingdom of God must be realised on earth.[9] The Gothic Westerner had a messianic impulse with his Crusades not only to secure the Holy Land from the Moor, but to make Jerusalem the centre of the Kingdom of God. The

---

5   Lev Gumilev, *Ethnogenesis and the Biosphere*, http://gumilevica.kulichki.net/English/ebe2a.htm

6   Mark Bassin, *The Gumilev Mystique*, (Cornell University Press, 2016).

7   Schubart was professor of sociology and philosophy at the Latvian State University. Dismissed by the Germans in 1941, his fate is unknown.

8   (W. Schubart, *Russia and Western Man* ([1938] New York: Frederick Ungar, 1950), 72-73).

9   Ibid., 74.

gothic epoch was the high point of western culture, and the impulse has long since passed. The Russian has yet to fulfil his analogous epoch of the 'Gothic', and Schubart saw this yet-to-be mission as the means by which Russia could reinvigorate Europe with a new spiritual awakening, while Europe could impart to Russia a sense of Promethean order. This seems akin to the dichotomy that existed between two strains that formed Greek culture; what Nietzsche called the *Apollonian* and the *Dionysian*, the first being the impulse to harmony and logic, the second that of emotion and enthusiasm.[10]

The contrast now between the West and Russia is that 'Promethean' (*Faustian*) man seeks only to exploit and rule the earth,[11] which Spengler saw as the final epoch of the Late West's domination by the machine.[12] The Westerner seeks as an end goal 'middle class comfort'. The Russian is impelled to sacrifice 'in a final dramatic scene'.[13] The Russian is the collective *Katechon*, holding back the Antichrist. The West has *become* the Antichrist. The Russian is a martyr. He accepts his fate Christ-like. Rather than submit to Napoleon, the Russians set their Holy City, Moscow, ablaze. The sight forever affected Napoleon.[14]

The Russian mission is to liberate the world from the contagion of the Late West, or to liberate Europe from its own terminal Western hubris; to 'redeem' the West or to 'replace it'.[15] This sense of mission has long been conscious among Russian thinkers and holy men. In 1852, seventy years before Spengler, Ivan Kireyevsky, the *Slavophil* philosopher, wrote of the decline of the West: 'The spiritual development of Europe has already passed in zenith. In atheism and materialism it exhausted the only powers at its disposal – those of abstract rationalism – and now it is approaching bankruptcy'.[16]

Schubart cited ethnologist and philosopher-historian Nikolay Danilevski's *Russia and Europe* (1871) as anticipating Spengler on

---

10   Friedrich Nietzsche, *The Birth of Tragedy* (1872).

11   Schubart, op. cit., 80.

12   Spengler, *The Decline...*, op. cit., XIV, 'The Form-World of Economic Life (B) The Machine', Vol. II, 499-507

13   Schubart, 80.

14   Ibid., 83-84.

15   Ibid., 191.

16   Quoted by Schubart, ibid.

organic culture cycles, in which the replacement of the West by Russia as the next world-civilisation was part of the ongoing cyclic historical process.[17] Danilevski had also critiqued the Westernisation of Russia by Peter the Great (*Petrinism*) as ill-fated. Foreshadowing Spengler, Danilevski's culture epochs are those of youth, adulthood, and old age. He saw the Slavic as being in the youth phase, and that with its capital in Constantinople, the Slavic would be considered by a decaying world as its redeemer. Konstantin N. Leontiev, at about the time of Danilevski, advanced the idea of 'the law of cyclicity of historical development'.

Schubart believed there was after the crisis of World War I a revival of religion in the West. Spengler also stated that during the epochal crisis of a Late Civilisation there is a 'second religiousness'.[18] Materialism, secularism, rationalism and scientism, do not satisfy an innate religious yearning, and themselves must assume religious forms. Note how zealous atheists and Darwinists are in defending their faith. Now there are a proliferation of cults and religions throughout the West, symptomatic of existential crisis, of a yearning for a return to the nexus with the divine that is lost during the 'Winter' epoch. At the time Schubart saw Western man 'approaching closer to the spirit' of Russia. 'While the night of decline is descending upon Western culture, which is destined to perish, the dawn of the Millennium is colouring the distant horizon...'[19] 'The approaching collapse of Western culture is unavoidable, and we may even ask ourselves whether it would be desirable to avoid it'.[20]

Neither Spengler nor Schubart believed it organically possible to return the West to a 'Spring' epoch, any more than it is possible for a geriatric to return to youth, despite whatever cosmetic and medicinal efforts are made. What Schubart did hope for was a chastising of the Late West's *hubris*, which we see in our collapsing societies, and existential angst, that would lead to the liberation of religious feeling without which 'no new creation can become possible'.[21] In this 'apocalyptic age' Schubart saw the promise of 'new life', while in Russia a new type emerges that is transforming what is of value in Western culture, without being retarded or distorted by it, despite the

---

17   Ibid., 192.

18   Spengler, *The Decline...*, op. cit., Vol. II, 455.

19   Schubart, op. cit., 284.

20   Ibid., 293.

21   Ibid.

conscious efforts of inner and outer enemies. 'This new type, while truly Russian, is yet heir to the eternal values of the West'.[22] This re-shaping of foreign elements that in a weaker culture would distort and even destroy that culture, but only contributes to the strength of the host culture, is what Spengler observed as *historical pseudomorphosis*. Again, we might be reminded of a dictum used by Nietzsche: 'that which does not destroy makes stronger'. As will be considered in a proceeding chapter,[23] the alien import of Marxism for example, was transformed so thoroughly by the impress of the Russian soul, that it became a veneer for a renewed Russian messianism in the guise of redeeming the proletariat. 'For although the Russian of today is not yet the Man of the Millennium, yet it is he – and only he – who will succeed in evolving him; the Russian will purify himself until he has attained the height of development necessary to produce him'.[24]

Schubart wrote that 'The spiritual Russian needs practical qualities; the practical European is in need of a new humanity'. Schubart called it a 'synthesis'.[25] The remaining option is for the Late West to continue as an animated zombie at the call of the USA, as a carrier of culture-pathogens.

A new Apocalypse is approaching with a Last Judgement – and a Resurrection! Promethean man already bears upon his brow the sign of Death. Now let the Man of the Millennium be born![26]

---

22   Ibid., 295.

23   'Messianic Tradition within Russian Bolshevism'.

24   Schubart, op. cit., 295.

25   Ibid., 297.

26   Ibid., 300

Wall Street and the Russian Revolution

A Review of Dr. Richard Spence's book
Wall Street and the Russian Revolution.

Even prior to the triumph of the Bolshevik revolt, the Provisional government and others were accusing the Bolsheviks of being in the pay of the German High Command, to take Russia out of the war. After the war the allegations intensified, and the notion of a 'German-Bolshevik conspiracy' became widespread, often with an anti-Semitic premise added. This was more than fringe agitation. Such ideas were commonly held in political, military intelligence, and diplomatic circles. The best-selling author Nesta H. Webster, today generally discounted as a 'conspiracy theorist', lectured British military intelligence on 'world revolution', was acclaimed as an historian from notable as diverse as Churchill and H. G. Wells, and wrote a book detailing collusion between Lenin and the Germans entitled *Boche and Bolshevik*.[1] Also notable was a collection of documents purchased by a U.S. diplomat in Russia, Edgar Sisson, in 1918, commonly referred to as the 'Sisson documents', and published by the U.S. Committee on Public Information, the propaganda arm of the U.S. Government, as *The German-Bolshevik Conspiracy.*[2]

In 1956 the Sisson documents, whose authenticity had been questioned from the start, were subjected to a now generally accepted scrutiny by George F. Kennan, U.S. diplomat and expert on Russia, discounting them as a hoax.[3] The documents purported to show that not only were the Bolsheviks funded by the German High Command, but that they were under orders from the Germans. Although the latter claim was spurious, it is now relatively well-known that the Germans did facilitate Lenin's return to Russia on the famous so-called 'sealed

1   Nesta H. Webster, *Boche and Bolshevik* (New York: The Beckwith Co., 1923).

2   The German-Bolshevik Conspiracy, Committee on Public Information, Washington, 1918, online: https://archive.org/details/germanbolshevikc00unit

3   George F. Kennan, 'The Sisson documents', *Journal of Modern History*, Vol. 28, no. 2, June, 1956, 130-154. Online: http://wiki.istmat.info/_media/%D0%B4%D0%BE%D0 %BA:sisson:the_sisson_documents.pdf

train,[4] and that he did receive funding from some of those mentioned in the Sisson documents, including millionaire Menshevik and German agent, Parvus; German banker Max Warburg, and Olof Aschberg of the Nya Banken, Stockholm. Clearly those who contrived the Sisson documents did have inside knowledge of certain transactions.

Ironically George F. Kennan was born (1904) near the time when his second cousin, the explorer and writer George Kennan, was being funded by banker Jacob Schiff of Kuhn, Loeb & Co., Wall Street, to distribute Left-wing propaganda among Russian prisoners of war being held by the Japanese. It is the year 1905, the year of the first revolt against the Czar, that begins Richard Spence's study of the relationship between Wall Street and Russian revolutionaries.

Spence is well placed to provide a detailed and documented study of this arcane aspect of history that is too readily dismissed as 'conspiracy theory'. Spence, starts by pointing out that while there is 'conspiracy theory' there is also 'conspiracy fact'.[5] While it might be opportune for academia to discount any notion of the latter, such a dogmatic attitude is hardly scholarly, and Spence is a scholar, not a fringe internet theorist. He has been professor of history at the University of Idaho since 1986. He is also an authority on the history of espionage, which provided an added advantage for such a study insofar as spies and double-agents are an important element of this study.

Spence dedicates this book to Dr. Antony Sutton, himself a renegade among academics, despite his acknowledged expertise in the field of Soviet technology as a Research Fellow at the Hoover Institution, Stanford University. Sutton produced a three-volume study of Western technological trade with the USSR, covering the years 1917 to 1965, *Western Technology and Soviet Economic Development*, summarised in *National Suicide*.[6] This research prompted Sutton to write *Wall Street and the Bolshevik Revolution*, based on contemporary newspaper accounts, military intelligence and diplomatic reports;[7] the inspiration for Spence's book. Sutton arguably devolved from 'conspiracy fact' to 'conspiracy theory' in attempting to explain why business would fund

4   Michael Pearson, *The Sealed Train* (London: Macmillan, 1975).

5   Spence, *Wall Street*, 3.

6   Antony C. Sutton, *National Suicide: Military Aid to the Soviet Union* (New Rochelle, NY: Arlington House, 1973).

7   Sutton, *Wall Street and the Bolshevik Revolution* (New Rochelle, NY: Arlington House, 1974).

their avowed enemies. He chanced upon a Yale fraternity, the crypto-Masonic Lodge 322, which he came to regard as an all-encompassing conspiracy for global domination, and felt that he had found the explanation: Hegelian dialectics – the backing of opposites to create a synthesis from conflict.[8]

Spence has a more plausible explanation, and rejects the notion of a 'Grand Unified Wall Street Conspiracy' to dominate Russia: simply, profit. The Wall Street concerns that sought the Russian market were as competitive there among themselves as in any other business venture, and rival consortiums to promote Russian trade were constantly being formed between 1917 and 1925. There were other variables. For example Jacob Schiff of Kuhn, Loeb & Co., was avid in wanting the overthrow of an anti-Semitic regime, and funding revolution was one among several strategies, the others including successfully lobbying against U.S. trade and loans, and funding Japan's war against Russia.[9] There were those who combined socialism with business, including the American Raymond Robbins, the German agent and Marxist Israel Helphand (Parvus), Julius Hammer, a founder of the Communist Party USA and his famous son Armand,[10] among the first to obtain commercial concessions from the Bolshevik government; and Olof Aschberg of the Nya Banken, Stockholm.[11] All of these were prominent in fostering economic dealings with Soviet Russia, which also happened to be personally lucrative, and afforded comrade Julius Hammer and comrade Parvus brazenly opulent lifestyles. Germany funded Bolsheviks to undermine the morale of the Russian soldiers, while Lenin stated he would take Russia out of the war. Max Warburg, head of the German branch of the Warburg banking family, undertook such arrangements. On the other side, banker and mining magnate William Boyce Thompson gave a personal fortune to the Bolsheviks to fund defeatist propaganda among the Central Powers, and toured the USA assuring Americans that the Bolsheviks had the highest motives of idealism and could be trusted.

It is with Schiff that Spence begins his history at 1905 when the Friends of Russian Freedom (FRF) in the USA, founded to support the overthrow of the Czar, had Schiff among their primary patrons.

---

8   Sutton, *How the Order Creates War and Revolution* (Western Australia, Veritas Publishing Co., 1984).

9   Spence, 38.

10   Ibid., 93-95.

11   Ibid., 118.

Another FRF luminary was George Kennan, who in 1917 at an FRF victory celebration for the February Revolution, publicly declared that it was thanks to funding from Schiff that he had been able to revolutionise 50,000 Russian POWs in 1905. This was reported in 1917 by *The New York Times*, and Schiff issued statements to the press praising the revolution as the culmination of long years of work.[12] A result of this propagandising was the abortive 1905 revolt, in which Trotsky and his mentor Parvus were involved.[13] The Friends of Russian Freedom continued to play a major role in sponsoring Russian revolutionaries,[14] including Socialist Revolutionaries such as Alexis Aladin and Nicholas Chaikovsky, who undertook lectures in the USA in 1907 under the FRF banner, and talked at exclusive clubs such as the Manhattan and Century Clubs, before the likes of Rockefeller and Vanderlip. [15]

In 1917 it was noted by U.S. military intelligence that Felix Warburg handled the dispensing of funds to Schiff's 'charities',[16] while it is interesting to recall that his brother Max in Germany was involved in similar undertakings with revolutionaries on behalf of the German military.[17] J. P. Morgan business interests were another major factor in dealings with Russia, with Nya Banken facilitating money transfers, its pro-Bolshevik director Aschberg being well connected with financial interests.

Among the most interesting characters that Spence profiles is Abram Zhivotovsky. The name perhaps first appears in connection with Bolshevism in a 1918 report to the U.S. State Department polemically entitled 'Bolshevism and Judaism'.[18] This, it should be kept in mind, was at a time when Jews were being widely identified with Bolshevism among prominent circles. Winston Churchill, for example, wrote of Bolshevism as 'this movement among the Jews'.[19] According to Sutton,

---

12   Spence, 39.

13   Ibid., 67-68.

14   Ibid., 74-76.

15   Ibid., 81-82.

16   Ibid., 41.

17   Ibid., 177.

18   'Bolshevism and Judaism', 13 November 1918, U.S. State Department Decimal File, 861.00/5399. Cited by Sutton, *Wall Street.*, op. cit., 186-187.

19   Winston Churchill, 'Zionism versus Bolshevism', *Illustrated Sunday Herald*, 8 February 1920, 5.

the report was written by 'a Russian employed by the U.S. War Trade Board',[20] which would strongly suggest Boris Brasol, a Czarist jurist of international repute, fixated with Jews, who promoted *The Protocols of the Learned Elders of Zion* in the USA. Brasol was in the USA at the time of the Bolshevik Revolution and was employed by the War Trade Board. Sutton, eager to eschew anti-Semitism, is too hasty in dismissing the report, which has accurate references to Schiff, Olof Aschberg, and Max Warburg as being involved in the funding of Bolshevism. The report alludes to a banker, 'Jivotovsky' (sic), stating that his daughter, Sedova married Trotsky, supposedly cementing an alliance between Jewish bankers and Jewish revolutionaries, although Sutton neglects to mention this reference. Spence does not mention this report, but he does identify this 'Jivotovsky' as Abram Zhivotovsky, having written of him in 2008.[21] Spence scrupulously traces the route of Trotsky to the USA and back to Russia to foment the October Revolution. Spence develops this research in *Wall Street and the Russian Revolution*. Abram Zhivotovsky was Trotsky's maternal uncle,[22] well connected to international business, a major figure in Russian banking,[23] close to Trotsky throughout his career, and a central figure in funding Bolshevism and Soviet Russia.

Another enigmatic and central figure is the so-called 'ace of spies', Sidney Reilly. Spence is an expert on Reilly's complex life of international intrigue. Reilly was not only a spy for the British, albeit to many in British intelligence, of highly questionable loyalty, but a globe-trotting businessman. What Spence convincingly shows is that Reilly, despite supposedly being at the centre of a plot to overthrow the Soviet Government, which involved British agent H. Bruce Lockhart, was linked with the Trotskyite faction. He was murdered not because he was an anti-Bolshevik but because he was part of the Trotskyite faction. Reilly had been employed by Zhivotovsky, and had worked with a Trotsky cousin, Joseph Davidovich Zhivotovsky, a known 'revolutionary sympathiser', in 1914.[24] Reilly was regarded widely as

---

20 Sutton, *Wall St.*, op. cit., 187.

21 Richard B. Spence, 'Hidden Agendas: Spies, Lies and Intrigue Surrounding Trotsky's American Visit of January-April, 1917, Revolutionary Russia, Vol. 21, No. 1, June 2008, 33-55. Online: h<u>http://www.academia.edu/14833068/hidden_agendas_spies_lies_and_intrigue_surrounding_trotskys_american_visit_of_january-april_1917_-_richard_b._spence</u>

22 Spence, *Wall Street*, op. cit., 107.

23 Ibid., 108.

24 Ibid., 112.

a criminal and a con man,[25] but was very well connected in Russia.[26] Other business colleagues in New York were Benjamin Sverdlov, brother of future Soviet eminence Jacob Sverdlov; Zhivotovsky's former London agent Alexander Weinstein, who had been associated with Bolshevik representatives Ludwig Martens and Maxim Litvinov;[27] and Samuel McRoberts of National City Bank, close to Olof Aschberg.[28] Reilly was an agent for the American International Corporation, a consortium that included Morgan, Rockefeller, and Kuhn, Loeb interests, among others.[29]

Reilly was also close to Sir William Wiseman, the head of British intelligence in New York during the war. Wiseman was also a key player in Wall Street connections with Bolshevism. When Trotsky arrived in New York he and his family were well looked after. Some unfounded rumours have entered legend that Trotsky was provided with $20,000,000 by Schiff, and was facilitated back to Russia with an American passport, along with an entourage of hundreds of 'Jewish Bolsheviks' from Lower East End New York. Trotsky did board the *Kristianiafjord* with his family and a few colleagues under the watch of William Wiseman. Not only were there commercial considerations but Trotsky had stated, in contrast to his old rival Lenin, that Russia would continue fighting Germany. Indeed, that he was the 'go-to' man for British agent R. H. Bruce Lockhart, is clear from Lockhart's memoir, while Lockhart himself was regarded in British circles as having 'gone Bolshevik'.[30] *En route* the *Kristianiafjord* was stopped at Halifax, and Trotsky was detained on suspicion of working for Germany. The order came from British Naval Attaché Captain Guy Gaunt in the USA.[31] Between Wiseman and Gaunt there was a mutual loathing, and Gaunt, among others, later accused Wiseman of treason.[32] Spence cites cables by Wiseman to London that indicate Trotsky and other socialists should be permitted to proceed to Russia to counteract the influence of the anti-war party,[33] led by Lenin. Spence suggests that

---

25 Ibid., 113.

26 Ibid., 114.

27 Ibid.

28 Ibid., 117.

29 Ibid., 116.

30 R. H. Bruce Lockhart, *Memoirs of a British Agent* (London: Putnam, 1934).

31 Spence, *Wall Street*, op. cit., 159.

32 Ibid., 160.

33 Ibid., 161.

Trotsky might have made a deal with Wiseman, which would have been no different from the deal Lenin had made with the Germans. An additional factor might have been that Wiseman was ingratiating himself with certain business interests. At any rate, after the war Wiseman became a partner in Kuhn, Loeb & Co., and foreswore his allegiance to the Crown. [34]

With Russia in turmoil following the February Revolution, a curious party was dispatched. The Amercian Red Cross Mission included few medical personnel and a majority of Wall Street agents, funded by William Boyce Thompson. While Sutton was possibly the first to detail this,[35] Spence elaborates and calls this mission 'by far the most important and controversial' of sundry business-orientated missions to be sent to Russia after the revolution.[36] The Thompson mission will be considered further in the following chapter. Meanwhile, Wiseman sought funds from Britain, and from Schiff and other banking interests in the USA, for a propaganda drive,[37] at the time Trotsky was arriving in Russia. Wiseman stated that Bolshevism was inevitable, and averred to having well placed agents within the Bolsheviki.[38] Lack of diplomatic recognition of the Bolshevik government by the USA until 1933 (a public relations problem) did not hinder business undertakings. Various other delegations from the USA proceeded to Russia, while in New York Ludwig Martens established the Soviet Bureau to cultivate trade.

One significant windfall for Wall Street from the Bolshevik victory was the shipment of Russian gold bullion out of Russia to U.S. vaults. Again the press of the time reported this. This was undertaken via Olof Aschberg's Nya Banken, and the Guaranty Trust at Wall Street. Melted down in Sweden the gold proceeded to London, Paris and especially New York, to Morgan interests and Kuhn, Loeb.[39]

One of the most interesting contentions of Spence, and the reason why his study ends at 1925, is that in that year there was a fundamental change in direction for Soviet Russia. While Sutton saw the transfer of technology and credits to the USSR as proving a continuous

---

34   Ibid.

35   Sutton, *Wall Street & the Bolshevik Revolution*, op. cit., chapter 5.

36   Spence, Wall Street, op. cit., 167.

37   Spence, op. cit., 176.

38   Ibid., 178.

39   Ibid., 222.

relationship between the Soviet state and Western capital, and in later years regarded the Cold War as a dialectical ploy, Spence contends that with the deposing of Trotsky by Stalin, the hopes that what Reilly called the 'Occult Octopus' of international capitalism[40] were ended. Trotsky had aptly become the Commissar for Foreign Concessions; a demotion, which was a prelude to his elimination from the party and the state. But 1925 was the launch at the 14th Party Congress of Stalin's 'socialism in one country', which meant that the Soviet Union would pursue economic self-development and would, as they stated it, stop being a 'raw materials appendage of Western Capitalism'. During that year industrial output had revived and owed less than 1% to foreign concessions, and that was of a small and temporary character. Instead 'technical assistance agreements' were negotiated for training and advice, but the foreign firms did not own any rights. Trotsky being deposed of all influence, uncle Abram provided the money to get his nephew out of Russia.[41] Again we can turn to other sources as indicative: while in Russia in 1921 on business Armand Hammer met Trotsky who sought to assure American capitalists that they could trust the Soviet regime with their investments.[42] In contrast, Hammer said that by 1930 it was obvious that Stalin did not want foreign concessionaires, and Hammer left Moscow.[43] Spence concludes that it would be sixty-six years before Wall Street saw another chance to get into Russia, but that failed, alluding to Putin, and the Cold War has returned.[44]

Wall Street and the Russian Revolution is an important reference. It has been seldom in recent decades that any attention has been brought to the machinations of business interests and revolution. While certain aspects were openly reported in the press at the time, and noted among diplomatic and military intelligence sources, lack of research has caused these aspects of history to be forgotten and obscured. Yet today it should not seem so incredible that business interests might fund revolutions for 'regime change', as it is now called, in order to secure better possibilities for investment. The funding of the so-called 'colour revolutions' is well-known, and undertaken by financiers who are reminiscent of Schiff, Aschberg, et al. The motives remain.

---

40   Ibid., 235.

41   Ibid., 252-255.

42   Armand Hammer, *Witness to History* (London: Coronet Books, 1988), 160.

43   Ibid., 221.

44   Spence, *Wall Street*, 255.

Globalist Response to the Revolution

Monopoly capitalism and socialism are by no means irreconcilable. There are sufficient historical examples of a cordial relationship between the two to question the universal validity of the 'socialism versus capitalism' dichotomy. There have also been circumstances in which monopoly capitalism has not been adverse to even violent social revolutions in order to overthrow systems that were considered economically antiquated and not suitable for allowing the full potential for industrialisation and capital investment. This chapter examines the response of significant sections of international capital towards both the March and the November 1917 Revolutions in Russia.

Funding of Revolutionary Cadres

The first process for the overthrow of the Czarist regime was to turn the outside world, and in particular the USA, against its traditional friendship with Russia, and to portray the Czar as a tyrant. The individual most responsible for turning American opinion, including government and diplomatic opinion, against Czarist Russia was the journalist George Kennan[45], who was sponsored by Jacob Schiff, a senior partner in Kuhn, Loeb & Co., New York. Robert Cowley states that during the Russo-Japanese War Kennan was in Japan organising Russian Prisoners Of War into "revolutionary cells" and Kennan claimed to have converted '52,000 Russian soldiers into 'revolutionists'. Cowley also adds, significantly, 'Certainly such activity, well-financed by groups in the United States, contributed little to Russian-American solidarity'. [46]

The source of the revolutionary funding 'by groups in the United States' was explained by Kennan at a celebration of the March 1917 Russian Revolution, reported by *The New York Times*:

> Mr. Kennan told of the work of the Friends of Russian Freedom in the revolution. He said that during the Russian-Japanese war he was in Tokyo, and that he was permitted to make visits

---

45   Robert Cowley, *'A Year in Hell', America and Russia: A Century and a Half of Dramatic Encounters*, ed. Oliver Jensen (New York: Simon and Schuster, 1962), pp. 92- 121. Cowley quotes historian Thomas A. Bailey as stating of Kennan: 'No one person did more to cause the people of the United States to turn against their presumed benefactor of yesteryear'. (A reference to Czarist Russia's support for the Union during the American Civil War). Cowley, ibid., 118.

46   Ibid., 120.

among the 12,000 Russian prisoners in Japanese hands at the end of the first year of the war. He had conceived the idea of putting revolutionary propaganda into the hands of the Russian army.

The Japanese authorities favoured it and gave him permission. After which he sent to America for all the Russian revolutionary literature to be had...

'The movement was financed by a New York banker you all know and love', he said, referring to Mr Schiff, 'and soon we received a ton and a half of Russian revolutionary propaganda. At the end of the war 50,000 Russian officers and men went back to their country ardent revolutionists. The Friends of Russian Freedom had sowed 50,000 seeds of liberty in 100 Russian regiments. I do not know how many of these officers and men were in the Petrograd fortress last week, but we do know what part the army took in the revolution.' Then was read a telegram from Jacob H Schiff, part of which is as follows:

'Will you say for me to those present at tonight's meeting how deeply I regret my inability to celebrate with the Friends of Russian Freedom the actual reward of what we had hoped and striven for these long years'.[47]

The reaction to the Russian revolution by Schiff and by other bankers in the USA and London, was one of jubilation. Schiff wrote enthusiastically to *The New York Times*:

May I through your columns give expression to my joy that the Russian nation, a great and good people, have at last effected their deliverance from centuries of autocratic oppression and through an almost bloodless revolution have now come into their own. Praised be God on high! Jacob H. Schiff.[48]

Writing to *The Evening Post* in response to a question about revolutionary Russia's new status with world financial markets, Schiff wrote:

---

47   *New York Times*, 24 March, 1917, 1-2.

48   Jacob H Schiff, 'Jacob H. Schiff Rejoices, By Telegraph to the Editor of The New York Times', *New York Times*, 18 March, 1917. *The New York Times* online archives: http://query.nytimes.com/mem/archive-free/pdf?

Replying to your request for my opinion of the effects of the revolution upon Russia's finances, I am quite convinced that with the certainty of the development of the country's enormous resources, which, with the shackles removed from a great people, will follow present events, Russia will before long rank financially amongst the most favoured nations in the money markets of the world.[49]

Schiff's reply reflected the general attitude of London and New York financial circles at the time of the revolution. John B. Young of the National City Bank, who had been in Russia in 1916 in regard to a US loan, stated in 1917 of the revolution that it had been discussed widely when he had been in Russia the previous year. He regarded those involved as 'solid, responsible and conservative'.[50] In the same issue, *The New York Times* reported that there had been a rise in Russian exchange transactions in London 24 hours preceding the revolution, and that London had known of the revolution prior to New York. The article reported that most prominent financial and business leaders in London and New York had a positive view of the revolution.[51] Another report states that while there had been some disquiet about the revolution, 'this news was by no means unwelcome in more important banking circles'. [52]

These bankers and industrialists are cited in these articles as regarding the revolution as being able to eliminate pro-German influences in the Russian government and as likely to pursue a more vigorous course against Germany in the war. Yet such patriotic sentiments cannot be considered the sole or primary motivation behind support for the revolution. While Max Warburg of the Warburg banking house in Germany advised the Kaiser and while the German Government arranged for funding and safe passage of Lenin and his entourage from Switzerland across Germany to Russia[53]; his brother Paul[54], an associate of Schiff's, looked after the family interests in New York.

---

49 'Loans easier for Russia', *The New York Times*, 20 March 1917. http://query.nytimes.com/mem/archive-free/pdf

50 'Is A People's Revolution', *The New York Times*, March 16, 1917.

51 'Bankers here pleased with news of revolution', ibid.

52 'Stocks strong – Wall Street interpretation of Russian News', ibid.

53 Michael Pearson, *The Sealed Train: Journey to Revolution: Lenin – 1917* (London: Macmillan, 1975).

54 Paul Warburg, prior to immigrating to the USA, had been decorated by the Kaiser in 1912.

The factor that was behind this banking support for the revolution whether from London[55], New York, Stockholm[56] or Berlin, was that of the largely untapped resources that would become available to the world markets.

This common interest in the exploitation of Russian resources beyond any national consideration was discerned by two widely different sources, Henry Wickham Steed of *The London Times*, and Samuel Gompers, the US labour leader[57]. On May 1, 1922 *The New York Times* reported that Gompers, reacting to negotiations at the international economic conference at Genoa, declared that a group of 'predatory international financiers' were working for the recognition of the Bolshevik regime for the opening up of resources for exploitation. Despite the rhetoric by New York and London bankers during the war, as noted above, that a Russian revolution would serve the Allied cause against Germany, Gompers opined that this was an 'Anglo-American-German banking group', and that they were 'international bankers' who did not owe any national allegiance. He also noted that prominent Americans who had a history of anti-labour attitudes were advocating recognition of the Bolshevik regime.[58]

What Gompers claimed was similarly expressed by Henry Wickham Steed, editor of *The London Times*, based on his own experiences. In a first-hand account of the Paris Peace Conference of 1919, Steed stated that proceedings were interrupted by the return from Moscow of William C. Bullitt and Lincoln Steffens, 'who had been sent to Russia towards the middle of February by Colonel House and Mr. Lansing, for the purpose of studying conditions, political and economic, therein

---

55 From London on May 1, 1918 Col. William Wiseman, cabled House that the allies should intervene at the invitation of the Bolsheviks and help organise the Bolshevik army then fighting the White Armies in a bloody Civil War at a time when the Bolshevik hold on Russia was doubtful. Edward M. House, ed. Charles Seymour, *The Intimate Papers of Col. House* (New York: Houghton, Mifflin Co., 1926), Vol. III, 421.

56 Olof Aschberg became head of the first Soviet international bank, Ruskombank. On September 6, 1948 *The London Evening Star* commented on Aschberg's visit to Swiss bankers that he had 'advanced large sums to Lenin and Trotsky in 1917. At the time of the revolution Mr. Aschberg gave Trotsky money to form and equip the first unit of the Red Army'.

57 Gompers was president of the American Federation of Labor.

58 Samuel Gompers, 'Soviet Bribe Fund Here Says Gompers, Has Proof That Offers Have Been Made, He Declares, Opposing Recognition. Propaganda Drive. Charges Strong Group of Bankers With Readiness to Accept Lenin's Betrayal of Russia', *The New York Times*, May 1, 1922. Online at Times' archives: http://query.nytimes.com/gst/abstract.html

for the benefit of the American Commissioners plenipotentiary to negotiate peace'.[59] Steed also refers to British Prime Minister Lloyd George as being likely to have known of the Mission and its purpose. Steed states specifically and at some length that international finance was behind the move for recognition of the Bolshevik regime and other moves in favour of the Bolsheviks, and specifically identified Jacob Schiff as one of the principal bankers 'eager to secure recognition':

> Potent international financial interests were at work in favour of the immediate recognition of the Bolshevists. Those influences had been largely responsible for the Anglo-American proposal in January to call Bolshevist representatives to Paris at the beginning of the Peace Conference — a proposal which had failed after having been transformed into a suggestion for a Conference with the Bolshevists at Prinkipo... The well-known American Jewish banker, Mr. Jacob Schiff, was known to be anxious to secure recognition for the Bolshevists...[60]

In return for diplomatic recognition Tchitcherin, the Bolshevist Commissary for Foreign Affairs, was offering 'extensive commercial and economic concessions'.

Steed in alliance with *The London Times*' proprietor Lord Northcliffe campaigned to expose the machinations going on to secure recognition of the Bolsheviks by international finance, on the premise that the post-war peace being inaugurated by President Woodrow Wilson under the banner of high moral principles, and a League of Nations, would appal American, British and other public opinion.

Steed next relates that he was called upon by President Wilson's confidante, Edward Mandel House, who was concerned at Steed's exposé of the relationship between the Bolshevists and international financers:

> That day Colonel House asked me to call upon him. I found him worried both by my criticism of any recognition of the Bolshevists and by the certainty, which he had not previously realized, that if the President were to recognize the Bolshevists in return for commercial concessions his whole "idealism"

59 Henry Wickham Steed, *Through Thirty Years 1892-1922 A personal narrative,* The Peace Conference, The Bullitt Mission, Vol. II. (New York: Doubleday Page and Co., 1924), 301.

60 Henry Wickham Steed, op. cit.

would be hopelessly compromised as commercialism in disguise. I pointed out to him that not only would Wilson be utterly discredited but that the League of Nations would go by the board, because all the small peoples and many of the big peoples of Europe would be unable to resist the Bolshevism which Wilson would have accredited.[61]

Steed then stated to House that it was Jacob Schiff, Warburg and other bankers who were behind the diplomatic moves in favour of the Bolsheviks:

> I insisted that, unknown to him, the prime movers were Jacob Schiff, Warburg, and other international financiers, who wished above all to bolster up the Jewish Bolshevists in order to secure a field for German and Jewish exploitation of Russia.[62]

Steed here reveals an uncharacteristic naiveté in stating that Edward House would *not* have known of the plans of Schiff, Warburg, et al. House was throughout his career close to these same bankers and was involved with them in setting up the influential think tank, the Council on Foreign Relations immediately following the world war, in order to help shape post-war U.S. foreign policy in favour of an international orientation. It was Schiff, Paul Warburg and other Wall Street bankers who called on House in 1913 to secure his support for the creation of the Federal Reserve Bank.[63]

House disingenuously asked Steed to compromise; to support a move that would supposedly secure benefits for both the pro-Bolshevik and non-Bolshevik Russian masses in terms of humanitarian aid. Steed agreed to consider this, but soon after talking with House found out that British Prime Minister Lloyd George and Wilson were to proceed with recognition of the Bolsheviks the following day. Steed therefore wrote the leading article for the Paris *Daily Mail* of March 28th, exposing the manoeuvres and asking where a pro-Bolshevik stance stood with Wilson's high moral principles for the post-war world?

---

61   Ibid.

62   Ibid.

63   Charles Seymour, op. cit., 165-166. House was assigned by Wilson to draw up the constitution for the League of Nations, and in 1918 formed a think tank at Wilson's request, called The Inquiry, to advise on post-war policy. This became the Council on Foreign Relations. House was the U.S. chief negotiator at the Peace Conference in Paris, 1919-1920.

...Who are the tempters that would dare whisper into the ears of the Allied and Associated Governments? They are not far removed from the men who preached peace with profitable dishonour to the British people in July, 1914. They are akin to, if not identical with, the men who sent Trotsky and some scores of associate desperadoes to ruin the Russian Revolution as a democratic, anti-German force in the spring of 1917.[64]

What is of special interest in this passage is that Steed identified Schiff, Warburg, et al as similar to or identical with those prominent individuals who allowed Trotsky in New York and Lenin in Switzerland to proceed to Russia in 1917 to foment the Bolshevik Revolution.

Charles Crane[65], who had recently talked with Wilson, related to Steed that he was concerned that Wilson was about to recognise the Bolsheviks, which would result in negative public opinion in the USA and destroy Wilson's post-War internationalist aims. Significantly Crane also identified the pro-Bolshevik faction as being that of Big Business, stating to Steed: 'Our people at home will certainly not stand for the recognition of the Bolshevists at the bidding of Wall Street'. Steed was again seen by House, who stated that Steed's article in the Paris *Daily Mail*, 'had got under the President's hide'. House asked that Steed postpone further exposés in the press, and again raised the prospect of recognition based on humanitarian aid. Lloyd George was also greatly perturbed by Steed's articles in the *Daily Mail* and complained that he could not undertake a 'sensible' policy towards the Bolsheviks while the press adopts an anti-Bolshevik position. [66]

As mentioned, House attempted to persuade Wickham Steed on the idea of relations with Bolshevik Russia ostensibly for the purpose of humanitarian aid for the Russian people. This is the type of activity that had already been undertaken just after the Bolshevik Revolution. Col. William Boyce Thompson, a director of the New York Federal Reserve Bank, organised the American Red Cross Mission to Russia, funded mainly by Thompson, and by International Harvester, which gave $200,000. According to Thompson's assistant, Cornelius

---

64 Henry Wickham Steed, 'Peace with Honour', Paris *Daily Mail*, 28 March 1922; quoted in Steed (1924).

65 Crane was a member of a 1917 Special Diplomatic Mission to Russia, and a member of the American Section of the Paris Peace Conference in 1919.

66 Steed, 1924, op.cit.

Kelleher, the mission was 'nothing but a mask' for business interests.[67] Of the 24 members, five were doctors and there were two medical researchers. The rest were lawyers and businessmen associated with Wall Street. Dr. Billings nominally headed the mission.[68] Professor Antony Sutton of the Hoover Institute stated that the mission provided aid for the assistance of the revolutionaries:

> We know from the files of the U.S. embassy in Petrograd that the U.S. Red Cross gave 4,000 roubles to Prince Lvoff, president of the Council of Ministers, for 'relief of revolutionists' and 10,000 roubles in two payments to Kerensky for 'relief of political refugees'.[69]

The original intention of the Red Cross Mission, hastily organised by Thompson in light of revolutionary events, was 'nothing less than to shore up the Provisional regime', according to the historian William Harlane Hale, formerly of the United States Foreign Service.[70]

Thompson set himself up in royal manner in Petrograd reporting directly to Wilson and bypassing U.S. Ambassador Francis. Thompson provided funds from his own money, first to the Social Revolutionaries, to whom he gave one million roubles,[71] and shortly after $1,000,000 to the Bolsheviks to spread their propaganda to Germany and Austria.[72] Thompson met Thomas Lamont of J.P. Morgan Co. in London to persuade the British War Cabinet to drop its anti-Bolshevik policy. On his return to the USA Thompson undertook a tour pleading for U.S. recognition of the Bolsheviks.[73] Thompson's deputy, Raymond Robbins, had been pressing for recognition of the Bolsheviks. Thompson agreed that the Kerensky regime was doomed and consequently 'sped to Washington to try and swing the Administration onto a new policy track', meeting resistance

67   Antony Sutton, *Wall Street and the Bolshevik Revolution* (New York: Arlington House Publishers, 1974), 71.

68   Ibid., 75.

69   Ibid., 73.

70   William Harlan Hale, "When the Red Storm Broke," *America and Russia: A century and a half of dramatic encounters*, ed. Oliver Jensen, (New York: Simon and Schuster, 1962) 150.

71   Ibid., 151.

72   'Gives Bolsheviki a Million', *Washington Post*, 2 February 1918, cited by Sutton, ibid., pp. 82-83.

73   Sutton, ibid., p. 8.

from Wilson, who was being pressured by Ambassador Francis.[74]

The 'Bolshevik of Wall Street'

Such was Thompson's enthusiasm for Bolshevism that he was jocularly nicknamed 'the Bolshevik of Wall Street' by others on Wall Street. Thompson gave a lengthy interview with *The New York Times* just after his four month tour with the American Red Cross Mission, lauding the Bolsheviks and assuring the American public that the Bolsheviks were not about to make a separate peace with Germany.[75] The article is an interesting indication of how Wall Street viewed their supposedly 'deadly enemies', the Bolsheviks at the time the Soviets were still far from secure. Thompson stated that while the 'reactionaries' if they assumed power might seek peace with Germany, the Bolsheviki would not. 'His opinion is that Russia needs America, that America must stand by Russia', states the *Times*. Thompson is quoted: 'The Bolshevik peace aims are the same as those of the Untied States'. Thompson alluded to President Wilson's speech to the United States Congress on Russia as 'a wonderful meeting of the situation', but that the American public 'know very little about the Bolshevik'. *The Times* states:

> Colonel Thompson is a banker and a capitalist, and he has large manufacturing interests. He is not a sentimentalist nor a 'radical'. But he has come back from his official visit to Russia in absolute sympathy with the Russian democracy as represented by the Bolsheviks at present.

While Thompson did not consider Bolshevism the final form of government, he did see it as the most promising step towards a 'representative government' and that it was the 'duty' of the USA to 'sympathise' with and 'aid' Russia 'through her days of crisis'. He stated that in reply to surprise at his pro-Bolshevik sentiments he did not mind being called 'red' if that meant sympathy for 17,000,000 people 'struggling for liberty and fair living'. Thompson also saw that while the Bolsheviki had entered a 'truce' with Germany, they were also agitating Bolshevism among the German people, which Thompson called 'their ideals of freedom' and their 'propaganda of democracy'. Thompson lauded the Bolshevik Government as being the equivalent

---

74   William Harlan Hale, op. cit., 151.

75   Trotsky while still in the USA had made similar claims. 'People War Weary. But Leo Trotsky Says They Do Not Want Separate Peace', *The New York Times*, March 16, 1917.

to America's democracy, stating:

> The present government in Russia is a government of workingmen. It is a Government by the majority, and, because our Government is a government of the majority, I don't see how it can fail to support the Government of Russia.[76]

Thompson saw the prospects of the Bolshevik Government being transformed as it incorporated a more Centrist position and included employers. If Bolshevism did not proceed thus, then 'God help the world', warned Thompson. The *Times* article ends: 'At home in New York, the Colonel has received the good-natured title of "the Bolshevik of Wall Street"'.[77] It was against this background that it can now be understood why Samuel Gompers denounced Bolshevism as a tool of 'predatory international finance', while Thompson lauded it as 'a government of working men' with the same peacetime ideals as the USA. The pro-Bolshevik efforts of both William B. Thompson and his deputy Raymond Robins were favourably noticed by General William V. Judson of the U.S. Army, who recommended both for the Distinguished Service Medal 'for their effective work with Bolshevism'.[78]

CFR Report

The Council on Foreign Relations (CFR) had been established in 1921 by President Wilson's chief adviser Edward Mandel House out of a previous think tank called The Inquiry, formed in 1917-1918 to advise President Wilson on the Paris Peace Conference of 1919. It was this conference about which Wickham Steed had detailed his observations when he stated that there were financial interests trying to secure the recognition of the Bolsheviks.[79]

Peter Grosse in the semi-official history of the CFR writes of this enduring globalist think tank that, 'It began with ... high-ranking officers of banking, manufacturing, trading and finance companies, together with many lawyers. Its purpose was to convene dinner meetings, to make contact with distinguished foreign visitors under

---

76 Ibid.

77 'Bolsheviki Will Not Make Separate Peace: Only Those Who Made Up Privileged Classes Under Czar Would Do So, Says Col. W B Thompson, Just Back From Red Cross Mission', *The New York Times*, 27 January 1918.

78 U.S. Adjutant General's Office A.G. 095 Thompson Wm b 6/18/19. Cited by Sutton, National Suicide, Ibid., 76.

79 Robert S. Rifkind, 'The Wasted Mission,' America and Russia, op. cit., 180.

conditions congenial to future commerce'.[80] Hence, the CFR's report on Soviet Russia at an early stage indicates the relationship that influential sections of big business wished to pursue in regard to the Bolshevik regime. Grosse writes of this period:

> Awkward in the records of The Inquiry had been the absence of a single study or background paper on the subject of Bolshevism. Perhaps this was simply beyond the academic imagination of the times. Not until early 1923 could the Council summon the expertise to mobilize a systematic examination of the Bolshevik regime, finally entrenched after civil war in Russia. The impetus for this first study was Lenin's New Economic Policy, which appeared to open the struggling Bolshevik economy to foreign investment. Half the Council's study group were members drawn from firms that had done business in pre-revolutionary Russia, and the discussions about the Soviet future were intense. The concluding report dismissed 'hysterical' fears that the revolution would spill outside Russia's borders into central Europe or, worse, that the heady new revolutionaries would ally with nationalistic Muslims in the Middle East to evict European imperialism. The Bolsheviks were on their way to 'sanity and sound business practices', the Council study group concluded, but the welcome to foreign concessionaires would likely be short-lived. Thus, the Council experts recommended in March 1923 that American businessmen get into Russia while Lenin's invitation held good, make money on their investments, and then get out as quickly as possible. A few heeded the advice; not for seven decades would a similar opportunity arise.[81]

This is not to say that certain corporations had not already, at the earliest stages of the Bolshevik regime, sought concessions with the new government.

H. G. Wells observed first-hand a certain accord between Communism and big business when he had visited Bolshevik Russia. Travelling to Russia in 1920 where he interviewed Bolshevik luminaries including Lenin, Wells hoped that the Western Powers and in particular the USA would come to the Soviets' aid. Wells also met there a 'Mr. Vanderlip' who was in the Soviet Union to try and negotiate business

---

80   Peter Grosse, *Continuing The Inquiry: The Council on Foreign Relations from 1921 to 1996*, (New York: Council on Foreign Relations, 2006); online: Council on Foreign Relations: http://www.cfr.org/about/history/cfr/index.html

81   Ibid. Chapter: 'Basic Assumptions'.

contracts with the Bolshevik Government. Wells commented of the situation he would like to see developing, and as a self-described 'collectivist' (Fabian Socialist) made a telling observation on the relationship between Communism and 'Big Business':

> The only Power capable of playing this role of eleventh-hour helper to Russia single-handed is the United States of America. That is why I find the adventure of the enterprising and imaginative Mr. Vanderlip very significant. I doubt the conclusiveness of his negotiations; they are probably only the opening phase of a discussion of the Russian problem upon a new basis that may lead it at last to a comprehensive world treatment of this situation. Other Powers than the United States will, in the present phase of world-exhaustion, need to combine before they can be of any effective use to Russia. Big business is by no means antipathetic to Communism. The larger big business grows the more it approximates to Collectivism. It is the upper road of the few instead of the lower road of the masses to Collectivism.[82]

In addressing concerns that were being expressed among Bolshevik Party 'activists' at a meeting of the Moscow Organisation of the party, Lenin sought to reassure them that the Government was not selling out to foreign capitalism, but that, in view of what Lenin believed to be an inevitable war between the USA and Japan, a U.S. interest in Kamchatka would be favourable to Soviet Russia. Lenin said of Vanderlip:

> We must take advantage of the situation that has arisen. That is the whole purpose of the Kamchatka concessions. We have had a visit from Vanderlip, a distant relative of the well-known multimillionaire, if he is to he believed; but since our intelligence service in the Choke, although splendidly organised, unfortunately does not yet extend to the United States of America, we have not yet established the exact kinship of these Vanderlips. Some even say there is no kinship at all. I do not presume to judge: my knowledge is confined to having read a book by Vanderlip, not the one that was in our country and is said to be such a very important person that he has been

---

82   H. G. Wells, *Russia in the Shadows*, Chapter VII, 'The Envoy'. Wells went to Russia in September 1920 at the invitation of Kamenev, of the Russian Trade Delegation in London, one of the leaders of the Bolshevik regime. *Russia in the Shadows* appeared as a series of articles in *The Sunday Express*. The book can be read online at: *gutenberg.net. au/ebooks06/0602371h.html*

received with all the honours by kings and ministers—from which one must infer that his pocket is very well lined indeed. He spoke to them in the way people discuss matters at meetings such as ours, for instance, and told then in the calmest tones how Europe should be restored. If ministers spoke to him with so much respect, it must mean that Vanderlip is in touch with the multimillionaires.[83]

Of the meeting with Vanderlip, Lenin indicated that it was based on a secret diplomacy that was being denied by the U.S. Administration, while Vanderlip himself returned to the USA – like sundry other capitalists before him – praising Lenin:

...I expressed the hope that friendly relations between the two states would be a basis not only for the granting of a concession, but also for the normal development of reciprocal economic assistance. It all went off in that kind of vein. Then telegrams came telling what Vanderlip had said on arriving home from abroad. Vanderlip had compared Lenin with Washington and Lincoln. Vanderlip had asked for my autographed portrait. I had declined, because when you present a portrait you write, 'To Comrade So-and-so', and I could not write, 'To Comrade Vanderlip'. Neither was it possible to write: 'To the Vanderlip we are signing a concession with' because that concession agreement would be concluded by the Administration when it took office. I did not know what to write. It would have been illogical to give my photograph to an out-and-out imperialist. Yet these were the kind of telegrams that arrived; this affair has clearly played a certain part in imperialist politics. When the news of the Vanderlip concessions came out, Harding—the man who has been elected President, but who will take office only next March issued an official denial, declaring that he knew nothing about it, had no dealings with the Bolsheviks and had heard nothing about any concessions. That was during the elections, and, for all we know, to confess, during elections, that you have dealings with the Bolsheviks may cost you votes. That was why he issued an official denial. He had this report sent to all the newspapers that are hostile to the Bolsheviks and are on the pay roll of the imperialist parties...[84]

---

83   V. I. Lenin, December 6, 1920, *Collected Works*, 4th English Edition (Moscow: Progress Publishers, 1965), Volume 31, 438-459 http://www.marxists.org/archive/lenin/works/1920/dec/06.htm

84   Ibid.

This mysterious Vanderlip was in fact Washington Vanderlip who had, according to Armand Hammer, come to Russia in 1919, although even Hammer does not seem to have known much of the matter.[85] Washington Vanderlip was an engineer whose negotiations with Russia drew considerable attention in the USA. *The New York Times* wrote that Vanderlip speaking from Russia denied that reports of Lenin's speech to 'Moscow activists' regarding the concessions as serving Bolshevik geopolitical interests were untrue, with Vanderlip declaring that he had established a common frontier between the USA and Russia and that trade relations must be immediately restored.[86] *The New York Times* reporting in 1922: 'The exploration of Kamchatka for oil as soon as trade relations between this country and Russia are established was assured today when the Standard Oil Company of California purchased one-quarter of the stock in the Vanderlip syndicate'. This gave Standard Oil exclusive leases on any syndicate lands on which oil was found. The Vanderlip syndicate was comprised of sixty-four units. Sixteen were owned by Los Angeles capitalists. The Standard Oil Company had purchased sixteen units. However, the Vanderlip concessions could not come into effect until Soviet Russia was recognised by the USA.[87]

> The Vanderlip syndicate holds concessions for the exploitation of coal, oil and timber lands, fisheries, etc., east of the 160th parallel in Kamchatka. The Russian Government granted the syndicate alternate sections of land there and will draw royalties amounting to approximately 5 per cent. on all products developed and marketed by the syndicate.[88]

Ruskombank

In 1922 Soviet Russia's first international bank was created, Ruskombank, headed by Olof Aschberg. The predominant capital represented in the bank was British. The foreign director of Ruskombank was Max May, vice president of the Guaranty Trust Company,[89] a J. P. Morgan interest.

---

85   Armand Hammer, *Witness to History* (Reading, England: Hodder and Stoughton, 1988), 151-152.

86   'Vanderlip's Empire', *The New York Times*, December 1, 1920, 14.

87   'Standard Oil Joins Vanderlip Project', *The New York Times*, January 11, 1922, 1.

88   Ibid.

89   Antony Sutton, *Wall Street and the Bolshevik Revolution* (New York: Arlington House Publishers, 1974), 62-63.

Guaranty Trust Company became intimately involved with Soviet economic transactions. A *Scotland Yard Intelligence Report* stated as early as 1919 the connection between Guaranty Trust and Ludwig C. A. K. Martens, head of the Soviet Bureau in New York when the bureau was established in that year.[90] When the Soviet Bureau offices were raided on May 7, 1919 by representatives of the Lusk Committee investigating Bolshevik activities in the USA, files of communications with almost a thousand firms were found. Basil H. Thompson of Scotland Yard stated in the special report that, despite denials, there was evidence in the seized files that the Soviet Bureau was being funded by Guaranty Trust Company.[91]

Guaranty Trust along with other firms including Standard Oil and Kuhn, Loeb, established the Amercian International Corporation (AIC), represented in Russia at the time of the revolutionary tumult by its executive secretary, William Franklin Sands. Sands was asked by U.S. Secretary of State Robert Lansing for a report on the situation and what the U.S. response should be. Sands' attitude toward the Bolsheviks was enthusiastic. He wrote a memorandum to Lansing in January 1918, at a time when the Bolshevik hold was still far from sure, that there had already been too much of a delay by the USA in recognising the Bolshevik regime. The USA had to make up for 'lost time'. Like William B. Thompson, Sands compared the Bolshevik Revolution with the American.[92] In July 1918 Sands wrote to U.S. Treasury Secretary McAdoo that a commission should be established by private interests with government backing, for 'economic assistance to Russia'.[93]

Hammer – First Concessionaire

One of those closely associated with Ludwig Martens and the Soviet Bureau was Dr. Julius Hammer, an emigrant from Russia who was a founder of the Communist Party USA. There is evidence that Julius Hammer was the host to Leon Trotsky when the latter with his family arrived in New York in 1917, and that it was Dr. Hammer's chauffeured car that provided transport to the Trotsky family. The Trotsky's were met on disembarkation at the New York dock by Arthur Concors, a

---

90 'Scotland Yard Intelligence Report', London 1919, US State Dept. Decimal File, 316-22-656, cited by Sutton ibid., 113.

91 Basil H. Thompson, British Home Office Directorate of Intelligence, 'Special Report No. 5 (Secret)', Scotland Yard, London, July 14, 1919; cited by Sutton, ibid., 115.

92 Sands memorandum to Lansing, p. 9; cited by Sutton, ibid., 132, 134.

93 Sutton, ibid., 135.

director of the Hebrew Sheltering and Immigrant Aid Society, whose advisory board included Jacob Schiff of Kuhn, Loeb and Co.[94] Dr. Hammer was the 'primary owner of Allied Drug and Chemical Co.', and 'one of those not so rare creatures, a radical Marxist cum wealthy entrepreneur', who lived an opulent lifestyle, according to Professor Spence.[95]

The intimate association of the Hammer family with Soviet Russia was to be maintained from start to finish, with an interlude of withdrawal during the Stalinist period. Julius' son Armand, chairman of Occidental Petroleum Corporation, was the first foreigner to obtain commercial concessions from the Soviet Government. Armand was in Russia in 1921 to arrange for the reintroduction of capitalism according to the new economic course set by Lenin, the New Economic Policy. Lenin stated to Armand Hammer that the economies of Russia and the USA were complementary, and in exchange for the exploitation of Russia's raw materials he hoped for America's technology.[96] This was precisely the attitude of significant business interests in the West. Lenin stated to Hammer that it was hoped the New Economic Policy would accelerate the economic process 'by a system of industrial and commercial concessions to foreigners. It will give great opportunities to the United States'.[97] As shown in the preceding chapter, this course was stymied by Stalin in 1925. Armand Hammer met Trotsky, who asked him whether 'financial circles' in the USA regard Russia as a desirable field of investment? Trotsky continued:

> Inasmuch as Russia had its Revolution, capital was really safer there than anywhere else because, whatever should happen abroad, the Soviet would adhere to any agreements it might make. Suppose one of your Americans invests money in Russia. When the Revolution comes to America, his property will of course be nationalised, but his agreement with us will hold good and he will thus be in a much more favourable position than the rest of his fellow capitalists.[98]

---

94   Richard B. Spence, 'Hidden Agendas: Spies, Lies and Intrigue Surrounding Trotsky's American Visit, January-April 1917', Revolutionary Russia, Vol. 21, #1 (2008).

95   Ibid.

96   Armand Hammer, *Witness to History* (Reading, England: Hodder and Stoughton, 1988) 143.

97   Ibid.

98   Ibid., 160.

Hammer related of his experiences in the young Soviet state that although lengthy negotiations had to be undertaken with each of the trades unions involved in an enterprise, 'the great power and influence of the trade unions was not without its advantages to the employer of labor in Russia. Once the employer had signed a collective agreement with the union branch there was little risk of strikes or similar trouble'.

Breaches of the codes as negotiated could result in dismissal, with recourse by the sacked worker to a labour court which, in Hammer's experience, did not generally find in the worker's favour, and which would mean that there would be little chance of the sacked worker getting another job.[99]

As the Council on Foreign Relations report of 1923 had warned, however, matters favourable to foreign capital might not last indefinitely. Under Stalinism Russia did not develop as individuals such as William Boyce Thompson had hoped. As for Hammer, the veteran concessionaire, despite his greatly expanding and diverse businesses in the Soviet Union, after Stalin assumed power Hammer packed up and left, not returning until Stalin's demise. Hammer opined decades later:

> I never met Stalin – I never had any desire to do so – and I never had any dealings with him. However it was perfectly clear to me in 1930 that Stalin was not a man with whom you could do business. Stalin believed that the state was capable of running everything without the support of foreign concessionaires and private enterprise. That is the main reason I left Moscow. I could see that I would soon be unable to do business there and, since business was my sole reason to be there, my time was up.[100]

Foreign capital did nonetheless continue to do business with the USSR[101] as best as it was able, but the promising start that some capitalists saw in the March and November revolutions for a new Russia that would replace the antiquated Czarist system with a modern economy from which they could reap the rewards was, as the 1923 CFR report warned, short-lived. Gorbachev and Yeltsin provided a brief interregnum of hope for foreign capital, to be disappointed again with the rise of Putin. The policy of continuing economic relations with

---

99   Ibid., 217.

100   Ibid., 221.

101   Charles Levinson, *Vodka-Cola* (West Sussex: Biblias, 1980). Sutton, *National Suicide: Military Aid to the Soviet Union* (New York: Arlington House, 1973).

the USSR even during the era of the Cold War was promoted as a strategy in the immediate aftermath of World War II when a CFR report by George S. Franklin recommended attempting to work with the USSR as much as possible, 'unless and until it becomes entirely evident that the U.S.S.R. is not interested in achieving cooperation...'

> The United States must be powerful not only politically and economically, but also militarily. We cannot afford to dissipate our military strength unless Russia is willing concurrently to decrease hers. On this we lay great emphasis.

> We must take every opportunity to work with the Soviets now, when their power is still far inferior to ours, and hope that we can establish our cooperation on a firmer basis for the not so distant future when they will have completed their reconstruction and greatly increased their strength.... The policy we advocate is one of firmness coupled with moderation and patience.[102]

Since Putin, the CFR again sees Russia as having taken a 'wrong direction'. The current recommendation is for 'selective cooperation' rather than 'partnership, which is not now feasible'.[103]

---

102 Peter Grosse, op.cit., 'The First Transformation', <http://www.cfr.org/about/history/cfr/first_transformation.html>

103 Jack Kemp, et al, Russia's Wrong Direction: What the United States Can and Should do, Independent Task Force Report no. 57 (New York: Council on Foreign Relations, 2006) xi. The publication can be downloaded at: http://www.cfr.org/publication/9997/

How America Helped to Bolshevise Russia

One of the primary elements in the analysis of 20th century history has been the assumption of an almost Zoroastrian 'tremendous dichotomy'[1] of 'good versus evil' manifested in the conflict between the 'Free World' and communism. Hence, the eminent Russian expert for the US State Department, George F. Kennan, writes in his seminal book on the Allied intervention in Russia during the Civil War that:

> there are those today who see the winter of 1917–1918 as one of the great turning points of modern history, the point at which there separated and branched out, clearly and for all to see, the two great conflicting answers — totalitarian and liberal — to the emerging problems of the modern age...[2]

However this epochal event, 'clearly and for all to see', is largely a myth. The assumption that the 'Cold War' was the continuation of a conflict between capitalism and communism that had been going on since the October 1917 Revolution does not take into account the new situation that was presented when Stalin declined to continue his wartime alliance with the USA and support American plans for a new world order which hinged on (1) The United Nations Organisation General Assembly functioning as a 'world parliament'[3] and (2) the 'Baruch Plan' for the internationalization of atomic energy.[4] The USSR was to perceive both these twin pillars of post-war US global policy as a

---

1   George F. Kennan, *The Decision to Intervene* (New Jersey: Princeton University Press, 1958), 13.

2   Ibid., p. 13.

3   Andrei Gromyko, Soviet Foreign Minister, recalled: 'The US position in fact allowed the UN to be turned into an instrument for imposing the will of one group of states upon another, above all the Soviet Union as the sole socialist member of the [Security] Council'. Andrei Gromyko, *Memories* (London: Hutchinson, 1989).

4   Gromyko stated of the 'Baruch Plan': 'The actual intention was to be camouflaged by the creation of an international body to monitor the use of nuclear energy. However, Washington did not even try to hide that it intended to take the leading part in this body, to keep in its own hands everything to do with the production and storage of fissionable material and, under the guise of the need for international inspection, to interfere in the internal affairs of the sovereign nations'. Gromyko, *Memories, Ibid.*

guise for American global hegemony.[5] Hence, the perception that the "Cold War" was a continuation of Allied policy since the 1917–1920 intervention in Russia is incorrect, and rests on the assumption that the intervention was motivated by anti-Bolshevism, which it was not.

Not only was Cold War American foreign policy *not* 'anti-communist', but it proactively supported *certain types* of Leftism that could be utilized in its fight against what might more accurately be regarded as *Russian national-collectivism*,[6] starting from the assumption to power of Stalin and ending with the assumption to power of Gorbachev.[7]

The purpose of Allied intervention in the Civil War was not to defeat Bolshevism, but to maintain Allied interests at a time when the Great War was still being fought and when the Bolshevists seemed to be inclined towards a separate peace with Germany. Nor did this Allied intervention, once Russia had been taken out of the war, and America had entered, transform at any stage into a determined effort by capitalism to destroy the very precarious Bolshevik regime.

Yet the myth of Allied anti-Bolshevism remains a subject of much study. For example David S. Foglesong, having alluded to American President Woodrow Wilson's penchant for secrecy and the lie, states of American intervention:

> From the Bolshevik Revolution to the end of the Civil War the United States sought to encourage and support anti-Bolshevik movements in a variety of secretive and semi-secret ways. Constrained by a declared commitment to the principal of self-determination and hemmed by idealistic and later isolationist

---

5   K. R. Bolton, "Origins of the Cold War' in *Stalin: The Enduring Legacy* (London: Black House Publishing, 2012), 125-139.

6   The epochal fight between Stalin and Trotsky over the question of who would rule Soviet Russia was ideologically that of 'socialism in one country' versus 'world revolution', respectively.

7   The manner by which the USA sought to recruit anti-Stalinist Leftists, including of course Trotskyites, is exemplified by the Congress for Cultural Freedom, sponsored by the CIA, which launched the careers of such anti-Soviet, pro-Marxist luminaries as the feminist guru Gloria Steinem. See: Frances Stonor Saunders, The Cultural Cold War: the CIA and the World of Arts and Letters (New York, The New Press, 2000). The subversive role of the Congress for Cultural Freedom has now been taken over by the National Endowment for Democracy, another institution with US official backing, which also has a noticeable Trotskyite foundation. See for example on the founder of the NED, Tom Kahn: Rachelle Horowitz, "Tom Kahn and the Fight for Democracy: A Political Portrait and Personal Recollection", *Dissent Magazine*, pp. 238-239. <http://www.dissentmagazine.org/democratiya/article_pdfs/d11Horowitz.pdf>

sentiments, Wilson and his advisors pursued methods of assisting anti-Bolshevik forces that evaded public scrutiny and avoided the need for congressional appropriations.[8]

While maintaining diplomatic relations with the representative in the USA of the deposed Provisional Government, Foglesong states that Wilson's policy was one of covertly providing funds and other support to anti-Bolshevik forces, particularly in Siberia, where Wilson sanctioned American troops in 1918. Foglesong describes this as an 'undeclared war against Bolshevism' which continued even after the defeat of the remaining White armies in Russia in 1920.[9] However, Foglesong also alludes to the manner by which the US intervention embittered anti-Bolsheviks who considered it to be inadequate meddling and 'irresolute'.[10]

Foglesong quotes Ludwig Martens, who was representing Bolshevik interests in the USA, as publicly condemning the U.S. intervention against the Soviets as tantamount to 'waging war against the Russian people'.[11] Yet that does not explain the situation. As we have seen previously, Martens had set up the Soviet Bureau at the World Tower Building in New York in 1919, and had successfully engaged in extensive deals with American firms. A British intelligence report noted that the, Guaranty Trust Company of New York was funding Martens.[12]

Foglesong states that despite the U.S. involvement in the Allied intervention, the Soviet regime considered the USA to be the most likely source from which to secure diplomatic and commercial relations.[13] Given the duplicitous nature of President Wilson, mentioned by Foglesong as being at the back of a covert anti-Bolshevik policy, placed in the context of other aspects of the US involvement in Russia, the assumption that Wilson was intent on a secret anti-Bolshevik policy might not be so convincing.

---

8   David S. Foglesong, *America's Secret War Against Bolshevism: US Intervention in the Russian Civil War,* (University of North Carolina Press, 1995), 5.

9   Ibid.

10   Ibid., 6.

11   Ibid.

12   Basil H. Thompson, Special Report No. 5 (Secret), British Home Office Directorate of Intelligence, Scotland Yard, London July 14, 1919; US State Dept. Decimal File, 316-22-656.

13   Foglesong, op. cit., 6.

Reasons for Allied Intervention

The reasons for Allied intervention had nothing to do with 'stopping Bolshevism.' The original concerns involved Russia in the war against Germany. Kennan states that when the Americans sent their first representative to Archangel in 1917, 'At the time of the Bolshevik seizure of power in Petrograd the allies were interested in Archangel not only for its importance as a channel of entrance and egress for European Russia but that also for the fact that here too, as at Vladivostok, war supplies shipped to former Russian governments had accumulated in large quantities'.[14] This material included 2,000 tons of aluminium, 2,100 tons of antimony, 14,000 tons of copper, 5,230 tons of lead, etc.[15] With the possibility of Russia concluding an armistice with Germany the Allies were anxious to recover the stocks. The Bolsheviks dispatched a commission to the region to secure Archangel and deliver the war materials to the interior.[16] Despite the arrival of two British ships, the British sat by for several months while the Bolsheviks removed the war materials.[17]

The second factor was to ensure the safety of Czech soldiers who had been prisoners-of-war in Russia and wished to fight Germany with the aim of securing a sovereign Czech nation in the post-war world. Their release was sanctioned by the Bolshevik regime and the Americans and Japanese were responsible for their transport by rail to Vladivostok. They were to become a major catalyst in the eruption of the Civil War as they fell afoul firstly of the Soviets, and finally with the White Russian leader Admiral Kolchak, ending with the giving over of Kolchak to the Soviets by his Czech "protectors." General William S. Graves, commander of the American Expeditionary Force in Siberia, explained:

> It should be remembered that the main reason advanced by those interested in military intervention in Siberia, was the immediate and urgent need for protection of the Czechs who were supposed to be trying to get through Siberia to Vladivostok and then to the Western front where they could join the Allies.[18]

---

14   Kennan, *The Decision to Intervene*, op. cit., 17.

15   'Memorandum regarding allied war stores lying at Archangel', US National Archives, Foreign Affairs Branch, Petrograd Embassy, 800 File; March 20, 1918.

16   Kennan, *The Decision to Intervene*, op. cit., 20.

17   Ibid., 21.

18   William S Graves, *America's Siberian Adventure 1918–1920* (New York: Peter Smith,

The position of the Bolsheviks in regard to Germany was at the time by no means clear, as indicated by the release of the anti-German Czech soldiers. Robert Service states that 'most Bolshevik leaders... thought that a separate peace with the Central Powers was an insufferable concession to capitalist imperialism'.[19] The Bolsheviks were amenable to dealings with the Allies if there were assurances of help in the event of a German invasion. Despite Lenin's directions, Trotsky as People's Commissar for Foreign Affairs, had instead of signing a peace treaty at Brest-Litovsk, called for a revolution against Germany, and with Trotsky's intransigence the armistice broke, with the Germans launching another offensive on the Eastern Front, where they now fought the unprepared Red Army. This caused a sense of 'solidarity' between the Soviets and the Allied representatives.[20] The British, via War Cabinet special agent R. H. Bruce Lockhart, sought out Trotsky on the instructions of Lloyd George. So close were Lockhart and Trotsky to become that Lockhart's wife commented that he was getting the reputation as a 'Red' among his colleagues in Britain.

Trotsky's parting words to Lockhart at their first meeting at the Smolny were: 'Now is the big opportunity for the Allied Governments'. Thereafter Lockhart saw Trotsky on a daily basis.[21] Lockhart stated that Trotsky was willing to bring Soviet Russia over to Britain:

He considered that war was inevitable. If the Allies would send a promise of support, he informed me that he would sway the decision of the Government in favour of war. I sent several telegrams to London requesting an official message that would enable me to strengthen Trotsky's hands. No message was sent.[22]

With unwarranted fears of a German and possibly Finnish anti-Bolshevik attack on Murmansk, the Murmansk Soviet telegraphed the Petrograd Soviet that they were preparing for the defence of Murmansk and the railway, describing the attitude of the missions of

1941), 'Aid to the Czechs'.

19 Robert Service, *Trotsky: A Biography* (Oxford: Pan Books, 2009), 210.

20 Kennan, *The Decision to Intervene*, op. cit., 35.

21 R. H. Bruce Lockhart, *British Agent* (London: G. P. Putnam's Sons, 1933), Book Four, 'History From the Inside', Chapter 3.

22 Ibid. The failure of Britain to respond, despite Lloyd George's eagerness to deal with the Soviet regime, would indicate the dichotomy that exited within the Allied Governments regarding how the Soviets should be dealt with; particularly with the intransigent anti-Bolshevik position of Winston Churchill.

the 'friendly powers', the French, British and Americans, as 'inalterably well inclined towards us', and prepared to provide any wherewithal, from food to weapons.[23] Believing that negotiations for a peace treaty between Germany and Russia at Brest-Litovsk had broken down and that there would be an impending German advance on Petrograd, Trotsky's response was to state to the Murmansk Soviet that, 'You must accept any and all assistance from the Allied missions', and use any means to obstruct the German advance.[24]

Believing in a German attack the Allied missions formulated a program that included the recognition of the Soviet as the supreme political authority in Murmansk, and the creation of a military council comprising one representative each from the French, British and Soviets.[25] On this basis, Allied forces landed in Murmansk to support the Soviets. Kennan notes that this was probably the first Allied landing of forces on Russian territory, and it was undertaken at the invitation of the local Soviet authorities.[26] American military involvement in Murmansk proceeded on the basis of being suspicious of British interests,[27] not in opposition to Bolshevism.

In Vladivostok the Allied war supplies were four times the amount as that stored at Archangel.[28] In March 1918 Admiral Austin M. Knight, Commander-in-Chief of the Asiatic Fleet, landed in Vladivostok and reported to Washington that there was no danger of the Bolsheviks delivering the stores to the Germans.[29]

The Allies continued to hope for a Soviet pro-Allied response, and the acceptance of an Allied military presence in Russia. In April 1918 the Allied military attachés issued a declaration stating that Japan with the support of the other Allies should intervene in Russia to block Germany, but that this could only be undertaken with the support of the Bolsheviks. Allied contacts with Trotsky indicated

---

23 Kennan, *The Decision to Intervene*, op. cit., 45.

24 Trotsky to the Murmansk Soviet, March 1, 1918; cited by Kennan, *The Decision to Intervene*, Ibid., p. 31.

25 Kennan, Ibid., 49.

26 Ibid., 52.

27 Ibid., 55.

28 Ibid., 61.

29 Ibid., 61.

that the Commissar for Military Affairs[30] would be amenable to Japanese intervention. There should also be Allied assistance in the reorganization of the Red Army.[31]

Reasons for Allied Contact with White Armies

The threat of Admiral A. V. Kolchak to accept assistance from the Germans, despite his pro-British inclinations, if the Allies would not help him in his battle against the Soviet regime, accounts for Allied aid to the Whites rather than an anti-Bolshevik aim, but Wilson continued to resist intervention, despite British and French concern. [32]

Hope still rested on Bolshevik requests for assistance from the Allies, which would eliminate any reticence by Wilson, and Trotsky remained the focus of Allied lobbying, particularly by Bruce Lockhart.

Trotsky, as People's Commissar for Foreign Affairs, was by no means inclined towards Lenin's insistence that peace be sought at any price with Germany. Robert Service writes of this juncture: 'Diplomats and journalist of the great powers queued to interview [Trotsky] in his office in the Smolny Institute...'[33] While Trotsky's colleague Adolf Ioffe negotiated at Brest-Litovsk, Trotsky continued to cultivate contacts with the Allied Powers. Service comments that:

> Trotsky and Bruce Lockhart met regularly and got on splendidly. Trotsky also made overtures to the French and the Americans in Petrograd. He formed a warm relationship with French military attaché Jacques Sadoul; he even asked America's Red Cross leader, Colonel Raymond Robins, to use his good offices to get the US Railway Mission ... to give assistance to Sovnarkom.[34,35]

The relationship between Robins and Trotsky was cordial, as was that between Bruce Lockhart and Trotsky. Robins recalled 'winning Trotsky' to the Allied position. Trotsky stated to Robins that he was also anxious to keep war supplies out of the hands of the oncoming

---

30   Trotsky had resigned as Commissar for Foreign Affairs because of his opposition to the Brest-Litovsk Treaty and was persuaded to accept the post of Military Affairs.

31   Kennan, op. cit., 120.

32   Ibid., 345.

33   Service, Trotsky: A Biography, op. cit., 195.

34   Sovnarkom = Council of People's Commissars.

35   Service, Trotsky: A Biography, op. cit., 196.

Germans, and immediately worked out a plan with Robins to safeguard the stocks.[36] However, under the insistence of Lenin, the Soviets also continued to pursue peace negotiations with Germany, much to Trotsky's chagrin, which saw him soon resign as Commissar for Foreign Affairs. In the meantime, while he was obliged to deal with the Germans and Austrians, Trotsky appealed to Robins to, 'send your officers, American officers, Allied officers, any officers you please. I will give them full authority to enforce the embargo against goods into Germany all along our whole front.'[37]

General Judson, at the time one of the few men from American officialdom on the scene at Petrograd, agreed with Robins. This pro-Bolshevik attitude was at variance with US Ambassador Francis, who pursued his own policy of contacting the embryonic White Army.[38]

The Allied governments had prevaricated, however, not certain as to the trustworthiness of the Bolsheviks, particularly since the German General Staff had facilitated the return of Lenin and his entourage to Russia.[39] From the opposite belligerents in the Great War, there is reason to believe that the British might have similarly facilitated Trotsky's return to Russia from New York in the hope of serving their interests.[40] While in New York Trotsky had stated that although the Russian people were 'war-weary' and desired peace they would not make a separate peace with Germany and did not wish to see Germany win.[41] The fear that the Bolsheviks were actually German agents seemed to many to have been proven by a collection of documents by American diplomat Edgar Sisson which purported to show that the Bolsheviks were virtually tools of the German High Command.[42] However, while the Germans encouraged certain

---

36   William Harlan Hale, 'When the Red Storm Broke', Oliver Jensen (Ed.) *America and Russia: A Century and a Half of Dramatic Encounters* (New York: Simon & Schuster, 1962), 154.

37   Ibid., 155.

38   Ibid., 155–156.

39   Michael Pearson, *The Sealed Train: Journey to Revolution: Lenin – 1917* (London: Macmillan, 1975).

40   While en route from New York to Russia to 'complete the revolution', Trotsky was detained at Halifax, Nova Scotia, Canada, by the local British authorities who suspected him of being a German agent.

41   'Calls People War Weary. But Leo Trotsky Says They Do Not Want Separate Peace', *New York Times*, March 16. 1917.

42   Edgar Sisson, The German-Bolshevik Conspiracy: A Report by Edgar Sisson,

Russian revolutionaries, what is even less known is the role the chief of British intelligence operations in the USA, William Wiseman, played in cultivating revolutionists for a pro-Allied course. It is only in recent years that much light has been thrown on this and on the activities of Trotsky leading up to his return to Russia in 1917. Professor Spence, states that:

> It was the prospect of a Russian defection from the Allied cause, not revolution, that worried Wiseman and his superiors in London. Wiseman believed he could do something to prevent that occurrence. In the immediate wake of the [March] Revolution, he hatched a plan to mount a propaganda campaign from America aimed at influencing political currents in Russia. He hoped to counter German influence and "guide the storm" by supporting the more responsible elements", including those of the revolutionary left, perhaps especially those. In this he might have been guided by [Sidney] Reilly's belief that the political contest in Russia was among rival variants of socialism, not revolution vs. reaction.[43]

By mid-April Wiseman acknowledged contact with "anarchist revolutionary socialists" in New York and was encouraging them, with financial incentive, to write comrades in Russia and lobby against pacifist, defeatist tendencies. An overriding concern was that this support be kept secret; the British hand was not to be visible in any respect.

> Trotsky was anti-war, but was not a defeatist; not pro-ally, but neither pro-German, and he was opposed to the most immediate danger, a separate peace. This clearly separated him from the likes of Lenin who was indeed backed by the Germans. Given his strong influence in revolutionary circles, Trotsky would have been an ideal asset for Wiseman's scheme. If Wiseman did not try to recruit him, he certainly should have.[44]

Spence states that Wiseman in a report, 'Intelligence and Propaganda Work in Russia', alludes to 'one of our agents from America… a well-known international socialist… at once accepted into the Bolsheviks

---

Special Representative in Russia, War Information Series, No. 20, October 1918, (Washington: Committee on Public Information, 1918).

43   This is also an interesting comment in regard to Reilly, the so-called 'British Ace of Spies', usually simplistically portrayed as anti-Soviet.

44   Richard B. Spence, University of Idaho, 'Interrupted Journey: British Intelligence and the Arrest of Leon Trotsky April 1917', Revolutionary Russia, 13(1), June 2000.

circles and admitted to their conferences'. Spence suggests that this 'agent' could have been Trotsky.[45] The description seems to fit well. Spence also suggests the possibility that Trotsky's brief detention by the British authorities at Halifax could have served as a ruse to throw any suspicion from Trotsky's use by the British.

With the conclusion of the Treaty of Brest-Litovsk withdrawing Russia from the war against Germany, an added worry for the Allies was the freeing of 1,600,000 mostly Austrian prisoners-of-war in Russia, and particularly in Siberia. US Secretary of State Robert Lansing for the first time argued in favour of Allied — specifically Japanese — intervention, for the purpose, not of overthrowing Bolshevism but of ensuring Russian authority in Siberia.[46] However President Wilson did not yet think the time was right for such a policy. There were however already both American and Japanese ships anchored off Vladivostok. When the local Bolsheviks seized power in March 1918 the only concern of the Americans was the brief interruption in telegraphic services (which was soon restored).[47]

While the Treaty of Brest-Litovsk between Soviet Russia and the Central Powers was ratified by the Soviets in March 1918, with Trotsky in the event resigning his position as Commissar for Foreign Affairs,[48] the intentions of the Germans towards Russia were uncertain. The Bolsheviks continued to put out feelers towards the Allies. Robert Service writes:

> [Trotsky] continued to talk to representatives of the Western Allies and on 5 March, only a couple of days after the signing of the separate peace, he asked the Americans whether they would give assistance in the event that Sovnarkom chose to go to war against Germany. The Bolsheviks knew they could not fight unaided. Trotsky was eager to keep up such contact since he still believed the Brest-Litovsk treaty a mistake. He was willing to resume operations against the Germans. Allied diplomats and officers in Moscow understood this and very readily talked to him...[49]

---

45   Ibid.

46   Papers Relating to the Foreign Relations of the United States: The Lansing Papers 1914–1920 (Washington: US Government Printing Office, 1940), Vol. 2, 358.

47   Kennan, op. cit., 96.

48   Trotsky assumed the position of People's Commissar for Military Affairs.

49   Service, Trotsky: A Biography, op. cit., 218.

While the British had sent troops to Archangel to guard military supplies and the French had landed in Odessa, Trotsky utilized his contacts with Lockhart, Sadoul and Robins to seek Allied assistance in reorganizing the Red Army, which was in disarray. He employed Captain G. A. Hill of the British Special Intelligence Service to organize the air force. Robert Service points out that Trotsky did not mention anything of this in his memoirs.[50] The legend of a Bolshevik struggle against 'reactionaries' who were backed by the capitalist, imperialist powers, had to be maintained as one of the central myths of the Soviet regime.

In April 1918 British Foreign Secretary Arthur Balfour, on the basis of encouraging reports from Lockhart, suggested joint Allied intervention in co-operation with the Soviets.[51] Colonel William Wiseman of the British Secret Service was of the same opinion, cabling President Wilson's confidante 'Colonel' Edward House from London on May 1 1918 that the Allies should intervene at the invitation of the Bolsheviks and help organize the Red Army[52], which was already fighting anti-Soviet forces.

However, the Allies remained unsure of the reliability of Soviet attitudes, and were cautious about the possibility of alienating the many factions vying for control of Russia at a time when the Soviet sphere of authority was still small and precarious. In particular the Socialist Revolutionaries remained a major factor politically, and it is incorrect to perceive the anti-Soviet forces as representing capitalism or a return to Czarism. Also at the time Ataman Semenoff's anti-Bolshevik Cossacks were successfully pushing through Siberia, and it might transpire that this force would be the best option for blocking a German invasion.[53] Therefore, it was out of caution in regard to alienating factions and thereby serving Germany that Balfour favoured Allied intervention with Soviet support while refraining from recognizing the Bolshevik regime diplomatically.[54] US Secretary of State Lansing expressed concern that if the Allies sided with Reds or Whites "we would probably find ourselves in hot water."[55]

---

50   Ibid., 218.

51   Kennan, op. cit., 346.

52   Charles Seymour (ed.), The Intimate Papers of Colonel House (New York: Houghton, Mifflin Co.), Vol. III, 421.

53   Kennan, op. cit., 350.

54   Ibid., 348.

55   Ibid., 350.

On the other hand, there was a danger that if the Bolsheviks invited Allied intervention, the Germans would occupy Moscow and Petrograd and the Bolshevik regime would fall. This was the opinion expressed by Wiseman to Edward House.[56] The Allied presence in Murmansk and Archangel were now causes of concern for the Germans who raised the issue in the course of the Brest-Litovsk negotiations, although the actual Allied presence was insignificant.[57]

In early 1918 American munitions from Archangel were shipped to the Bolsheviks, Raymond Robins informing US Ambassador Francis:

> Munitions that are being evacuated from Archangel are sent to Moscow, the Urals and Siberian towns. Soviet government desires to take up the matter of payment for these munitions, and expects to pay for them in raw materials, but asks for time to reorganize the economic resources of the country.[58]

Civil War

The catalyst for the outbreak of hostilities involved a dispute between the Czechs and the Soviets. By agreement with the Allies, Trotsky had allowed the Czech prisoners-of-war to leave Russia and join the Allies fighting the Germans in France. *En route* along the Trans-Siberian railway an order came from Trotsky for the Czechs to hand over their weapons. The Czechs believed this to be of treacherous intent and a revolt broke out in May, the Czechs turning back into Russia and on reaching Samara on the River Volga offered their services to the Socialist-Revolutionary "Committee of Members of the Constituent Assembly", a rival Government formed on the basis that the Party of Socialist-Revolutionaries had won more seats to the Consequent Assembly than the Bolsheviks and were thus the legally elected Government of Russia. The battle-hardened Czechs defeated the Red Army and the entire Volga region came under the control of the Socialist-Revolutionaries. Russia was in disarray, with industrial strikes, peasant resistance, and opposition to the Bolsheviks ranging from anarchists and Socialist-Revolutionaries to liberals and Czarists. Additionally fighting soon broke out between the Bolsheviks and

---

56   Ibid., 348.

57   Ibid., 370.

58   Raymond Robins to Ambassador Francis, April 4, 1918. Cited by Sutton, National Suicide, op. cot., 76.

their partners, the Left Socialist-Revolutionaries.[59] The Bolshevik regime, which had not extended far beyond Petrograd and Moscow, was ripe for defeat.

After months of procrastination, American troops landed in Siberia and North Russia in July 1918, without advising the French and British who had been pushing for decisive action. Here Admiral A. V. Kolchak had formed a White Army.

Encouraged by Allied troop landings, an anti-Bolshevik *coup* in Archangel succeeded in driving out the Soviets. A small American force led by a lieutenant chased the Soviets for seventy-five miles south along the Archangel-Vologda railroad. However, it is important to realize that military engagement against the Bolsheviks contravened US policy, and such actions were undertaken by enthusiastic military men at the scene, in disregard for Wilson's directive of *not* engaging the Red Army.

General William S. Graves in Russia

In September General William S. Graves arrived in Vladivostok to take over command of the American Expeditionary Force in Siberia. Graves maintained an antagonistic attitude towards the White movement for the entirety of his service in Siberia. From the start Graves' attitude towards the White movement was one of contempt, the commander later sneeringly writing of the officers:

> At the time of my arrival in Vladivostok, when the Allied representatives spoke of Russians, they meant the old Czarist officials, who felt it was then safe enough for them to appear in their gorgeous uniforms every evening, and parade down Svetlanskaya, the principal thoroughfare.[60]

Kolchak had staged a *coup* against the governing 'Directorate' with the encouragement of British commander, General Knox. Graves saw this as nothing other than a revival of Czarist 'autocracy', and Graves makes the claim that the Kolchak Government treated the war-weary peasants with brutality because of their lack of desire to

---

59   Service, op. cit., 220. The 'Left Socialist Revolutionaries' were an originally pro-Bolshevik faction that had broken away from the Party of Socialist Revolutionaries over the issue of supporting the Bolsheviks.

60   Graves, op. cit., 'Before the Armistice'.

take up arms for any faction.[61] It is noticeable that even in 1931, when Graves wrote his reminisces of the 'Siberian adventure', there is not a single reference to the 'Red Terror' or any criticism of the Bolsheviks. Rather, Graves emphasizes the "autocratic" nature of the Kolchak regime without a word about the character of the Soviet regime, even with the advantage of hindsight over a decade later:

> No one in Siberia, excepting those belonging to the Kolchak supporters, enjoyed any of the boons of modern civilization, such as freedom of speech, freedom of press, freedom of assembly, and freedom of legal action, which are well-recognized heritages of all civilized people.[62]

Graves' hatred of Semenoff seems to have been even more intense than the hatred he had towards Kolchak, years later expressing his indignation that a representative of the Cossack Ataman had been permitted entry into the USA in 1919 to lecture on the situation in Siberia from the White perspective.[63]

General Gayda, commander of the Czech soldiers in Siberia, urged Graves to support Kolchak and to assist the Czechs and the White armies to destroy Bolshevism, and had a plan to march on Moscow. According to the pro-Soviet American authors Sayers and Kahn, citing Graves, the American commander told Gayda that 'as long as he was in command no American soldiers would be used against the Bolsheviks'.[64] Sayers and Kahn quote Graves as concluding soon after his arrival in Vladivostok:

> The word 'Bolshevik', as used in Siberia, covers most of the Russian people and to use troops to fight Bolsheviks or to arm, equip, feed, clothe or pay White Russians to fight them was utterly inconsistent with "non-interference with the internal affairs of Russia."[65]

Graves was to write of his refusal to act against the Bolsheviks that this was in strict accord with his orders:

---

61   Ibid., 'After the Armistice'.

62   Ibid.

63   Ibid.

64   Sayers and. Kahn, op. cit., 64.

65   Ibid., 65.

The United States never entered into a state of war with Russia, or any faction of Russia. It was equally as unconstitutional to use American troops in hostile action in Siberia against any faction of Russia, as it would have been to send them to Russia with a view to using them in hostile action against the Russians. If I had permitted American troops to be used in fighting 'Red armies,' as stated, I would have taken an immense responsibility upon myself, as no one above me, in authority, had given me any such orders. The fact that I did not permit American troops to be so used was responsible for nine-tenths of the criticism directed against us, while in Siberia. I was told by General Leonard Wood, upon my return from the Far East in December, 1920, that if I did not have copies of my papers I would be "torn limb from limb, in the United States, because I did not take part in fighting bolshevism."[66]

The attitude of Graves was alarming to Britain's General Knox, who was one of those among the Allies on the scene who did genuinely want to defeat Bolshevism, and he expressed concern to Graves that the American General already had a pro-Soviet reputation.[67]

'Bolshevik Americans'

To many Russians, the Americans who came to their land seemed to be imbued with a Bolshevistic attitude. The ideals of Wilson's 'Fourteen Points' for post-war world re-organization could be interpreted as having a Bolshevistic ideology, not only by Russian 'autocrats' but by conservatives throughout the world. Wilson's blueprint was certainly intended to destroy the traditional order of Europe. Additionally, America's originally pro-Russian sentiments had long been soured by the anti-Czarist output of journalist George Kennan.[68] Kennan was

---

66   Graves, op. cit., 'Before the Armistice'.

67   Sayers and Kahn, op. cit., 65.

68   Not to be confused with a relative, George F. Kennan, the US State Department strategist and expert on Russia, cited in this paper. According to Robert Cowley, editor of *American Heritage*, 'An American journalist, George Kennan, became the first to reveal the full horrors of Siberian exile and the brutal, studied inhumanity of Czarist 'justice', and as having exposed the allegedly 'brutal police state', the 'deep seated sickness of an entire nation'. During the years following the American Civil War there had been "a kind of golden age" of Russo-American relations, and 'scarcely blemished good-fellowship."' The anti-Czarist publicity began when *Century Magazine* published 'a long and highly sensationalised' series of articles by Kennan, who had spent two years in Siberia. These articles formed the basis of his book *Siberia and the Exile System*, which Cowley states 'were devastating in their effect' on American attitudes

funded by Jacob Schiff of Kuhn, Loeb and Co., one of those bankers who, according to H. Wickham Steed, were eager for the recognition of the Soviet regime at the 1919 Paris conference. Schiff, a leader of the organized Jewish community in the US, financed Russian radical movements directed at overthrowing the Czar[69] had provided the money for Kennan to distribute revolutionary propaganda to Russian prisoners-of-war in Japan during the 1904–1905 Russo-Japanese War, these revolutionized soldiers providing the cadres for the first anti-Czarist revolution in 1905, and for the 1917 Revolution.

Perhaps Americans could more readily identify with the Bolsheviks and other socialist revolutionaries because of their own revolutionary and anti-monarchical tradition. Their President, Woodrow Wilson, touted as a great idealist despite being surrounded by the 'vested interests' he feigned to denounce,[70] stated at the Paris Peace Conference in 1919, in terms reminiscent of the Bolsheviks:

There is throughout the world the feeling of revolt against vested interests which influence the world in both economic

---

towards Russia. The book became what Mikhail Kalinin, Chairman of the Presidium of the Supreme Soviet under Stalin, years later described as 'a kind of "Bible" to his generation of revolutionaries'. Robert Cowley, 'A Year in Hell', in Oliver Jensen (Ed.) *America and Russia, Ibid.*,, 93–121. Conversely, the descriptions of the Russian prison system and Siberian exile for even the Czar's most avid opponents seem relatively enlightened and humane for the times when reading of the treatment meted out to Trotsky and his comrades, as related in Robert Service's recent biography of Trotsky. Certainly Trotsky was accorded better treatment than that provided for by the system he established under Bolshevism. Trotsky was even accorded conjugal rights when in jail. Robert Service, *Trotsky: A Biography*, op. cit., pp. 50-95.

69 Judith S. Goldstein, *The Politics of Ethnic Pressure: The American Jewish Committee Fight against Immigration Restriction, 1906–1917* (New York: Garland Publishing, 1990), 26–27; Zosa Szajkowski, 'Paul Nathan, Lucien Wolf, Jacob H. Schiff and the Jewish revolutionary movements in Easter Europe' Jewish Social Studies 29(1), 1–15, 1967. The leaders of Western Jewish communities were highly committed to the overthrow of the czar. For example, in 1907 Lucien Wolf wrote to Louis Marshall of the American Jewish Committee that 'the only thing to be done on the whole Russo-Jewish question is to carry on persistent and implacable war against the Russian Government' (in Szajowski, ibid., 8). "Western Jewish leaders actively participated in general actions in favour of the liberal and revolutionary movements in Russia both during the revolution and after its downfall" (Szajkowski, obid., 9); http://www.jstor.org/pss/4466323

70 Wilson's confidante, Edward House, had during the war founded a think tank called 'The Inquiry' which after the war transformed into the Council on Foreign Relations, to advise on post-war policy. The CFR was, and remains, an influential nexus between businessmen and international bankers, politicians, and academics. See the official CFR history: Peter Grose, Continuing The Inquiry: The Council on Foreign Relations from 1921 to 1996. < http://www.cfr.org/about/history/cfr/>

and political spheres. The way to cure this domination is, in my opinion, constant discussion and a slow process of reform; but the world at large has grown impatient of delay. There are men in the United States of the finest temper, if not of the finest judgment, who are in sympathy with Bolshevism because it appears to them to offer that regime of opportunity to the individual which they desire to bring about.[71]

Hence, President Wilson had given the moral high ground to the Soviets. Wilson went further, and on his post-war sojourn to Europe unsuccessfully tried to speak with revolutionary rhetoric to crowds in Italy and France.[72] Wilson was aiming to create his own liberal-democratic "world revolution" that could accommodate socialist revolutionaries of all types, including Bolsheviks.

Wilson's 'Fourteen Points' to reorganize the world amounted to a revolutionary manifesto that gave notice to the old European order that America would lead the new. Explicating the ideology behind the 'Fourteen Points' it was stated in terms that seemed to coincide with the foreign policy of the Bolsheviks and would give reason for concern by the British, French and other colonial powers, that:

In regard to these essential rectifications of wrong and assertions of right we feel ourselves to be intimate partners of all the governments and peoples associated together against the Imperialists. We cannot be separated in interest or divided in purpose. We stand together until the end.[73]

The Wilsonian manifesto was a call for anti-imperialist solidarity led by America, against the powers that the US had supposedly entered the war to assist, and could easily be interpreted as including the Bolsheviks as comrades in a world anti-imperialist struggle.

With this US pro-revolutionist, anti-Czarist attitude in mind, while many were concerned at the sadism of the Reds, Graves' subordinates were bringing him daily intelligence reports on alleged White atrocities, and Graves expressed his abhorrence,[74] yet feigned ignorance as to the 'Red Terror'. The pro-Bolshevik attitude among the

---

71 Sayers and Kahn, op. cit., 74.

72 Ibid.

73 Woodrow Wilson, 'Fourteen Points', January 8, 1918.

74 Sayers and Kahn, op. cit., 66–67.

Americans was noted by the White Russian press in Siberia, Graves complaining that the White press was describing the Americans as being 'Bolshevistic', and White Russian reports from Vladivostok to Kolchak at Omsk warned that, 'The United States Soldiers are infected with Bolshevism'. [75]

General Graves' Antagonism Towards Kolchak

Of General Ivanoff-Rinoff, one of Kolchak's commanders, whom Graves was to describe as the 'Dictator of Eastern Siberia',[76] Graves stated to British High Commissioner Sir Charles Eliot, that, 'As far as I'm concerned the people could bring Ivanoff-Rinoff opposite American headquarters and hang him to that telephone pole until he is dead — and not an American would turn his hand!'[77]

Graves' characterization of the Kolchak Government was that of 'a crowd of reactionaries', and Ivanoff-Rinoff was a 'typical Russian Czarist official'. These were the types of description Graves was dispatching to the US War Office.[78]

The antagonism between Graves and the White Russian press was to result in Graves' demand that Kolchak stifle the press, despite the supposed policy of 'non-interference' (sic) and Graves' supposed moral indignation at the 'autocratic' nature of the Kolchak regime, whose restrictions in regard to "free speech" so enraged him. In retaliation over the White Russian criticism of him and the Americans in general, Graves withheld 14,000 desperately needed rifles from Kolchak's forces, which had been bought and paid for by the White movement.[79]

When the American Red Cross, as a private agency, under the direction of Dr Teusler, whom Graves slanders as having 'no sympathy for the aspirations of the Russian people', was found to be providing Kolchak's forces with warm underwear, and running hospitals for Kolchak, Graves put Teusler on notice that no further guards would be available for Red Cross trains unless this support ceased.[80]

---

75   Graves, op. cit., 'After the Armistice'.

76   Ibid., "Mobilization of Russian Troops."

77   Sayers and Kahn, op. cit., 69.

78   Graves, op. cit., 'Mobilization of Russian Troops'.

79   See below.

80   Graves, op. cit., 'The Railroad Agreement'.

Another example of American 'non-interference' was the efforts made to undermine Kalmikoff, Graves insisting that the Japanese disarm the Ussuri Cossack Ataman, writing to Japanese Headquarters, 'that the excesses of Kalmikoff should be stopped and that his actions were a disgrace to civilization....'[81] Indignantly replying to the US Military Attaché in Tokyo in regard to allegations that American deserters had joined the Red Army[82] and that the US had stood by while Japanese forces had been attacked by the Reds, Graves stated: 'There is not a man in the bolshevik, or any other army, worse than Kalmikoff'.[83]

Red Atrocities Ignored

Yet in his condemnation of Ivanoff-Rinoff, Kolchak, Semenoff, Kalmikoff and others, Graves could not have been unaware of the atrocities being committed by the Reds. The so-called 'Red Terror' included forms of sadism that have the symptoms of mass psychosis, and were being reported both in the Western press and in dispatches by Allies on the scene.

After Denikin's White forces defeated the Bolsheviks at Odessa in August 1919, Rev. R. Courtier-Forster, Chaplain of the British forces at Odessa and the Black Sea ports, who had been held captive by the Bolsheviks, reported the horrors of Bolshevism, relating how on the ship Sinope, the largest cruiser of the Black Sea Fleet, some of his personal friends had been chained to planks and slowly pushed into the ship's furnaces to be roasted alive. Others were scalded with steam from the ship's boilers. Mass rapes were committed, while the local Soviet press debated the possibilities of nationalizing women. The screams from women being raped and from other victims in what Rev. Courtier-Forster called the 'Bolshevik's House of Torture' at Catherine Square, could be heard for blocks around, while at Catherine Square the Bolsheviks tried to muffle the screams with the noise of lorries thundering up and down the street.[84]

Lenin used the Allied intervention as a rationalization for the 'Red Terror' stating in 1919 that, 'The Terror was forced on us by the

---

81 Ibid., 'After the Armistice'.

82 Graves insisted that the Japanese could not know that American deserters had joined the Bolsheviks, but wrote also that he did not know their whereabouts either. Graves, ibid., 'Mobilization of Russian Troops'.

83 Ibid.

84 R. Courtier-Forster, 'Bolshevism, Reign of Torture at Odessa', *London Times*, December 3, 1919, 2, 3, 4.

Entente'.[85] However the plan for a 'Red Terror' was already drafted on the orders of Lenin in December 1917 for the *Cheka*, the secret political police.[86] The People's Commissary for the Interior, Ptervosky, sent a communiqué to all Soviets not to flinch from the "mass execution by shooting" of hostages to achieve their aims.[87] Of the Civil War period, Melgunoff states that the number of 'hostages' shot by the Bolsheviks in the autumn of 1918 cannot be estimated.[88] The number of victims of the Bolsheviks in South Russia during the period 1918–1919, was estimated by the Denikin Commission to be 1,700,000, a total with which Melgunoff concurs.[89] When the Rohrberg Commission of Enquiry entered Kiev, after the Soviets had been driven out in August 1919, it described the 'execution hall' of the *Cheka* as follows:

> All the cement floor of the great garage (the execution hall of the departmental Cheka of Kief) was flooded with blood. This blood was no longer flowing, it formed a layer of several inches: it was a horrible mixture of blood, brains, of pieces of skull, of tufts of hair and other human remains. All the walls were bespattered with blood; pieces of brains and scalps were sticking to them. A gutter twenty-five centimetres wide by twenty-five centimetres deep and about ten metres long ran from the centre of the garage towards a subterranean drain. This gutter along its whole length was full to the top with blood. ... Usually as soon as the massacre had taken place the bodies were conveyed out of the town in motor lorries and buried beside the grave about which we have spoken; we found in a corner of the garden another grave which was older and contained about eighty bodies. Here we discovered on the bodies traces of cruelties and mutilations the most varied and unimaginable. Some bodies were disembowelled, others had limbs chopped off, some were literally hacked to pieces. Some had their eyes put out and the head, face, neck and trunk covered with deep wounds. Further on we found a corpse with a wedge driven into the chest. Some had no tongues. In a corner of the grave we discovered a certain quantity of arms and legs.[90]

85   S. Melgunoff, 'The Record of the Red Terror,' 198. http://www.paulbogdanor.com/left/soviet/redterror.pdf

86   Ibid.

87   Ibid., 199.

88   Ibid., 205.

89   Ibid., 205.

90   S. Melgunoff, Larreur rouge (Paris, 1927), cited by Vicomte Leon de Poncins, *The*

The nature of Bolshevism was understood in the West by the time Graves took command of the Americans in Siberia. However, of the leaders of the major powers only France's Clemenceau desired to see the elimination of Bolshevism, and introduced Wilson and Lloyd George to eyewitnesses in regard to the 'Red Terror'. Wilson however would not be moved by the testimony.[91] Amidst the numerous accusations by Graves regarding White atrocities, the only comment he makes on the 'Red Terror' is that:

> The foreign press was constantly being told that the Bolsheviks were the Russians who were committing these terrible excesses, and propaganda had been used to such an extent that no one ever believed that atrocities were being committed against the Bolsheviks.[92]

While Graves might have pleaded ignorance when he took command of the American forces in Siberia, these statements were made in his book *America's Siberian Expedition* published in 1931, and by that time there could be no excuse for ignorance, other than that of an apologist for Bolshevism.

'Very Largely Our Fault'

In March 1919 Captain Montgomery Schuyler, Chief of Staff of the American Expeditionary Force in Siberia, reporting from Omsk to Lt. Colonel Barrows in Vladivostok, wrote of his misgivings:

> You will feel I am being hot about this matter but it is I feel sure, one which is going to bring great trouble on the United States when the judgment of history shall be recorded on the part we have played. It is very largely our fault that Bolshevism has spread as it has and I do not believe we will be found guiltless of the thousands of lives uselessly and cruelly sacrificed in wild orgies of bloodshed to establish an autocratic and despotic rule of principles which have been rejected by every generation of mankind which has dabbled with them.[93]

Secret Powers Behind Revolution (California: Christian Book Club of America, n.d.), 149.

91   Sayers and Kahn, op. cit., 77–78.

92   Graves, op. cit., 'Kolchak and Recognition'.

93   Capt. Montgomery Schuyler, Report of March 1, 1919, Record Group 120, Records of the American Expeditionary Forces, 383.9 Military Intelligence Report, p. 2.

How America Helped to Bolshevise Russia

In the same month as Captain Schuyler was writing his report which confirms the widespread White Russian assertions, much to Graves' ongoing outrage, that the Americans were pursuing a policy helpful to Bolshevism, Graves cabled Washington to ensure that his actions were in accord with the US Administration. General March, Chief of Staff of the US War Department, replied: 'Your action as reported in the cablegram was in accordance with your original instructions and is approved, and you will be guided by those instructions until they are modified by the President'.[94]

Wilson had urged 'evacuation of all Russian territory' by foreign troops as the sixth of his 'Fourteen Points', which would hardly encourage confidence among the White movement in regard to the intentions of the USA, the implications of Wilson's statement again being pro-Soviet:

> The evacuation of all Russian territory and such a settlement of all questions affecting Russia as will secure the best and freest cooperation of the other nations of the world in obtaining for her an unhampered and unembarrassed opportunity for the independent determination of her own political development and national policy and assure her of a sincere welcome into the society of free nations under institutions of her own choosing; and, more than a welcome, assistance also of every kind that she may need and may herself desire. The treatment accorded Russia by her sister nations in the months to come will be the acid test of their good will, of their comprehension of her needs as distinguished from their own interests, and of their intelligent and unselfish sympathy.[95]

Therefore, when authorizing American troops to enter Russia, Wilson stated of the US forces in North Russia at the time of their landing that:

> military intervention there would add to the present sad confusion in Russia rather than cure it. ... Whether from Vladivostok or from Murmansk and Archangel, the only legitimate object for which the American or Allied troops can be employed... is to guard military stores which may subsequently be needed by Russian forces and to render such aid as may be acceptable to

---

94   Graves, op. cit., 'Mobilization of Russian Troops'.

95   Woodrow Wilson, 'Fourteen Points', January 8, 1918.

the Russians in the organization of their own self-defence.[96]

This was at variance with the British military's understanding of the meaning of intervention, and the British military, which had command of the Allied Supreme War Council, wished to pursue an anti-Bolshevik policy, albeit at variance with Prime Minister Lloyd George. They had supported an anti-Soviet *coup* in Archangel the following month (August). Hence, there was no common agreement as to the meaning of intervention, and Allied military action against the Red Army was more likely to arise from the initiative of Allied officers on the scene. This is acknowledged by George F. Kennan when he writes of the *coup* in Archangel:

> That the participants in this happy escapade had any knowledge of the President's recent expression of unwillingness to have American troops participate in organized intervention into the interior from Murmansk and Archangel, or that it would have meant much to them had they known it, seems doubtful in the extreme.[97]

Japanese Factor

Although both Trotsky and Allied military attachés were urging Japanese assistance in the intervention,[98] Japanese aims in Russia's Far East became problematic to the Allies.

Kolchak had established his Government in Omsk, but was opposed by pro-Japanese officers, and by the powerful Cossack Ataman Semenoff, who had established his domain in the Far East with Japanese support. The Western Allies became aware of Japan's intentions of keeping the region destabilized and of preventing a stable, united Russian authority, which was the aim of Kolchak, who was recognized by most of the other White leaders as the "supreme Ruler of All the Russias." As early as 1918 US military intelligence had reported that the Japanese did not desire a stable order in Russia since this would eliminate the need for Japanese intervention under the pretext of maintaining stability.[99]

---

96   Woodrow Wilson, July 17, 1918. Cited by E M Halliday, 'Where Ignorant Armies Clashed by Night', in Jensen (ed.) America and Russia, op. cit., 166.

97   Kennan, *The Decision to Intervene*, op. cit., 425.

98   Ibid., 120

99   Jon Smele, Civil War in Siberia: The Anti-Bolshevik Government of Admiral Kolchak

How America Helped to Bolshevise Russia

The pro-British Kolchak's position was precarious in regard to Japanese-backed rival White leaders, such as Semenoff and Kalmikoff. The Japanese were seeking to establish their dominion over the Russian Far East and to keep Britain and America out.[100] The White forces were caught between the Red Army and inter-Allied post-war rivalry. This was a factor for an American business syndicate, with the support of the US Administration, being able to negotiate a concession from the Soviet regime over the Kamchatka Peninsula.

In 1920, when the Allies were ostensibly in Vladivostok to assist the Whites, an American businessman, Washington Vanderlip, representing a consortium of US business interests *and the US Government*, was negotiating a concession with Lenin for what would have virtually made the whole area a protectorate of the USA. This involved a sixty-year lease of the Far Eastern Kamchatka Peninsula to secure important oil and mining concessions.[101]

The British novelist, historian, and Fabian-socialist H. G. Wells, in Russia at the time to interview Lenin and other Bolshevik luminaries, met Vanderlip and expressed the hope that the USA and commercial interests would sustain Bolshevism:

> The only Power capable of playing this role of eleventh-hour helper to Russia single-handed is the United States of America. That is why I find the adventure of the enterprising and imaginative Mr. Vanderlip very significant. I doubt the conclusiveness of his negotiations; they are probably only the opening phase of a discussion of the Russian problem upon a new basis that may lead it at last to a comprehensive world treatment of this situation. Other Powers than the United States will, in the present phase of world-exhaustion, need to combine before they can be of any effective use to Russia. Big business is by no means antipathetic to Communism. The larger big business grows the more it approximates to Collectivism. It is the upper road of the few instead of the lower road of the masses to Collectivism.[102]

1918–1920 (New York: University of Cambridge, 1996), 192.

100 Ibid.

101 'The Vanderlip Concession, an alternate history', 26 December 2009, http://www.articlesbase.com/politics-articles/the-vanderlip-concession-an-alternate-history-1626435.html

102 H. G. Wells, *Russia in the Shadows*, Chapter VII, 'The Envoy'. Wells went to Russia in September 1920 at the invitation of Lev Kamenev, a member the Russian Trade

Vanderlip embarked on his mission at a time when the Soviets did not yet control the region, and undertook the trip with the authority of the US State Department. Lenin explained the lease to the Eighth All-Russia Congress of Soviets on December 21, 1920, replying to a question on the possibility of war with Japan, that Soviet Russia was now in a position to fight Japan with the help of America, and that 'an attack by Japan on Soviet Russia is much more difficult now than it was a year ago'.[103] Hence, the lease was intended to serve both Soviet and US geopolitical interests. Lenin, writing to Vanderlip in 1921, expressed the importance the Soviet regime attached to the lease:

I thank you for your kind letter of the 14th, and am very glad to hear of President Harding's favourable views as to our trade with America. You know what value we attach to our future American business relations. We fully recognise the part played in this respect by your syndicate and also the great importance of your personal efforts. Your new proposals are highly interesting and I have asked the Supreme Council of National Economy to report to me at short intervals about the progress of the negotiations. You can be sure that we will treat every reasonable suggestion with the greatest attention and care. It is on production and trade that our efforts are principally concentrated and your help is to us of the greatest value.[104]

At the time the 'ownership' of Kamchatka was not even known to Lenin, but the Japanese were in possession, and did not withdraw until signing a treaty with the USSR in 1925. Lenin pointed out that an American presence, including a naval base, would act as a 'buffer' to Japanese aggression, stating: 'Actually the Japanese are in possession, and they do not relish the idea of our giving it away to the Americans'.[105] Hence the statement often made that the Vanderlip

---

Delegation in London and one of the leaders of the Bolshevik regime. *Russia in the Shadows* appeared as a series of articles in *The Sunday Express*. The whole book can be read online at: *gutenberg.net.au/ebooks06/0602371h.html*

103 Lenin, December 21, 1920, Eighth All-Russia Congress of Soviets, 'Reply To The Debate On The Report On Concessions Delivered To The R.C.P.(B.) Group At The Eighth Congress Of Soviets', Lenin: Collected Works (Moscow: Progress Publishers, 1971), Vol. 42, 239–267.

104 Lenin to Vanderlip, March 17, 1921; *Lenin: Collected Works* (Moscow: Progress Publishers, 1976), Vol. 45, 98.

105 Lenin, December 22, 1920; 'Speech To The R.C.P.(B.) Group At The Eighth Congress Of Soviets During The Debate On The Report Of The All-Russia Central Executive Committee And The Council Of People's Commissars Concerning Home And Foreign Policies', Lenin Internet Archive (2003) http://www.marxists.org/

concession never became operative because of opposition from the US Government and 'big business' is incorrect.[106] Japan held possession until 1925, the U.S. Government did not feel enabled to officially recognize the USSR until 1933, but American 'big business' initiated commercial relations with the Bolsheviks as early as 1920.[107]

'Poorly Armed and Equipped'

The reliability of assistance not only for military but also for civil administration relied on recognition of Kolchak's Omsk administration as the *de jure* authority. But neither *de jure* nor *de facto* recognition was ever forthcoming. 'Such assistance could not be relied on without recognition', recalled Kolchak's Foreign Minister, Sukin.[108] Since the 1918 armistice between Soviet Russia and Germany the Allied policy was indefinite and vacillating, writes Smele,[109] who succinctly explains the situation:

> By November 1918 there had been Allied troops on Russian territory for the best part of a year. Soviet historians, of course, consistently construed this intervention and the concomitant sponsorship of counter-revolution in Siberia and European Russia as being purely anti-Bolshevik in origin and inspiration. Unfortunately for Kolchak and the Whites, however, this was far from being the whole story.[110]

Wilson at Paris stated that the Allied troops were 'doing no sort of good' in Russia and should be withdrawn. Churchill, one of the few politicos who sought the overthrow of the Bolsheviks, worried that communism would triumph and reduce all of Russia to misery. He urged a detailed study be made to determine what force was needed to defeat Bolshevism. Wilson immediately repudiated Churchill and,

---

archive/lenin/works/1920/dec/x01.htm

106 The Vanderlip project was still proceeding in 1922, when Standard Oil purchased one-quarter of the stock and exclusive rights for oil exploration in the area. However the concession could not become operative until diplomatic recognition. 'Standard Oil Joins Vanderlip Project', *New York Times*, January 11, 1922, p. 1.

107 That year the press reported that on the initiative of American businessmen a 'new international organization had been formed in Denmark to exchange raw materials for manufactured goods after lengthy discussions with Maxim Litvinoff', Commissar for Foreign Affairs. 'Americans to Trade with Reds', *New York Times*, February 15, 1920.

108 Smele, op. cit., 200.

109 Ibid.

110 Ibid. 201.

without American support, there could be no offensive to defeat the Soviets.[111] The attitude of Churchill's Prime Minister, Lloyd George, was in agreement with that of Wilson, and both desired the Allies to meet with Soviet representatives, Lloyd George stating at the Paris conference in 1919 in terms that could only give comfort to the Bolsheviks:

> The peasants accepted Bolshevism for the same reason that peasants accepted it in the French Revolution, namely that it gave them land. The Bolsheviks are the *de facto* Government. We formerly recognized the Czar's Government, although at the time we knew it to be absolutely rotten. Our reason was that it was the *de facto* Government ... but we refuse to recognise the Bolsheviks! To say that we ourselves should pick the representatives of a great people is contrary to every principle for which we have fought.[112]

Lloyd George was wrong on several historical points: the peasants had not accepted Bolshevism. Ironically, the peasants at the time were in revolt against Bolshevism,[113] just as they had been the foundation for a resistance to the proto-"Bolshevism" of Revolutionary France, to which George alludes.[114] Describing the Czar's regime as *de facto* and 'rotten' and no more legitimate that the precarious Soviet regime based around Moscow and Petrograd was sending a negative message to many of those resisting the Red Army. In March 1918, Kolchak was informed of the Bullitt mission to Moscow, which had come back with a favourable view of the Soviet regime.[115]

---

111   E. M. Halliday, 'Where Ignorant Armies Clashed by Night', in Jensen (ed.) *America and Russia*, op. cit., 177.

112   Quoted by Sayers and Kahn, op. cit., 76–77.

113   The "Green" army for example was a large-scale manifestation of peasant resistance.

114   The uprising of the Vendee Province in France.

115   William C. Bullitt, an aide with the US State Department, and a member of the American delegation at the 1919 Paris conference, was secretly sent to Russian to make contact with the Bolsheviks, with a brief from Edward House, who told Bullitt that terms could include Allied withdrawal, and the establishment of economic relations. Among Bullitt's choices for his delegation was a journalist, Lincoln Steffens, 'an outspoken admirer of the Soviets'. However, the conservative press was still a major factor in publicizing the manoeuvres to recognize the Bolsheviks, and questions were asked in the British Parliament, to Lloyd George's dismay. The Bolsheviks did not help their cause, or that of statesmen such as Wilson and Lloyd George who were trying to sell the idea of accommodating the Bolsheviks to anti-Bolsheviks such as France's Clemenceau, by continuing their revolutionary rhetoric against the West. See: Robert S. Rifkind, 'The Wasted Mission', in Jensen (Ed.) *America and Russia*, op. cit.,

In April the Allies announced food relief to central Russia, thereby helping to stem popular resentment against the Soviet regime.[116] The aid from the Allies to Kolchak continued, the purpose as explained by Lloyd George in the House of Commons being not due to any anti-Bolshevik policy, but because British prestige would suffer if it was seen that the anti-Soviet forces were being abandoned to their fate now that they had served their purposes in regard to the World War. There was also increasingly widespread horror in Britain once the facts in regard to the "Red Terror" and the bestial nature of Bolshevism became known.[117] It should also be recalled, as previously noted, that Wickham Steed of *The London Times* had conducted a highly effective campaign against recognizing the Soviets that, as Lloyd George complained, was preventing him from recognizing the Soviets.

In October another blow was struck at Kolchak when Canada, whose troops comprised a major component of the Allied forces, announced it was withdrawing from Siberia.

The prospect of continued Allied aid to Kolchak was pegged to the Admiral's commitment to establishing a liberal order and on pursuing a policy that was in accord with the Wilsonian ideals for the post-war world which, as alluded to previously, were analogous to Bolshevik ideology. Hence the US sought commitments from Kolchak that he would not only establish a democratic regime in Russia, but that Russia would join the League of Nations and honour foreign debts.[118] It was made sufficiently clear that if Kolchak was not willing to adopt these post-war aims aid would be curtailed.

Kolchak felt that with military success he would be able to eventually establish his own terms for the governance of Russia. During 1919, despite the demoralizing Allied actions of the previous year, it looked possible that the Red Army might be defeated, and it seemed prudent for the US to maintain its connections with the Omsk regime. There was a danger that the Whites might defeat the Reds with or without Allied aid, and that if without, any subsequent non-Soviet Government would view the Allies with resentment. Another major factor was the possibility that any such Government would turn to

---

180–196.

116   Smele, *Civil War in Siberia*, op. cit., 209.

117   Ibid., p. 210.

118   Ibid., pp. 214-215.

Germany, which is what the Soviet regime did under the Treaty of Rapallo in 1922.

Yet, despite the initial successes of Kolchak, in August 1919 *The New York Times* was already reporting that he was in retreat, with 100,000 'poorly armed men' facing a well-equipped Red Army of 500,000. The White Army was 'still fighting bravely, but they are poorly armed and equipped', states a *New York Times* report. The report refers to Kolchak's forces being 'partially armed and equipped':

> The defeat of the Omsk Government is authoritatively attributed to the lack of trained soldiers and the lack of military supplies. The setback suffered in the field by the Kolchak army is believed to make more uncertain if not positively unlikely the early recognition of the Omsk Government by the United States and the allied powers.[119]

Contemporary reports confirm White allegations that Allied support had always been inadequate. Wilson had already determined in early 1919 that American troops would leave Russia. One historian of the period comments: 'Having undertaken to lead the White Russians against the Bolsheviks, the Allies were now about to leave them holding a bag of very dubious tenability'.[120] General Ironsides, the British commander at Archangel, had anticipated such a scuttle and had done what he could to outfit and 'partially train' 15,000 White Russian troops, but rumors of an impending American withdrawal destroyed anti-Bolshevik morale, mutinies spread from April 1919, and hundreds of Whites began deserting to the Red Army after killing their officers.[121] Although the Americans were replaced by 10,000 British troops 'it was soon clear that the intervention was in effect over. ... The Allies were on their way out'.[122] The British replacements were at Archangel for only three months, before the Whites were left to their own devices, and at first fared quite well against the Reds.

By this time the reputation of the Americans in Siberia was so low

---

119 'Kolchak Army in Serious Straits; Disaster Feared. Sadly Lacks Munitions. 100,000 Men Poorly Armed and Equipped Unable to Withstand Red Onrush'; *The New York Times*, August 12, 1919, 1, 5.

120 E. M. Halliday, in *America and Russia*, op. cit., 178.

121 Ibid., 178.

122 Ibid., 178.

that the Kolchak Government requested the American forces *not* to advance into Siberia any further lest the extension of the American presence further aggravated the low opinion the Russians held for the Americans.[123]

In July 1919 General Graves called in the Japanese Chief of Staff and the American commander at Sviagina to condemn the Japanese execution of five suspected Bolsheviks, and reprimanded the American commander for not having forcibly prevented the Japanese from doing so. Graves was to write of this incident:

> I felt so strongly about this murder that I brought the commanding officer of Sviagina to American Head-quarters at Vladivostok and, in the presence of the Japanese Chief of Staff, told him he should have used force to prevent it. I also told the Japanese Chief of Staff that if such a thing was ever attempted again in American sectors of the railroad, it would bring on a conflict between Japanese and American troops.[124]

The New York Times again reported on the routing of Kolchak by the Red Army and placed the blame on the Allies, and particularly on the US Administration. The Admiral's White Army had been beaten back over 800 miles, 'because he had not sufficient gun power, no airplanes, no tanks, and little food'.

> The Allies withheld the necessary supplies, especially the supplies of arms and ammunition from the Omsk Government. ... [T]he Allies have given no officers to Kolchak, not even a non-commissioned officer to train the undisciplined privates he has in some fashion dragged together.

> So Kolchak, without ammunition, food or other supplies, and with a patriotic mob he cannot discipline by himself without aid, has done wonders and has finally been routed...[125]

The following day *The New York Times* was reporting that the US Administration had finally agreed to allow the release to Kolchak, in the midst of his retreat, some of the American-made arms and ammunition the US had gone into Russia to guard from German

---

123 'Asks Graves to Stop American Advance. Omsk Government Says Undefined Attitude of United States Causes Trouble in Siberia', *New York Times*, May 19, 1919.

124 Graves, op. cit., 'Japan, The Cossacks and Anti-Americanism'.

125 'Kolchak Beaten', *The New York Times*, Editorial, August 13, 1919.

capture in the closing months of World War I, after financial arrangement had been made by White Russian representatives. Diplomatic recognition remained elusive however,[126] despite the urgent plea by Robert S. Morris, American Ambassador to Japan, reporting on his mission to Siberia, that US recognition would be vital for the survival of Kolchak's authority, and that had it been given three months previously, the Omsk Government would not have been in its perilous situation.[127] It is notable that even then, and with disquiet from those on the scene regarding the possibility that the White movement might be forced into alliance with Germany and Japan, the arms were only belatedly forthcoming because White Russian agents in the USA had arranged for payment. After several years, and awaiting arms that had to be paid for by the White movement, Graves still ensured that even now there were delays and ill-will attached to the late delivery, *The New York Times* reporting of the situation that:

> Major General Graves recently refused delivery of the arms to the Russian authorities at Vladivostok, his action resulting in criticism of the American command by the Russian authorities in the Far East, as well as by General Knox, chief of the British Military Mission at Omsk, who said that General Graves had held up the delivery of arms which the Russians had bought and paid for.[128]

Graves had been piqued by criticism of American forces in an article in a Vladivostok newspaper and had demanded Kolchak suppress the newspaper. When Kolchak refused, the General decided that withholding 14,000 arms would be apt punishment. The US State Department intervened, *The New York Times* reporting:

> In advising General Graves to permit the resumption of arms shipments to the Kolchak forces, state department officials took the position that withholding the rifles now, with a wide offensive against the Bolsheviki starting, might prove fatal to the success of the operation.[129]

---

126 'Arms to Kolchak now being rushed by United States', *New York Times*, August 14, 1919, 1, 4.

127 'Envoy Morris Attributes Kolchak's Reverses to Failure to Recognize Him 3 months Ago', *New York Times*, August 28, 1919, 1.

128 'Semenoff demanded arms of Americans,', *New York Times*, November 2, 1919.

129 'Released Rifles Held Up by Graves', *New York Times*, October 3, 1919.

That month also (October 1919) when the situation for Kolchak was dire, the Allied authorities demanded that he withdraw from Vladivostok due to the shooting of a drunken American solider by a Russian officer, who had been struck at by the American after demanding that the soldier desist from anti-Government statements.[130] One might think that in such a situation the Allies would be concerned with the actions of their subordinates, rather than with using the incident as a pretext to yet again try and hamstring Kolchak. The Admiral replied that Vladivostok is a defensive position and that the Allied demand was an intrusion on Russian sovereignty, and refused to comply.[131]

In November General Semenoff attempted to acquisition for his Cossack forces 15,000 of the 68,000 firearms *en route* to Kolchak under American guard, but the small American contingent was under orders not to provide Semenoff with any arms under any circumstances.[132] Semenoff was again confronted by American troops as he sought to assist Kolchak in his final days.

Revolutionists Thankful for American Help

In December 1919 a revolt by an army regiment against Kolchak in Irkutsk resulted in the proclamation of a revolutionist Government, whose forces proceeded to capture the railway station. Kolchak threatened to bomb the station but was prevented from doing so by the Allies, and the station was declared 'neutral'. Kolchak succeeded in driving the revolutionists across the Irkutsk River. However several days later Kolchak was detained at Nijnie Udinsk after the establishment of a revolutionary authority. Several hundred of Semenoff's soldiers arrived and clashed with the revolutionists.

On January 12, 1920 American troops clashed with Semenoff's

---

130 The way Graves later explained the incident was that an American soldier was drunk and was called a 'Bolshevik' by a Russian officer, whom he lunged at, the American being shot in response. The Russian turned himself over to a Russian court, which Graves described as "fake", and was acquitted of wrongdoing. Graves does not mention that the Allies used this as a pretext for demanding Kolchak's withdrawal from Vladivostok. Graves, America's Siberian Adventure, op. cit., 'Japan, The Cossacks, and Anti-Americanism'.

131 'American Soldier Killed by Russian. Shot by Officer he Struck when Ordered to Desist from Agitation. It is Said', *New York Times*, October 11, 1919.

132 'Semenoff demanded arms of Americans', *New York Times*, November 2, 1919.

troops, which had also fought with the Czechs.[133] Thus, one of the final acts of the American forces had been to clash with the remnants of the White movement under Semenoff, who had been designated by Kolchak as his successor as commander of the White Armies,[134] as he sought to assist Kolchak.

With the end of the Kolchak Government in sight, the US succeeded in persuading Japan to adhere to the US position that the purpose of the Allied presence in Siberia should be to do nothing more than guard the Trans-Siberian railroad.[135] The US had ensured prior to its withdrawal that Kolchak would be left without support.

On entering Vladivostok the revolutionists sought to capture the Russian Governor, General Rozanov, but were prevented from entering his house by Japanese troops. The Americans responded with a Marine detachment whose commanding officer stated to the Japanese that 'interference' would not be tolerated. 'The Japanese then withdrew and all foreign forces observed a neutral attitude'.[136] The American forces guarding the Trans-Siberian railway left Vladivostok amidst wild acclaim from the revolutionist regime. *The New York Times* reported:

> Parades, street meetings and speechmaking marked the second day today of the city's complete liberation from Kolchak authority. Red flags fly on every Government building, many business houses and homes.

---

133 'Says Kolchak's Staff Joined Revolution. Happenings in Irkutsk Region Before and After Admiral's Overthrow', *New York Times*, January 25, 1920,

134 'Revolt in Irkutsk. Admiral Kolchak Resigns Command. Russian Leader said to be Ill, Names Semenoff as Military Successor', *New York Times*, December 28, 1919.

135 'America and Japan Agree on Siberia Plan. Tokio Modifies Policy — will now Protect Railways as First Priority, Regardless of Kolchak', *New York Times*, December 27, 1919.

136 'Americans Block Japanese Action. Prevent Attempt by Mikado's Troops to Save Gen. Rozanov from Revolutionists', *New York Times*, February 8, 1920. Fortunately, Rozanov escaped and took refuge on a Japanese cruiser; otherwise he would presumably have been dragged from his house and killed within the environs of Allied 'neutrality', although Graves never seemed to have accepted that the revolutionists would be capable of such actions.
Graves was later to recall the Rozanov incident in terms at variance with contemporary press reports, and stated that a single field artillery shot fired at the General's house was sufficient to scare his Japanese guards, who promptly got Rozanov out in disguise. Graves, op. cit., 'Japan, The Cossacks, and Anti-Americanism'. Such jitteriness of the Japanese military seems out of character.

There is a pronounced pro-American feeling evident. In front of the American headquarters the revolutionary leaders mounted steps of buildings across the street, making speeches calling the Americans real friends, who at a critical time saved the present movement. The people insist upon an allied policy of no interference internationally in political affairs.

The General Staff of the new Government at Nikolsk has telegraphed to the American commander, Major Gen. Graves, expressing its appreciation for efforts toward guaranteeing an allied policy of non-interference during the occupation of the city, also in aiding in a peaceful settlement of the local situation.[137]

Despite the lengths that Graves went to both during and subsequent to his command in Siberia to repudiate the contention of not only the Whites but also of General Knox that 'by not supporting Kolchak you are encouraging the Bolsheviks to think the United States is supporting them', he conceded that 'There were some truths in this claim'.[138]

In 1920, in the midst of defeat, Kolchak stated that, 'the meaning and essence of this intervention remains quite obscure to me',[139] as his forces were left fleeing for their lives in disarray, abandoned to their fate by the Allies. Kolchak was captured after being betrayed by his Czech guard and was shot by the Revolutionist regime on February 7.[140] Graves, while being appalled at the reports of the punishments allegedly meted out by the White regime, excused the execution of Kolchak as being the result of justified 'resentment by the people', and as having been properly tried and convicted by a 'military court'.[141]

The New York Times editorialized with some pertinent analysis of the Allied intervention and the impending collapse of the White remnants, with Denikin's forces in retreat and Semenoff only maintained by the Japanese:

---

137 'Vladivostok Pro-American. Revolutionist Staff Thanks Graves for Preserving Neutrality', *New York Times*, February 15, 1920.

138 Graves, op. cit., 'Japan, The Cossacks, and Anti-Americanism'.

139 Smele, op. cit., 201

140 'Kolchak Sought to Save Companions. 48 Officers and Civilians Refused to Leave Him when Miners Halted Train. Czech Guard Gave Him Up', *New York Times*, February 22, 1920.

141 Graves, op. cit., 'The Gaida Revolution'.

There can be no doubt that the allied Governments must bear a large part of the blame for the collapse of this movement. As *The New Europe* recently observed, 'the publicly proclaimed vacillations of our statesmen are worth a whole army corps to the Bolsheviki'.[142]

An inherent weakness in the position of the White movement was also comprehended by the *Times'* editorial as being a lack of unity of ideas, having to 'harmonize political factions running all the way from rather extreme Socialists to supporters of the old autocracy'.[143]

Sayers and Kahn, remarking on the Civil War, stated that the aims of the White movement were to restore the old order — but that 'the war aims of the Allies in Russia were less clear. ... The intervention was finally presented to the world by allied spokesmen, in so far as its motives were publicized at all, as a political crusade against Bolshevism. Actually, "anti-Bolshevism" played a secondary role'.[144] But what Sayers and Kahn could not say was that business interests in the West were as willing to reach accord with the Soviets as with anyone else; hence the lack of any mention by the pro-Soviet American authors of the Vanderlip concession or of the unnamed Americans reported by *The New York Times* as having formed a consortium for Soviet trade as early as 1920, or of the extensive commercial and financial relations Britain, the USA and Germany soon established with the Soviets.

CONCLUSION

The Allied intervention served Soviet purposes. Such a crisis was required in order to consolidate the Bolshevik position. Luckett in his history of the Civil War states that the Allied intervention had 'helped the Soviets' by making the Soviet cause appear to be 'patriotic rather than factional'.[145] Of the Great Powers, only Japan and France had the aim of eliminating Bolshevism, while Britain sought to get out without being seen as dishonourable, and America's presence served as nothing other than a menace to the White movement.

---

142 'Kolchak's Fall', *New York Times*, December 30, 1919.

143 Ibid.

144 Sayers and Kahn, op. cit., 107.

145 Richard Luckett, *The White Generals: The White Movement and the Russian Civil War* (London: Longman, 1971), 386.

Robert Service writes that:

> Lenin and Trotsky had wanted a civil war in order to have the chance to carry out their irreversible suppression of the enemies of the October Revolution. Neither of them said this directly in public. A secret telegram that Trotsky had sent to Lenin on 17 August 1918 summed up their attitude:

> I consider it unacceptable to let steamers sail [the Volga] under a Red Cross flag. The receipt of grain will be interpreted by charlatans and fools as showing the possibility that agreement can be made and that civil war is unnecessary. The military motives are unknown to me. Air pilots and artillerymen have been ordered to bomb and set fire to the bourgeois district of Kazan and then to Simbirsk and Samara. In these conditions a Red Cross caravan is inappropriate.[146]

Luckett states that, 'The Civil War removed from Russia, through death or exile, the greater part of the upper and middle classes. It polarized the political conflict and reinforced the monolithic structure of the emergent state'.[147]

Of particular interest is that Luckett contends that rather than a commitment to the restoration of monarchy being a weakness or a cause of divisiveness, had the White movement from the start declared its commitment to Czarism it would have initially lost 'some of their adherents' but that in the long run the gains 'could have been very considerable'.[148] Not surprisingly, the 'White movement' having embraced sundry elements from Socialist Revolutionaries to Czarists, with the bizarre situation of great Czarist military leaders such as Kolchak having to offer their services to Socialist Revolutionaries, had no positive unifying factor. Of course, the Allies, led by Wilson and Lloyd George, were unrestrained in their contempt for Czarism.

The elimination of the Bolshevik regime was not a doomed cause, despite the wishful thinking of many Allied representatives and businessmen. Far from it. The Bolsheviks started with a precarious hold that did not extend far beyond Moscow and Petrograd. Luckett concludes in his study that although the White army made many

---

146 Service, op. cit., 223.

147 Luckett, op. cit., 387.

148 Ibid., 388.

strategic blunders, 'the Reds made mistakes also: in exclusively military matters they made far more than the Whites. ... Given the White failure to organise politically, their achievements are all the more remarkable'.[149]

In October 1919, although Kolchak was being pushed back in Siberia, Yudenich's forces came within eight miles of Petrograd and the Soviet regime had moved its seat of power to Moscow.[150] Although the Red Army pushed Yudenich back from the verge of triumph, Robert Service writes:

> Armed conflicts continued to cover Russian and Ukrainian territory as peasants rose in revolt against the Soviet order with its expropriations and conscriptions. Scarcely had the Red Army defeated Yudenich than it was being sent out to crush the rebellions. The Greens[151] roamed across province after province. Mutinies broke out in Red Army garrisons. Industrial strikes broke out in an increasing number of factories and mines. Inter-ethnic and inter-religious clashes also continued to occur in outlying regions. The Bashkirs and Tatars were fighting each other in the southern Urals. Muslim communities fought with Russians in the province by the River Volga.[152]

Yet according to Graves' reminisces, written over a decade later and with the advantage of hindsight, the Russian peasants and workers were entirely in support of the Bolsheviks, and the White movement comprised a "crowd" of sadistic reactionaries and autocrats.

Service comments of this situation that while the White forces sought to regroup and challenge the Red Army, their hopes were undermined by the decision of the United Kingdom and France to halt their intervention in the Civil War. In December 1919 the British withdrew from Archangel, the French from Odessa. Neither Trotsky nor his leading comrades made much comment because they were wary of concluding that the threat of an anti-Bolshevik crusade was over... The Reds had come close to defeat several times since the Civil War.

---

149 Ibid.

150 Service, op. cit., 242.

151 Peasant partisans often led by anarchists.

152 Service, op. cit., 244.

... The Civil War was a close run conflict between the Reds and the Whites.[153]

The White forces were literally stabbed in the back by the machinations of the Allied politicians, and the 'vested interests', to use Wilson's term, that saw bright prospects for business dealings with their supposed arch-enemies.

The lessons of U.S. duplicity in regard to aiding supposed friends, and particularly those in conflict with Communism, could have been a warning to those finding themselves in similar circumstances and who succumbed because of American betrayal, from China[154] to Cuba[155] to Nicaragua[156] to Tibet,[157] where on each occasion the USA scuttled at the crucial juncture. The tendency towards treachery that remains a factor of American foreign relations, which continues the Wilsonian doctrine for 'world order', is something that still needs learning by those who would 'sup with the devil'.

The last Shah of Iran, Mohammed Reza Pahlavi, himself a victim of U.S. duplicity, summed up the policy of the USA that has been one of consistency no matter who the president, and what the party:

> America's post-war history is an uninterrupted demand that the rest of the world resemble America, no matter what the history - political, economic and social – of other nations might have been. The example of Vietnam haunts me still. Unlike the French, who had a sense of what could and could not be done, the U.S. set out to build a new nation in Vietnam modelled on itself. When Ngo Dinh Diem refused to bend his policies to an unrealizable democratic ideal .... The Administration ordered Diem's murder. It is worth noting that on the day he died, Diem

---

153 Ibid., p. 244-245.

154 Jung Chang and Jon Halliday, Mao: the Unknown Story (London: Jonathan Cape, 2005), Chapter 28, 'Saved By Washington', 292–303.

155 Mario Lazo, Dagger in the Heart: American Policy Failures in Cuba (New York: Twin Circle Publishing Co., 1968).

156 Anastasio Somoza and Jack Cox, Nicaragua Betrayed (Boston: Western Islands, 1980).

157 R. Sengupta, 'The CIA Circus: Tibet's Forgotten Army', Friends of Tibet (India), February 15, 1999. http://www.friendsoftibet.org/databank/usdefence/usd7.html
See also: K R Bolton, 'The Tragedy of Tibet: A Saga of Betrayal, Colonization and Exploitation', Foreign Policy Journal, June 25, 2010. http://www.foreignpolicyjournal.com/2010/06/25/the-tragedy-of-tibet-a-saga-of-betrayal-colonization-and-exploitation/

was on the offensive against the Communists, and that on the day afterwards the initiative had passed to the Vietcong and the North Vietnamese. Over the next twelve years the Americans and the South Vietnamese never regained it.[158]

The Vietnamese 'Communists', like the victorious section of the Bolshevik Party, more nationalist than Marxist, as the following chapter – 'Messianic Tradition within Russian Bolshevism – shows,[159] only nominally 'won'. Vietnam, however, exhausted by the war, succumbed to globalisation. In that sense, what global capital sought for Russia with Bolshevism, but failed, succeeded in Vietnam, despite the military loss by the USA. As the saying goes, North Vietnam 'won the war, but lost the peace'.[160] In 1986 North Vietnam embarked on a 'socialist-oriented market economy'.[161] Afghanistan was intended by the USA as Russia's Vietnam, to so exhaust the USSR to the point that Russia would succumb to globalisation, and hence the *Mujahidin* was established by the USA, and the *Jihadism* that emerged continues to be used to exhaust any state that does not embrace globalisation, from Serbia and Chechnya to Libya to present-day Syria. The Soviet bloc did implode, and the USA's proxy-war in Afghanistan played its part, along with the type of inner and outer subversion that will be examined in following chapters. Despite the brief interregnum of Boris Yeltsin, Russia narrowly escaped the enslavement of the global oligarchs thanks to Putin's intervention, just as Russia narrowly escaped with the intervention of Stalin. We shall next examine the historic background within Bolshevism itself of how this narrow escape by Russia came about.

---

158 Mohammed Reza Pahlavi, *The Sha's Story* (London: Michael Joseph, 1980) 231.

159 See also Bolton, *Stalin: The Enduring Legacy*, passim.

160 Bolton, 'Has Vietnam Lost the Struggle for Freedom?', *Foreign Policy Journal*, 10 June 2010; https://www.foreignpolicyjournal.com/2010/06/10/has-vietnam-lost-the-struggle-for-freedom/view-all/

161 Geoffrey Murray, (1997) *Vietnam: Dawn of a New Market* (New York: St. Martin's Press, 1979), 24-25.

Messianic Tradition within Russian Bolshevism

With the one hundredth anniversary of the Bolshevik Revolution in October 1917, Russia is still very largely the product of that legacy. But what of Bolshevism itself? Bolshevism unleashed conflicting forces. This article contends that the successful faction was not that of doctrinaire Marxism, but was shaped by "eternal Russia," and metamorphosed into something far removed from Marxism, as Trotsky and many other Marxists have lamented. In this article Bolshevism is re-examined as the product of a long-time tradition, focusing on the views of the Russian dissident Mikhail Agursky.

Russia stood at a cross-roads from the late 19th century, as she was beginning to industrialize and to "modernize." The political system was not keeping pace with these demands. Depictions of Czarism as a tyranny that brutalised its people is a myth, emanating from well-funded propaganda from the USA, courtesy of New York banker Jacob Schiff and his paid journalist George Kennan.[1] Much was achieved under Czarism in terms of workers' and peasants' welfare, but outside industrial and financial interests and inner unrest would not allow a peaceful and gradual transition. Agents of the German High Command, British military intelligence, and Wall Street finance scrambled over Russia in its time of chaos, each wanting to impose its will over the vast land, people and resources.[2]

The revolutions that occurred in February and October 1917 had within them several contending currents that at times converged. With the elimination of the old regime there ensued a decade of struggle within Bolshevism between what was later called 'rootless cosmopolitanism' and Russian messianism: the first under Trotsky, the second under Stalin. The Russian faction won, and the significance of that remains *the* primary factor in world politics. What is often overlooked or deliberately hidden, however, is that while Stalin is

---

1   K. R. Bolton, *Revolution from Above* (London: Arktos Media Ltd., 2011), 57-65.

2   Bolton, ibid. Also see Dr. Richard Spence's *Wall Street and the Russian Revolution 1905-1925* (Walterville, Oregon: Trine Day, 2017).

accused of "betraying the revolution" with his "socialism in one country," that course was initiated by Lenin.

Bolshevism contra Communism

From the start there was a wide perception among the Russian people that differentiated between Communism as foreign import, and Bolshevism as a Russian manifestation. Trotsky and Zinoviev were identified with the former, Lenin with the latter.[3] It was a dichotomy that was to culminate in the expulsion of Trotskyites, and under Stalin to reaffirm the Leninist national and imperial path. During the sailors' uprising at Kronstadt in 1921 against the Soviet government, the sentiments were against Trotsky and Zinoviev, not against Lenin.[4] Trotsky is remembered as the 'butcher of Kronstadt'.

The rivalry between German-Jewish and Russian socialism goes back to the days of Karl Marx and the First International. This factionalism, despite the vaunted 'internationalism' of the socialists, played along national lines. Marx and Engels maintained the traditional German animosity towards Slavs, while the Anarchist Mikhail Bakunin and other Russian socialists were pan-Slavic. This pan-Slavism and antagonism between Russian and German socialism had a primary impact on Bolshevism and the development of the USSR, where Bolshevism came to be seen even by proponents of the old regime as the only choice for liberation from foreign capital, German political influence, and Western liberalism.

Germany contended with Russia to be the world centre of socialism. For the faction of Bolshevism that triumphed in Russia this was a continuation of Russia's messianic outlook no less than the mysticism of Russian Christian Orthodoxy that sees Russia as having a mission to remake humanity. What was early called *National Bolshevism* developed as an intrinsic part of Russian socialism. Agursky contended that Marxist theory was 'historical camouflage' for 'deeper historical and geopolitical processes'. [5]

---

3   Mikhail Agursky, *The Third Rome: National Bolshevism in the USSR* (London: Westview Press, 1987), 233. Dr. Agursky was an adviser to the Soviet military industry, becoming a dissident who migrated to Israel and pursued a career in academia. His father, Solomon, had been leader of the Jewish section of the Bolshevik Party, and the party's official historian. Agursky's book is essential reading for understanding developments in the USSR.

4   Agursky, ibid., 234.

5   Ibid., xiii.

Marx Russophobic

Agursky refers to Lenin's 1912 eulogy to Alexander Herzen as the founder of Russian socialism. Herzen had been in conflict with Marx and Engels.[6] Lenin's eulogy to Herzen was therefore ideologically significant. Lenin concluded by emphasising the Russian character of Herzen's thinking: 'Herzen was the first to raise the great banner of struggle by addressing his *free Russian word* to the masses'.[7] This is far removed from Marx's attitude, when he wrote to Engels that he did not want to appear with Herzen, "not being of the view that Old Europe should be rejuvenated with Russian blood."[8] Lenin focused on repudiating liberalism which, as Agursky shows, was an antipathy that later provided common ground between the Bolsheviks and those who had at first reacted against Bolshevism, including former Czarist officers and emigres. It is this common antipathy to liberalism and a desire by the Bolsheviks to make Russia the centre of a new humanity, as does Orthodox Christianity, that enabled reconciliation with the new regime. Many returned to Russia to become prominent in Soviet culture in particular. Conversely Marxist internationalists, who were later called 'rootless cosmopolitans' by Stalin, those such as Trotsky and Zinoviev (head of the ill-fated Comintern) were purged in a process of what Agursky calls 'nationalisation', started by Lenin.

Trotskyite theorist Cyril Smith[9] contends that Russian socialism had nothing to do with Marx, who possessed the anti-Slavism of a German chauvinist. This rivalry between German and Russian socialism for supremacy was important in the development of Bolshevism. Smith writes:

> Russia has, inevitably, loomed large in this account of the development of Marxism, so it is important to clarify the relationship of Marx himself to the origins of "Marxism" in that country. As is well known, the hostility of Marx and Engels to Russia in their earlier political work was so deep that it sometimes approached anti-Slav racism. ... Marx detested those, like A. I. Herzen (1812-1870) and M. A. Bakunin (1814-

---

6 Ibid.

7 V. I. Lenin, "In Memory of Herzen," *Sotsial-Demokrat* No. 26, 8 May 1912; https://www.marxists.org/archive/lenin/works/1912/may/08c.htm

8 Agursky, 21.

9 John Plant, "Marking the Death of Cyril Smith," https://www.marxists.org/reference/archive/smith-cyril/obituary.htm

1876), who argued that there was a specific Russian national road to socialism, arising from some special qualities of the "Russian spirit". When socialist ideas developed in Russia, they had nothing to do with Marx ...[10]

Agursky stated that Russia had by 1917 become heavily influenced by a German-filled bureaucracy and foreign capital investment. Bolshevism was a revolt against foreign influences. The revolution was one of national liberation, not of international revolution inspired by a German-Jewish Slavophobe. Marx and Engels, as much as any German xenophobe, regarded a Russian invasion of Europe with dread, as the end of civilisation. 'Backward Russia', Marx stated, must be civilised by the West, that is, it must go through the phase of capitalism, before achieving socialism.[11] The necessity of a capitalist phase in a nation's development is an essential part of Marxist historical dialectics, and therefore slavery and colonialism were historically justified by Marxism, although it is no longer expedient for the Left to say so. During the Crimean War the Russophobia of Marx and Engels became particularly vehement.[12]

Russia's Mission

Conversely, Russians considered they had a mission to overcome and revivify the decrepit and decadent West with Russian vigour. The Bolsheviks were heirs to this messianic mission that had been proclaimed by Dostoyevsky and others. Dostoyevsky saw the Russian socialists becoming the "most fervent .... champions ... of the Russian spirit."[13] That they undertook this mission in the name of Bolshevism rather than Christian Orthodoxy was a matter of labelling rather than substance. This Russo-Slavic messianism had been advocated by Herzen, contending that Russians were still a race of youth and health.[14]

Such messianism, inherited by Russian socialism, and brought to fruition by Bolshevism, enabled a convergence even with widespread

---

10   Cryil Smith, "Marx at the Millennium" (1998) https://www.marxists.org/reference/archive/smith-cyril/works/millenni/smith2a.htm

11   Agursky, 17.

12   Ibid., 18-19. See: *Karl Marx and Frederick Engels, The Russian Menace to Europe*, edited by Paul Blackstock and Bert Hoselitz (London: George Allen and Unwin, 1953).

13   Dostoyevsky, *Diary of a Writer*, quoted by Agursky, 55.

14   Agursky, 11.

mysticism and gnosticism. The dualistic dichotomy of gnosticism translated readily into the dualistic dichotomy of Bolshevism. Gnostic and sectarian apocalyptic beliefs that the world was corrupt were translated into revolution. Agursky states that 'Russian mystical sects played an extremely important part in the Bolshevik revolution'.[15]

The USSR always referred to the 'decadent West' as did conservative historian Oswald Spengler. It is notable that Spengler's seminal *Decline of The West* was a best-seller in Soviet Russia as early as 1923, when it was translated.[16]

Herzen as the father of Russian socialism saw Russia having a mission to lead the universal revolution to renew humanity. German Marxism remained committed to the supremacy of the Fatherland. Hence, the German Social Democrats were among the most zealous supporters of militarism during World War I. Lenin's primary concern in dealing with Germany was to ensure that a socialist revolution did *not* occur there. German Communists for their part harboured the Russophobia of Marx and Engels. Liebknecht, leader of the German Social Democratic party, wrote in 'Must Europe become Cossack?' of Russia as semi-barbaric and a threat to European and especially German freedom. This Russophobia was continued by his successor, Bebel. During the 1880s Bebel affirmed the party's Russophobia, encouraged by Engels, who demanded a strong German military.[17]

Bolshevism

The character of Russia as an intrinsic superpower shapes the way that the head of Russia will develop his regime, unless one is like Yeltsin, for example, atypically interested in integrating Russia into a so-called "world community," politically, economically, and culturally, the short duration indicating the depth of Russian tradition. Lenin's Bolshevism became nationalist and geopolitical, and notions of world revolution expressed by foreign Communist parties[18] were pressed into the service of Russian foreign policy. Those who could not serve as such were scuttled, and this includes in particular the German Communists, and the Comintern. Since the conflict between Marx and Herzen, Agursky states that the 'national heritage of Russian

---

15   Ibid., 61.

16   Ibid., 229.

17   Ibid., 62-63, 65.

18   Ibid., 72.

socialism was absorbed by Lenin in its entirety, though transformed and synthesized'. [19]

Bolshevism despised liberalism, epitomised by the Constitutional Democrats or Kadets party. After the triumph of Bolshevism many even among Czarist officers and emigres were reconciled with Bolshevism because of its creation of a strong, centralised Russian state. Agursky shows that this Right-wing and ex-Czarist support for Bolshevism was sincere and principled, rather than opportunistic.

The *Okhrana*, Russian secret police, had cultivated contacts with the Bolsheviks, regarding them as preferable to Mensheviks, Socialist Revolutionaries, and Kadets. The editor of the Bolshevik organ, *Pravda*, was an *Okhrana* agent. The common ground between Bolsheviks and *Okhrana* was opposition to liberalism, with which the Mensheviks were aligned. The Bolsheviks with their opposition to German and other Western Marxists, were regarded by the *Okhrana* as fellow Russian patriots.[20] In comparison to these factions, Lenin and other Bolshevik leaders when prosecuted were favourably treated.[21]

In what Agursky calls 'God-building' among the Bolsheviks, Maxim Gorky, a *Russian* socialist in the manner of Herzen, and a primary influence on Soviet culture and ideology, refers to 'God [being] resurrected by the collective Russian soul expressed as a single popular will'.[22] He even regarded the 'Black Hundreds', a mass anti-Semitic movement of the ultra-Right among peasants and workers, as a nucleus for revolution. Many of them went over to Bolshevism, again opposition to liberalism and capitalism being the common factor.[23] Lenin and Stalin both stated that liberalism and the Kadet party were the enemy, not the 'Black Hundreds'.[24] Lenin, Stalin, Kamenev and Rykov, at the time of the February Revolution, spoke of a *national* revolution, and Stalin referred pointedly to the *Russian people* as the "only true ally" of a 'Russian revolution army'.[25] Agursky stated that the greatest allies of the Bolsheviks were 'the radical right', 'which made

---

19   Ibid., 73.

20   Ibid., 105.

21   Ibid., 102.

22   M. Gorky, Ispoved ("Confession," 1907), cited by Agursky, 88.

23   Agursky, 116-117.

24   Ibid., 118.

25   J. Stalin, Works, cited by Agursky, 150.

the Bolshevik revolution feasible'.[26] The 'Black Hundreds' were always anti-capitalist. Bolshevism for many Russians seemed preferable to the heavily Jewish Mensheviks and Socialist Revolutionaries, and a 'dictatorship of the proletariat' was preferable to the liberalism of the Kadets.[27] Lunatcharsky, first Soviet commissar for education, and a man of culture who ensured that the Russian heritage would not be ravaged by zealous Marxists and nihilists, was another prominent 'God-builder'.[28] Lunatcharsky as early as 1907 regarded Bolshevism as the restraining influence on revolutionary destruction.[29] In 1928 he cited the Bible at the 100th anniversary celebration of Tolstoy, stating that the Bible championed the right of the peasantry against capitalism.[30]

Lenin – Russian Patriot

Lenin himself was unequivocal in explaining that the Bolshevik revolution was required to redeem Russia nationally from degeneration, writing during World War I that "Great Russian proletarians" love their language and their country. The 'Great Russian masses' would lead the world to a new humanity. The revolutionary workers wanted a 'free, independent and proud Great Russia'.[31] He saw Russia as a world power, not as the centre of a world Marxist revolution. Lenin wrote of Russia ceasing to be 'wretched and impotent', to become 'mighty and abundant'. The revolution had unleashed the latent 'creative powers of the people ... to build a truly mighty and abundant Russia'.[32] Patriotism, so far from being a bourgeois sentiment to divide the working class was, Lenin wrote in *Pravda* in 1918, a 'deeply ingrained' sentiment, and 'fatherlands' were the product of millennia of development. The seeming betrayal of patriotism by the Armistice with Germany, the Treaty of Brest-Litovsk, was unfortunate but necessary, and did not indicate a departure of Bolshevism from patriotism. Lenin unequivocally stated that socialist revolution should be seen as a tactic

---

26   Ibid., 151.

27   Ibid., 152.

28   Ibid., 88.

29   Ibid., 92.

30   "Lunatcharsky Takes Bible as Tolstoy Celebration Text," Jewish Telegraphic Agency, 13 September 1928.

31   *V. I. Lenin, Collected Works*, quoted by Agursky, 144.

32   Ibid., quoted by Agurksy, 193.

to maintain Russian's 'independence and freedom'.[33] In 1919 Stalin repeated the Leninist principle, which was to become the Stalinist premise, that the Soviet Government is a truly 'national government', liberating Russia from 'world imperialism';[34] the globalisation of the day. Stalin, like Spengler, Jung, Fichte, or the Russian Berdyaev, wrote of folk-souls and of the American as an "industrial-commercial soul," while expressing the messianic tradition of the self-sacrificing, martyred Russian as the world saviour.[35]

Convergence with the Right

Agursky describes Bolshevism as a triumph of the popular will, in the tradition of Russian populism. Lenin and other Bolshevik leaders were carried along with it. Bolshevism became a populist revolt against foreign influences, economically, politically and culturally. The poet Riurik Ivnev lauded the Revolution as a messianic outcome: 'I was taught by Dostoyevsky to understand my Russia'.[36] Russia's literati went over the Bolshevism, seeing it in messianic, mystical and even Christian terms. This trend produced two collections of poetry in 1917, and 1918; *Skify* ('Scythians'). The editor was Ivanov-Razumnik, who regarded the revolution as genuinely 'Russian', not 'alien' or Marxist. These pro-Bolshevik *Slavophils* believed Russia was the new Scythia that would purge the world of decadence. Alexander Blok saw Russia in this way, declaring that the 'old world' would perish before the new Scythians. Andre Bely, a major and enduring influence on Soviet culture, an anthroposophist and friend of Rudolf Steiner, saw Bolshevism in mystical, Christian terms, writing of 'Russia the Godbearer, who defeats the serpent', crucified and resurrected.[37] Lunatcharsky saw Russia in Dostoyevskyan terms as the messianic world liberator.[38]

Among the first from the Right to praise Bolshevism was Vasily Sulgin who was, prior to the revolution, deputy chairman of the conservative All-Russian National Union. He saw the Red Army as invigorating the Russian military. He foresaw the emergence of a leader who would be energised by Bolshevism and motivated by nationalism.[39]

---

33   Ibid., quoted by Agursky, 204.

34   Agursky, 205.

35   Ibid., 207.

36   R. Ivnev, "Rossia," 1922.

37   A. Bely, Kristos voskrese, 1923.

38   Lunatcharsky, cited by Agursky 206

39   Ibid., 238-239.

The novelist and poet, Ieronim Yaskinsky, a nationalist, regarded the Bolsheviks as deeply rooted in Russia, making strong Russian heroes. He became a Soviet literary figure.

The Right-nationalist, Professor Nicholai Ustrialov, formerly of Moscow University, having supported the anti-Bolshevik redoubt of Admiral Kolchak in the Russian Far East, after 1920 started advocating National Bolshevism. He foresaw Bolshevism as moving towards nationalism.[40] He was a Hegelian who saw history unfolding dialectically.[41] Like other Right-nationalists who moved to Bolshevism, Ustrialov saw the Soviet state as having eliminated the rot of liberalism. The destruction wrought by Bolshevism was a historically necessary purgatory which resurrected Russia. The slogans about internationalism served Russian national and imperial interests.[42] Harbin, China, where he and other Russian emigres settled, became a centre of a National Bolshevik intelligentsia. Among the self-declared adherents of National Bolshevism was Vladimir L'vov, who had been procurator of the Russian Holy Synod.[43] Many returned to Russia and played an influential part especially in the culture of the USSR.[44]

Lenin's Legacy

Agurksy states that Stalin's 'socialism in one country' was not an innovation; it had even before 1917 been a major influence in Bolshevism. For 'the majority of Bolsheviks' the aim was not world revolution, but revolution dominated by Russia; the messianic yearning of Moscow as the 'Third Rome' reshaping humanity in the Russian's image.[45] The question was settled with the Great Purges of the 1930s. The Comintern was closed, foreign Communists, especially the German Communists, were scuttled, and most of the German party central committee who fled Hitler, were executed in the USSR.[46]

Perhaps the most symbolic move was the restoration of the Orthodox

---

40   Ibid., 240.

41   Ibid., 243.

42   Ibid., 245.

43   Ibid., 247-251.

44   Ibid., 257.

45   Ibid., 306.

46   K. R. Bolton, *Stalin: The Enduring Legacy* (London: Black House Publishing, 2012), 6-9

Church under Stalin, whose own commitment to 'Godless atheism' is doubtful, to the extent that today he is depicted as a saint on Orthodox icons, and in publications of the Church. The legacy remains. The Communist Party of the Russian Federation, led by Zyuganov, having maintained a major role in politics, with a National Bolshevik orientation, called on the Church to canonise Stalin in 2008.[47] In 2014, the Trinity Lavra of St. Sergius Monastery in Moscow, a centre of Orthodoxy, published a calendar commemorating the life of Stalin, starting from his days as a seminary student. Mikhail Babkin, a noted Russian historian specializing in Russian Orthodox Church studies, commented that 'The link between the Moscow Patriarchy of the Russian Orthodox Church and Stalin remains close to sacred'.[48]

Even many former supporters of the Czar came to regard the apocalypse of revolution that descended on Russia as dialectically an historical necessity, and the harbinger of a new beginning. Russia had become stagnant and was becoming a colony of outsiders, economically, politically and culturally. She needed drastic surgery. Reform was insufficient, much less Western liberalism. There remains a strong current of opinion among Zyuganov Communists, Eurasianists and others of both the Russian Right and Left, who believe that without Bolshevism Russia would have sunk into a quagmire of decay; that from the horrendous birth-pangs of revolution and civil war Russia was reborn, and restored to the possibilities of the destiny foretold by Dostoyevsky and other mystically and messianically inclined religious and literary figures over the centuries. It is a current that continues to exist in influential circles, and has persisted in Russia whether under Czarism, Bolshevism, or Putinism.

---

47   Adrian Blomfield, "Could Joseph Stalin Be Made a Saint?," *The Telegraph*, 22 July 2008; www.telegraph.co.uk/news/worldnews/europe/russia/2445683/Could-Josef-Stalin-be-made-a-saint.html

48   "Russian Orthodox Church Slammed for Stalin Calendar," Radio Free Europe, 8 January, 2014; www.rferl.org/a/russia-stalin-calendar/25224022.html

'Saint Joseph': Was Stalin Defender of the Church?

The upsurge of nostalgia for Joseph Stalin in Russia is a remembrance of the greatness that Russia achieved during that era, and one which many Russian's hope to see renewed. A notable seeming paradox is that this revival of Stalinism is related more to Russian messianic *Slavophilism*, which sees Russia has having a unique world-mission, than to Communism. The reconstituted Communist Party under Zyuganov is also notably of Stalinist orientation, and part of a patriotic resurgence that is inconsistent with the anti-national basis of Marxist dogma. The Russian Orthodox Church is the spiritual foundation of renewed Russian nationalism, although "nationalism" in the Western sense is here a misnomer, since the Russian outlook is universal, regardless of the ideological label. Orthodoxy and patriotism towards Holy Mother Russia are inseparable. There is a convergence of forces, and among this is the phenomenon of the Orthodox faithful embracing Stalin to the point of his being portrayed as a "Saint." How is it possible that the person assumed to be the most avid persecutor of the Church, could be portrayed in such a manner?

Stalin Revival

In 2008 the Communist Party petitioned the Orthodox Church to canonise Stalin. That the Communist Party should approach the Church in this manner is itself significant.[1] Not surprisingly attitudes among the faithful towards the idealization of Stalin are mixed. Controversially, in 2008 a priest displayed a painting, 'Matrona and Stalin' in his church in Saint Petersburg. The painting, by noted icon-artist Ilya Pivnik, depicts the alleged meeting of Stalin with 'the Blessed Eldress of Moscow',[2] a canonised Saint of the 20th century. Stalin is said to have spoken with the holy woman before the Battle

---

1   Adrian Blomfield, 'Could Joseph Stalin be made a Saint?', *The Telegraph*, July 22, 2008; http://www.telegraph.co.uk/news/worldnews/europe/russia/2445683/Could-Josef-Stalin-be-made-a-saint.html

2   'Matrona of Moscow', Orthodox Wiki, https://orthodoxwiki.org/Matrona_of_Moscow

of Moscow. Although the priest was dismissed he insisted that Stalin was a "man of faith."

In 2015 a monk priest prayed for Stalin and other World War II heroes as part of a military celebration that included an icon-style painting entitled "Sovereign Holy Mother." This included Stalin and his Generals, looked over from heaven by Mary, Christ and the saints.[3]

A calendar published in 2014, depicting Stalin throughout his life, including his time as a Seminary student, was published by the Trinity Lavra of St. Sergius Monastery in Moscow. This is significant because the monastery is the centre of Russian Orthodoxy, and was the seat of the Russian Patriarch until 1983. The Monastery had been closed by the Bolsheviks, but reopened by Stalin in 1945, and services resumed in 1946.

Mikhail Babkin, a noted Russian historian specializing in Russian Orthodox Church studies, commented that 'The link between the Moscow Patriarchy of the Russian Orthodox Church and Stalin remains close to sacred'.[4]

Revolution Betrayed

Stalin is surely one of the most enigmatic of historical figures. Did any 'anti-communist', from Hitler to Ronald Reagan, pursue an anti-Marxist policy so thoroughly as the man who is both heralded and damned as a leader of the first Communist state and of the "world revolution"? Other than the collectivization of the economy, Marxist doctrine had been progressively purged from the USSR. For those on the 'Right' whose ideology is a variation of economic reductionism (as is Marxism) any state that pursues a policy antithetical to the Free Market is an athema. For those looking beyond economics, there is much to be seen.

Trotsky lamented that Stalin was a 'Bonapartist' who 'betrayed the revolution'. The hatred of Stalin by Trotskyites and other Marxists was such that many became prominent Cold Warriors in the service of the USA, because they, like Trotsky's widow Sedova, saw Stalin's

---

3   "Russian Orthodox Church outraged by appearance of Stalin icon," Sputnik News, May 31, 2015; https://sputniknews.com/russia/201505311022778000/

4   'Russian Orthodox Church slammed for Stalin calendar', Radio Free Europe, January 8, 2014; http://www.rferl.org/a/russia-stalin-calendar/25224022.html

Russia as a bigger threat to world socialism than the USA.[5] Already in 1936 Trotsky had written *The Revolution Betrayed* in which he described how Stalinism had reversed many of the primary Marxist doctrines that had been implemented during the early years of Bolshevism. Stalin had also done a more thorough job of liquidating Bolsheviks than Hitler. This included the elimination of the Old Bolsheviks Association, the dismantling of the Comintern which he regarded as a nest of traitors, and the elimination of most of the leading Communist exiles who had sought refuge in the USSR from Hitlerism.[6] Trotskyites and other Marxists flocked to the CIA front, the Congress for Cultural Freedom, and they came to the fore in the fight against the USSR after World War II.[7] Their legacy is today's "neo-con" movement, and even without Stalin their bitterness towards Russia endures.

What incensed Trotsky most of all was Stalin's rehabilitation of family and of religion. One might regard Trotsky's primary motive in embracing Marxism as the destruction of those two institutions. The destruction of family and religion seems to be the *raison d'être* of Marxism for many revolutionaries. It was their psychological rationalization often arising from a deep personal hatred, projected onto Western Civilization. Among those with such pathologies who embraced Marxism were Marx himself and Trotsky. In China Mao vented his hatred of the family on the Confucian heritage that honoured parents.[8] Chapter 7 of *The Revolution Betrayed* is devoted to condemning Stalin's revival of family and religion.[9]

Why did Stalin 'betray the revolution'? There are several hypotheses: (1) Stalin was being dialectical, and hence what he undertook was in accord with Marxist dialectics in both theory and practice. (2) Stalin was forced by pragmatism to reverse the Marxian doctrines of the early Bolshevik years as unworkable and self-destructive. If this is so, then one might ask whether Stalin would have seen Marxism as intrinsically flawed and not worthy of pursuing on any basis, whether pragmatically or dialectically? (3) Stalin was an agent of the *Okhrara*,

5   Natalia Sedova Trotsky, May 9, 1951, Labor Action, June 17, 1951, quoted in Bolton, *Stalin: The Enduring Legacy* (London: Black House Publishing, 2012), 117-118.

6   Bolton, ibid., 3-92.

7   Frances Stonor Saunders, *The Cultural Cold War: The CIA and the World of Arts and Letters* (New York: The New Press, 1999). See also Bolton, ibid., 34-38.

8   Bolton, *The Psychotic Left* (Black House Publishing, 2013).

9   Leon Trotsky, *The Revolution Betrayed* (1936), Chapter 7, "Family, Youth and Culture."

Czarist secret police. If so, perhaps he was never committed to Marxism, but was swept along by history and obliged to work within the Bolshevik framework?[10]

Stalin the Christian?

Much has been written about Stalin's days at the Tiflis seminary school where he studied for the priesthood. It is said that he soon became a rebellious, avid Marxist who rejected Christianity after reading Darwin. The most widely held account is that he was expelled from Seminary along with other students because of their revolutionary beliefs. This is questionable. The reason for his expulsion from the seminary seems to have been, rather, the result of a feud with a priest nicknamed "Black Spot." Montefiore provides the background, stating that 'Soso' was not expelled for being a revolutionist, and remained in friendly contact with the seminary. The seminary regarded Soso as an excellent student, however Father Abashidze, "Black Spot," was determined to be rid of him. It was tuition fees that troubled Soso, and he appealed to the Rector:

> To Archimandrite Serafim, Very Reverend Rector of the Tiflis Orthodox Seminary from 2nd Grade student Josef Djugashvili: Your Reverence knows all about the pitiful circumstances of my mother who takes care of me. My father has not provided for me in three years. This is his way of punishing me for continuing my studies against his wishes… It is for this reason I am applying to Your Reverence for the second time. I beg you on my knees to help me and accept me on full public expense. Josef Djugashvili 25 August 1895.[11]

In 1899 'Black Spot' raised the school fees, Soso was unexpectedly invoiced 25 roubles for his tuition and left (he was not expelled). The seminary urged him to pursue a career in teaching, which he declined. There is also a question as to whether he was an informant in regard to the radical beliefs of other students.[12]

There are several anecdotes that attest to Stalin's personal views on Christ. Stalin's daughter, Svetlana Alliluyeva, according to her biographer Rosemary Sullivan, found *The Life of Christ* in her father's

---

10   Roman Brackman, *The Secret File of Joseph Stalin: A Hidden Life* (London: Frank Cass, 2001), 59-60.

11   Montefiore, *Young Stalin* (London: Orion Publishing, 2007), 28.

12   Ibid.

library when an adolescent. As an indoctrinated atheist she asked her father about the myth of Jesus. He replied that Jesus was no myth, but a real person and spent the day telling her about Christ from what he had learnt at seminary.[13] Dr. Erik van Ree of Amsterdam University, an expert on Stalin, quotes him as stating in 1952 in regard to the suffering of soldiers: 'Jesus Christ also suffered, and even carried his cross, and then he rose up to heaven. You, then, have to suffer too, in order to rise up to heaven'.[14]

Ilizarov, drawing on hitherto closed Russian archives, quotes Stalin as refusing to accept atheist literature into his personal library, calling it 'anti-religious waste-paper'. He addressed friends and comrades with Godly salutations, such as 'May God give you New Year every day'.[15] To American envoy W. Averill Harriman he remarked: 'Only God can forgive'. He maintained his friendship with old seminarian friends who became priests, such as Peter Kapanadze. When he sent a gift of fish to Alexei Kosygin after the Second World War he included a handwritten note: 'Comrade Kosygin, here are some presents for you from God! (I am an executor of His will)'.[16]

Failure of Godless Crusade

Even in the mid-1930s when Trotsky wrote *The Revolution Betrayed*, in condemning the restoration of family life by Stalin, he claimed that already the State was withdrawing from the campaign against religion:

> Concern for the authority of the older generation, by the way, has already led to a change of policy in the matter of religion. The denial of God, his assistance and his miracles, was the sharpest wedge of all those which the revolutionary power drove between children and parents. Outstripping the development of culture, serious propaganda and scientific education, the struggle with the churches, under the leadership of people of the type of Yaroslavsky,[17] often degenerated into buffoonery and mischief.

---

13   Rosemary Sullivan, *Stalin's Daughter: The Extraordinary and Tumultuous Life of Svetlana Alliluyeva* (Harper, 2015), 229.

14   Erik van Ree, *Political Thought of Joseph Stalin: A Study in Twentieth Century Revolutionary Patriotis*m (London: Routledge Curzon, 2002) chapter 14, footnote 41.

15   B. S. Ilizarov, *Secret life of Stalin* (2004), 434.

16   Stalin letter to Kosygin, 1948-10-22. Cited by Montefiore, *Young Stalin*, op. cit.

17   Head of the League of Militant Godless.

The storming of heaven, like the storming of the family, is now brought to a stop. The bureaucracy, concerned about their reputation for respectability, have ordered the young "godless" to surrender their fighting armour and sit down to their books. In relation to religion, there is gradually being established a regime of ironical neutrality. But that is only the first stage. It would not be difficult to predict the second and third, if the course of events depended only upon those in authority.[18]

The League of Militant Godless had been established in 1925 as an organization theoretically independent of the Communist Party. Trotsky alluded to this under the leadership of Yaroslavskii as being largely a manifestation of 'buffoonery', and it is generally regarded as having had the opposite of its intended aims. Yarosslavskii commented that 'when entire districts are declared Godless, in a region where there is nothing, no culture, no [antireligious] work - this is a joke'. In 1928 Anatolii Lunacharskii, minister of education, commented that 'religion is like a nail; the harder you hit it, the deeper it goes into the wood'. That seems to have been the result of the Militant Godless' campaigns. Daniel Peris shows from Soviet archives that entire districts of supposed organizational networks of the League of Militant Godless only existed on paper.[19] Persi calls the League "largely a house of cards,"[20] despite its claim of over 5,000,000 members, many of whom were simply trades unionists and members of party organs dragooned into the League *en masse*.

According to a January 1937 census, despite the totalitarian character of the USSR, and a decade of atheist crusading, only 42.9% of respondents claimed to be 'nonbelievers'. Peris suggests that where atheism was increasing this was not the result of Militant Godless campaigns, but a natural process of secularization caused by social and economic transformations.[21] The process of secularisation has been just as widespread in Western liberal societies under the impress of the social and economic developments of capitalism.

The Bolshevik terror against the Church started in 1918. Already there had been a series of murders against the faithful, prompting

---

18   Trotsky, *The Revolution Betrayed*, op. cit., 7: 1.

19   Daniel Peris, *Storming the Heavens: The Soviet League of the Militant Godless* (Ithaca: Cornell University Press, 1998), 114.

20   Ibid.

21   Ibid.

Patriarch Tikhon to proclaim his anathema on the Bolsheviks on January 19, 1918. The 1918 law separating church and state enabled nationalized church property to be turned over to registered communes of believers; hence it became a widespread practice to use Soviet laws to regain church property for the faithful.[22] The resistance of believers to Bolshevik efforts at the eradication of religion was not passive; years after the Civil War, into the early 1930s, thousands of believers could be readily mobilized to confront local anti-religious efforts. Atheist agitators were faced with violence and even death. Atheist clubs were attacked and ransacked. Clergy and believers even took over leadership of anti-religious clubs. [23]

In 1922 anti-Church actions intensified. A 'Resolution of the All-Union Central Executive Committee' (ACEC) ordered the removal of church valuables.[24] All valuables under 200 years old, such as bells, gold icon frames, and silver plates, had to be melted down. The Alexander Nevsky Lavra in St. Petersburg was plundered. These actions were undertaken on the pretext of funding famine relief. In 1922 Trotsky complained that *Pravda* and *Izvestiya* were not giving sufficient attention to the anti-religious struggle in their columns.[25] Had Trotsky triumphed in the leadership struggle against Stalin it is certain that he would have pursued the anti-Christian offensive to its completion.

Interestingly, believers often appealed to higher authorities, and in particular to Mikhail Kalinin, confidante of Stalin until his death in 1946, and head of state as chairman of the Supreme Soviet, to get decisions overturned, to the frustration of atheists.[26] In 1930 Kalinin ordered an investigation into reports of arbitrary methods being used against the faithful.[27] William Husband states:

At no time before 1932 did the Bolsheviks feel they controlled

---

22   Ibid., 87.

23   William B. Husband, "Soviet Atheism and Russian Orthodox strategies of resistance 1917-1932," Journal of Modern History, Vol. 70, No. 1, 74-107; https://ir.library. oregonstate.edu/xmlui/bitstream/handle/1957/21678/HusbandWilliamHistory. SovietAtheismRussian.pdf?sequence=19.

24   Resolution of the ACEC from February 23, 1922.

25   L. Trotsky, communique of May 14, 1922, cited by F. Corley, *Religion in the Soviet Union: An Archival Reader* (London: Macmillan, 1996), 32.

26   Husband op. cit., 89.

27   Ibid., 90-91.

the situation... During the second half of the 1920s, organs in Nizhnii Novgorod continued to encounter no shortage of religious groups that effectively circulated anti-Soviet political materials, and similar reports that legal organizations served as fronts for oppositional activity reached party leaders from other locales as well.[28]

William Husband concludes in regard to the conflict between believers and Bolsheviks:

> This battle of competing visions of truth and reality produced lessons of experience for all involved, but no definitive victor. Bolshevism proved to be no single-minded monolith determined to eradicate religion as an end in itself and at all cost. Despite the countless antireligious resolutions routinely passed at all levels of party and state work, the promotion of atheism was chronically underfunded, neglected by the very organs designated to carry it out, and left to amateurs and the least talented cadres. High officials made a sustained effort to maintain Soviet law and restrain crude attacks at the regional and local levels, but in the process they created avenues through and around Soviet policy...[29]

The dichotomy between the Soviet State and the Church is not as simple as 'Godless Bolshevism versus the Faith'. The Church, an integral part of the Czarist state, was a counter-revolutionary force. The Orthodox Church was also a mainstay of 'patriotism' and of the notion of 'Holy Mother Russia' with a world messianic mission. This mission is to remould a new humanity according to Christian brotherhood, and sees Russia as the *Katechon*, the means by which the unleashing of the Antichrist is being delayed. The German-Latvian scholar Walter Schubart wrote in his once influential book, *Russia and Western Man*, where he described this world mission, and noted even then (1938) that the world revolutionary mission of the USSR was a very Russian application of Marxism, and that the Bolshevik dogma would become increasingly reshaped into something far removed from the imported Marxist dogma.[30] Trotsky and the Bolshevik and other Marxist opposition against Stalin saw this already happening at the same time.

---

28 Ibid., 86.

29 Ibid., 106-107.

30 Walter Schubart, *Russia and Western Man* ([1938] English ed. New York: Frederick Ungar, 1950).

Corley comments that 'had it really had the desire, as Albania later did, the Soviet state could have extinguished all open expressions of religious faith. ... Issuing decrees and writing long reports was often a substitute for action which probably would have been only barely effective. Only in certain cases did the state resort to repression'. Corley comments that these reports could even be impartial and scholarly.[31]

Revival of Orthodox Church

In June 1941, with the attack of Germany on Russia, Stalin is said to have had a nervous breakdown and to have secluded himself in his *dacha* for three days. Another theory is that he was testing the loyalty of his confidantes to see whether they would accept his resignation.[32] Others claim that he retired to meditate and pray. At the same time Metropolitan Elias Karam of Lebanon was also praying for three days on the fate of Russia. He sent a telegram to Stalin asking that for Russia to be saved the Kremlin churches must be opened, and that a procession of the cross should carry the Kazan Icon of the Mother of God, the holiest icon of the Russian Orthodox Church. The icon was carried around Leningrad, and Moscow, was with the Russian troops at Stalingrad, and a prayer service was held prior to the battle. The icon was taken to all crucial points of the frontline. The priests carrying the icon led the troops under intense fire. The presence of the icon had an intense impact on the troops; even the sceptics. [33]

On September 4 1943, the exiled Metropolitan Sergei and two other Metropolitans were summoned to the Kremlin to meet with Stalin. He told them he had decided to restore the Patriarchate, reopen churches and seminaries, and resume the publication of *The Journal of the Moscow Patriarchate*. Stalin reminisced at length about his time at seminary. As for his intentions to restore the Patriarchate and churches, he said to Sergei, 'Your Grace, that's all I can do for you now'.[34] Daniela Kalkandijeva opines that, with the setting up of Moscow as the centre of world Orthodoxy at Stalin's suggestion, it would nonetheless 'be wrong to think that the church was just a pawn

---

31   F. Corley, op. cit., 2

32   Simon Sebag Montefiore, *Stalin: The Court of the Red Tsar* (Weidenfeld & Nicholson, 2003), Part 7, Chapter 33.

33   Lyubov Tsarevskaya, "The Wonderworking Icon of Kazan of the Most Holy Mother of God," Voices from Russia, January 15, 2008; https://02varvara.wordpress. com/2008/01/15/the-wonderworking-icon-of-kazan-of-the-most-holy-mother-of-god/

34   Montefiore, Young Stalin, op. cit., 36.

on Stalin's chessboard'.[35] The churches were already being reopened in 1941. This was not merely a strategy caused by the German invasion, to mobilise the Russian masses. In 1938 the Communist party declared that the faithful were also loyal Soviet subjects. Further, in a reversal of Bolshevist dogma, the party and the Soviet Academy of Sciences stated that the Church had provided a 'progressive role' in Russian history. In 1941 even Yaroslavsky, head of the Militant Godless, criticized those who still regarded the millions of faithful as superstitious fools.[36] The 1943 meeting with Sergei formalized the process. He was elected Patriarch by the Synod that year. The Council of the Russian Orthodox Church, headed by NKVD Colonel G.G. Karpov was established. Karpov, who had been responsible for the repression of religion during the 1930s, now worked for state support for the church.

In November 1943 the Council of People's Commissars adopted Decree No. 1325, 'On the Procedure for Opening Churches'. In 1944 206 churches were opened; in 1945, 510. The Orthodox Church flourished. On Easter night 1944 the thirty churches in Moscow were attended by 120,000. Attendance throughout Russia was overflowing. Worshippers included many Soviet officers. Even Communist party functionaries and NKVD agents had their children baptized. The historian of the Russian Orthodox Church, Vladislav Tsypin, estimated that the number of baptisms in the aftermath of the war was 150,000,000. By April 1946 the number of functioning Orthodox churches in the USSR had tripled to 10,437. By early 1949 there were 14,477 in the USSR. Karpov's office reported 22,000 functioning churches and prayer in 1946 in the USSR. By January 1948, 85 monasteries and convents, institutions hitherto all closed, had been opened. In 1945 Kalinin replied to a question from *Komsomol skaia pravda* that the State was 'not at war' with the Church, while alluding to atheist education. Balzer comments that "postwar atheism was to a greater degree a nod to the tradition that had arisen in the first years of Soviet power, rather than a policy objective." [37]

In 1947, the Metropolitan Elias (Karam) of Lebanon made a triumphal visit to the Soviet Union. He was presented with an especially crafted cross from the state.

---

35 Daniela Kalkandijeva, *The Russian Orthodox Church, 1917-1948: From Decline to Resurrection* (New York: Routledge, 2015), 180-181.

36 Denis R. Janz, *World Christianity and Marxism*, (Oxford University Press, 1998), 38.

37 Marjorie Mandelstam Balzer (ed.), *Religion and Politics in Russia: A Reader* (New York: Routledge, 2010), 8-9.

In 1946, the department of external relations of the Church, headed by Metropolitan Nicholas Yarushevich, was established. In July 1948, an international meeting of Orthodox churches was held in Moscow. The historian of the Russian Church, Johann Chrysostomus, commented:

> The Moscow Conference of the Orthodox Churches was to demonstrate the leading role of Moscow in world Orthodoxy. On this question the wishes of the Patriarchate and the Soviet government coincided, and both sides attached exceptional importance to the holding of this conference. Although the conference addressed a letter to Christians throughout the world, the attention of the conference organizers was centered on world Orthodoxy. It was to show itself as the moral force on which the Eastern bloc rested, contrary to other churches in the countries of the free world.[38]

Requiem Masses for Stalin

Requiem masses were said for Stalin on his death in 1953. Patriarch Alexy stated in the patriarchal cathedral on the day of Stalin's funeral:

> We, who gathered to pray for him, cannot pass in silence on his always benevolent, sympathizing attitude to our church needs. Any question which we addressed to him, was not rejected by him; he satisfied all our requests. And a lot that is good and useful, thanks to his high authority, has been done for our Church by our Government. The memory of him for us is unforgettable, and our Russian Orthodox Church, mourning over his leaving us, escorting him to his last journey.

> In these sad days for us, from different directions of our Fatherland from bishops, clergy and believers, and from heads and representatives of Churches, as orthodox and heterodox, from abroad, I receive a mass of telegrams telling of prayers for him and consoling us on the occasion of this sad loss. We prayed for him when the message about his serious illness had come. And now, when he is no more, we pray for his immortal soul. Yesterday our special delegation ... placed a wreath on his coffin and bowed on behalf of the Russian Orthodox Church to his dear body. The prayer, fulfilled with Christian love, reaches God.... And to our loved and unforgettable Joseph

---

38 Johann Chrysostomus, *Kirchengeschichte Russland dor heusten Zeit*, Munich-Salzburg, 1965-68, vol. 3, 119.

Vissarionovich we devoutly, with deep, passionate love proclaim his eternal memory.[39]

Stalin's family held a requiem, arranged by Vasily Stalin, in the Church of the Resurrection of Slovushchy. A State requiem was held at the Elohovsky Cathedral, led by patriarch Alexy. This was the first time requiems had been held for a Soviet leader.[40] The honor guard at the coffin during Stalin's funeral included Metropolitan Nicholas, Archbishop Nikon, and archpriest Nikolai Kolchitsky.[41]

With de-Stalinization the atheistic campaign resumed under Khrushchev, and those 'soft on religion' were regarded as 'Stalinists'.

In 1958, with Khrushchev's position consolidated the monasteries started to be closed, and those that remained were heavily taxed to raise the cost of religious accoutrements. The objections of Patriarch Alexy I were ignored. Karpov was removed from his position in 1960. That year the Communist Party Central Committee issued a declaration that 'The struggle against religion must not only be continued, but it must be enhanced by all possible means'.[42]

The original Bolshevist formulae of Trotsky and Lenin of storming heaven had been re-established. Again, churches were blown up, priests arrested, seminaries closed. Believers were registered, and subjected to dismissal from jobs and denied university entrance and careers. Priests were attacked. Atheist displays toured the USSR.

During the 1960s thousands of churches that had been opened during the war, were destroyed. In 1959 there had been 13,372 functioning churches; by 1963, 8,314, and 18 monasteries and convents remained. An active atheist campaign was resumed. However, in 1967 60,000,000 Soviet citizens still stated they were believers, and many more retained icons in their households.[43]

---

39   *Magazine Metropolitan Patriarchate*, No. 4, 1953.

40   "How Stalin died", documentary film, Russia, 2008, director Sergey Kostin.

41   *Journal of the Moscow Patriarchate*, No. 3, 1953. See: "Generalissimo Stalin funeral," Youtube, https://www.youtube.com/watch?v=7TXP9JLa6zs (19:57).

42   "On the aims of party propaganda in the contemporary conditions," Communist Party CC, January 9, 1960, quoted by Dimitry V. Pospielovsky, Soviet Antireligious Campaigns and Persecutions: Volume 2 of a *History of Soviet Atheism in Theory and Practice, and the Believer* (London: Macmillan 1988), 127.

43   Balzar, op. cit., 9-10.

On October 7, 1964 the USSR gave Israel land in Jerusalem that had been owned by the Russian State and the Orthodox Church since the 19th century, in exchange for several ton of rotting oranges.[44] Precisely a week later, on the Day of the Virgin, Khrushchev was deposed. A moderated policy was assumed.

Archbishop Anthony (Marchenko) returning after the war from emigration, wrote of the world-mission of Russian Orthodoxy in the journal of the Moscow patriarchate.

> Our native church life... fulfils not only its inner, ideological mission concerning the religious-moral education of our people, but also, which is most important, reveals its world-historical vocation, uniting the whole Orthodox world and all Slavonic peoples under the single common church-national slogan of Cyril and Methodius' great and undying idea. "Moscow - the Third Rome" remains as before the symbol of the universal collective idea, contraposed to the Papacy with its striving for spiritual autocracy, its episcopal aristocratism and its maniacal dreams of ruling the earth. The visit to Moscow by the Eastern Patriarchs, the visit to the Holy Land by His Holiness Patriarch Alexis, the coming to Moscow of a delegation from the Orthodox Czech Church and, as a result, the appointing of a Russian Orthodox Exarch there testify to an exceptional revival in the Orthodox Ecumenical Catholic Church under the actual leadership of Russian Orthodoxy: 'Moscow is the Third Rome, and a fourth there will not be' as our forefather said in the days of Ivan III ...[45]

This centuries-old world messianic mission of 'Moscow the Third Rome', or the *Katechon* resisting the Antichrist, has become again the state outlook under Putin.[46]

Bolshevism took messianic forms, as an integral part of the Russian character, and was united with Orthodoxy by Stalin. Contemporary

---

44 This was given back to Russia by Israel in 2008 as a goodwill gesture. See: Vladimir Putin and the Holy Land, *The Economist,* May 16 2013, http://www.economist.com/news/europe/21573600-warmer-relations-israel-do-not-stop-russia-backing-syria-and-iran-vladimir-putin-and-holy

45 Archbishop Anthony, Zhurnal Moskovskoy Patriarkhii, No. 9, 1946, 54-55.

46 Maria Engström, 'Contemporary Russian Messianism and New Russian Foreign Policy', *Journal of Contemporary Security Policy,* November 20, 2014; http://www.tandfonline.com/doi/full/10.1080/13523260.2014.965888

conservative scholars such as Oswald Spengler and Walter Schubart foresaw this reassertion of Russian character even under Bolshevism. Spengler foresaw that Bolshevism would clear the way for Russia to 'someday awaken between 'Europe' and East Asia. It is more a beginning than an end'. Beyond the superficiality of Marxist dogma lives the Russian peasantry, which will 'become conscious of its own will, which points in a wholly different direction.'[47] Schubart saw that 'even the Bolshevists' are imbued with the Russian messianic idea, and that their world revolution "unconsciously continues to maintain an old tradition – a fact which proves that the pull of the Russian soil is stronger than any cleverly devised artificial program."[48] This perhaps provides the explanation as to why Stalin reversed the Marxist doctrines and policies that had been inaugurated under Lenin; and that explanation is deeper than Stalinist pragmatism. Had Trotsky assumed leadership rather than Stalin the result would have been a messianism of an entirely different, and perhaps irremediable type.

Conclusion

Did Stalin consider Russia to be 'The Third Rome' rather than the centre of world proletarian revolution? Was his revival of Orthodoxy during the war something more than war strategy? He had dissolved the Comintern, and seen Moscow as the world centre of Orthodoxy. He released priests and liquidated 'Old Bolsheviks'. The revival of the family, outlawing abortion, and honouring motherhood complemented the revival of the Church. After the war the Orthodox revival did not abate; to the contrary. Why was it that Stalin did not revert, at least in stages, to the atheist campaign? Khrushchev undertook the task within several years of Stalin's death. Anecdotally there are suggestions that Stalin had a religious epiphany. Another possibility is that Stalin never did reject Christianity. The widely stated stories of his being expelled from Seminary for revolutionary activities after being converted to atheism by reading Darwin, are uncertain. Stalin as a supposedly feared dictator personally intervened to moderate and eventually reverse the atheist campaign. The German invasion gave him the justification to accelerate this to the point where the Church resumed its traditional role as the moral and spiritual foundation of the Russian State.

---

47   Spengler, "The two faces of Russia and Germany's Eastern problems," February 14, 1922; first published in *Politische Schriften*, Munich, 1932.

48   Schubart, op. cit., 188.

How the Soviet Bloc was Pushed from Within

I. GORBACHEV

When the news media touts an individual as a great human being, one should immediately become cynical. When Hollywood touts an individual as a great human being, one should immediately become cynical. When the news media and Hollywood, in conjunction with a bunch of other luminaries, celebrates the birthday of such an individual with universal applause, one might ask what manner of evil this individual has done. While the reference could apply to Nelson Mandela, who is lauded as a latter-day-saint (with due apologies to the Mormon church) for the unique achievement of delivering South Africa to predatory international capital[1] while not delivering an iota of benefit to the Black masses, despite the miracles that are supposed to invariably attend universal franchise and equal rights, the bouquets are on this occasion going to Mikhail Gorbachev.

Gorbachev earned his sainthood for his role in dismantling the USSR, and precipitating the fall of the Warsaw Pact. For this, people of goodwill throughout the world are supposed to be eternally grateful, as this ended the 'Cold War' and achieved 'peace', so long as one has a very skewered definition of the word. While conservatives quoted Lenin that 'peace simply means communist world rule', today we might paraphrase, 'peace simply means capitalist world rule', or alternatively, 'U.S. global hegemony'. We have 'peace' only insofar as there is no longer a spectre of nuclear holocaust poised over the world. Harmony between nations, tribes, ethnicities, cultures, and religions remains elusive, however, and this in no small measure because those who hurrahed the demise of the Soviet bloc have ever since been even more avid in promoting their globalist agendas by promoting wars, civil wars, and "spontaneous revolts" because they no longer have the restraining factor of the Soviet bloc. With the Soviet bloc gone the

---

1   "Privatisation is the fundamental policy of the ANC and will remain so." Lynda
     Loxton, "Mandela: We are going to privatise," *The Saturday Star*, May 25, 1996, p.1.

Yankee is now astride the Earth like a half-witted adolescent, devoid of tradition and High Culture;[2] a child cut free and told to do as it likes; a spoilt brat with weapons of mass destruction. So against this background, we come back to Gorbachev.

Eightieth Birthday Celebration

ABC News described the nature of the 'gala celebration', hosted by actors Sharon Stone and Kevin Spacey, aptly stating that the 'movie stars, singers and politicians' who turned out for the show, 'underlined the celebrity status Mr. Gorbachev enjoys in the West, where he is widely perceived as the man who freed Eastern Europe from Soviet rule and ended the Cold War'.[3]

Spacey opined that Gorbachev's actions in helping to dismantle the Soviet bloc continue to reverberate, the latest manifestation being the 'velvet revolutions' in the Near and Middle East. The analogy is apt, considering that the revolts that helped topple the Soviet regimes were encouraged, funded, and otherwise assisted by the same NGOs – with US Governmental backing – that are behind the present tumult in the Muslim states.[4]

The Reuters report states that the Russian view of Gorbachev is ambivalent. Quoted is a middle-aged Moscow lawyer who states: 'To me he is a good-for-nothing-man [who] simply betrayed his people, he destroyed the mechanism of the state and sold his country for nothing'.[5]

President Medvedev, on the other hand, awarded Gorbachev Russia's

2 "America is the only nation in history which miraculously has gone directly from barbarism to degeneration without the usual interval of civilization." George Clemenceau, Prime Minister of France.

3 Reuters, ABC News, "Stars honour Gorbachev at gala birthday bash," March 31, 2011, http://www.abc.net.au/news/stories/2011/03/31/3178823.htm).

4 K. R. Bolton, "The Globalist Web of Subversion," February 7, 2011 *Foreign Policy Journal*, https://www.foreignpolicyjournal.com/2011/02/07/the-globalist-web-of-subversion/
K. R. Bolton, "What's Behind the Tumult in Egypt?," *Foreign Policy Journal*, February 1, 2011, https://www.foreignpolicyjournal.com/2011/02/01/whats-behind-the-tumult-in-egypt
K. R. Bolton, "'Post-Qaddafi Libya': on the Globalist Road," *Foreign Policy Journal*, February 26, 2011, https://www.foreignpolicyjournal.com/2011/02/26/post-qaddafi-libya-on-the-globalist-road/

5 Reuters, ABC News, op. cit.

highest honours, yet enigmatically stated that the 'big work' Gorbachev did, 'can be assessed in different ways'. What might one think of this 'compliment' other than that Medvedev, while feeling obliged to pay tribute to someone so esteemed by the 'rich and famous', has to live with the quagmire that he inherited from Gorbachev.

From Communist Functionary to Global Elitist

The gala celebration at the Royal Albert Hall, London, for 'Gorby's' eightieth was accurately labelled 'The Man who Changed the World'. For his part, Gorbachev honoured as 'a man who changed the world' the 'founder of the internet', Sir Tim Berners-Lee. Others honoured by Gorbachev with the annual 'Gorbachev Awards' were CNN founder Ted Turner[6] and Kenyan engineer Evans Wadonongo. Lech Walesa, father of post-Soviet Poland, was also present.[7] *Y-Net News*, one of the large Israeli media outlets, stated of the Gorbachev festivities that among the attendees were Israeli President Shimon Peres, and unnamed 'oligarchs'. The Israeli account is more informative than other news outlets. Peres was a featured guest of the event, and presented the Kenyan engineer Wadonongo with his award. *Y-Net News* reporting on Peres' speech states:

> In his speech, the Israeli president said Gorbachev fought to regain what his country had lost to communism, adding that the former Soviet leader changed history. Peres also called Gorbachev a good friend to the Jewish people, saying many Soviet Jews were permitted to make *aliyah* under his rule.[8]

It is evident from Peres' statements that Gorbachev realigned the USSR in its official attitude towards Israel and Zionism, a factor in itself meriting his elevation to celebrity status among some influential quarters. Russia, more than any other state,[9] has historically given Jews

---

6   Turner, like all good billionaires, has his own globalist network. This includes the United Nations Foundation and the Better World Foundation. Turner Foundation Inc., http://www.turnerfoundation.org/about/ao.asp

7   'Gorbachev gala honours rich, famous and charitable', *Sydney Morning Herald*, April 1, 2011.

8   H Klaiman, "Peres attends Gorbachev's birthday bash in London," March 31, 2011, http://www.ynetnews.com/articles/0,7340,L-4050192,00.html

9   German Jewry was the most assimilated and nationally patriotic of any Jewish entity in the world, right up until the advent of Hitler. Zionists got a poor hearing among German Jews, and the Jewish population, anti-Semitic claims to the contrary, had figured heroically in World War I, and were prominent in the German Right

a lot of worry. The Menshevik and subsequent Bolshevik revolts were greeted by some sections of Jewry – high and low – with messianic fervour, but their hopes, along with those of international capital (Jewish and Gentile),[10] were soon dashed by the rise of Stalin and the exiling of Trotsky, et al. Especially after World War II and the creation of the Israeli State, the USSR viewed Zionism not only with suspicion, but as a primary world enemy. Soviet academe gave much attention to the international ramifications of Zionism. Just how well informed the Soviets were is indicated by the official publication of well-informed books such as *Caution: Zionism!* by Yuri Ivanov,[11] indicating that the upper echelons of the Soviet bloc knew precisely what the Zionists were up to. The Israeli media account continues:

> Leonid Shlachover, the event's general producer, said "this gala has been organized to honour Mikhail Gorbachev, a man who truly changed the world for the better through his actions and example. "This event will celebrate his achievements by bringing together major artists from East and West in a night of celebration."

Klaimant comments that Gorbachev's *perestroika* and *glasnost* reforms altered the course of history by burying the Soviet Union and liberating Eastern Europe. He turned 80 on March 2, marking the occasion by advising Russian Prime Minister Vladimir Putin against running for a third term as president and warning about the dangers of Arab-style social revolt.[12]

(e.g. Stahlhelm, National People's Party), despite the conspicuous appearance of Jews among communists and other anti-national groups. If it wasn't for Hitler's anti-Semitic policy, Zionism would have gotten nowhere among German Jews, which explains why the Zionists tended to have an optimistic view of Hitler's rise. (See Lenni Brenner, *Zionism in the Age of the Dictators* (Westport, Connecticut: Lawrence Hill, 1983). A good book on the history of German Jewry is: Amos Elon, *The Pity of it all: A History of the Jews in Germany 1743-1933* (New York: Metropolitan Press, 2002).

10   Jacob Schiff of Kuhn, Loeb and Co., for example, stated in messianic terms of the Menshevik Revolt: "May I through your columns give expression to my joy that the Russian nation, a great and good people, have at last effected their deliverance from centuries of autocratic oppression and through an almost bloodless revolution have now come into their own. Praised be God on high! Jacob H. Schiff." "Jacob H Schiff Rejoices, By Telegraph to the Editor of *The New York Times*", *New York Times*, March, 18, 1917. The globalists must have felt much the same way when Gorbachev sabotaged the USSR.

11   Y Ivanov, *Caution: Zionism! Essays on the Ideology, Organisation and Practice of Zionism* (Moscow: Progress Publishers, 1970). The entire document is online at: http://home.alphalink.com.au/~radnat/zionism/preface.html

12   Ibid.

Gorbachev's Ultimatum

Note the ominous warning from Gorbachev against Putin, the globalists' bugbear: do not run for the presidency again or you will face a "velvet revolution." In context, it could be seen as an ultimatum by the globalists. Since Yeltsin, matters have not gone at all as the globalist elite intended: Putin has been like the Bonaparte of the post-Soviet era, just as Trotsky accused Stalin of being the Bonaparte of the Bolshevik Revolution.[13] Putin halted the slide of Russia into globalization and has fought an ongoing battle with the oligarchs, whom those such as the National Endowment for Democracy portray as persecuted dissidents.

The globalists just cannot trust the Russians to keep to the script. Hence, the globalist think tank, the Council on Foreign Relations,[14] opines that 'Russia is heading in the wrong direction'.[15] One of the CFR recommendations is to directly interfere with the Russian political process, urging US Congress to fund opposition movements by increased funding for the *Freedom Support Act*, in this instance referring specifically to the 2007-2008 presidential elections.[16] Authors of the CFR report include Mark F Brzezinski, who served on the National Security Council as an adviser on Russian and Eurasian affairs under Clinton, as his father Zbigniew served in the Carter Administration; Antonia W. Bouis, founding executive director of the Soros Foundations; and James A Harmon, senior advisor to the Rothschild Group, et al.

The U.S. 'Establishment' has boasted of its subversive role in out-bolshying the bolshies. The U. S. globalists had been working away subverting the Soviet bloc since the aftermath of World War II, when Stalin repudiated the wartime alliance and rejected US proposals for both the United Nations Organization and for the 'internationalisation'

---

13   Leon Trotsky, *The Workers' State, Thermidor and Bonapartism* (1935), http://www.marxists.org/archive/trotsky/1935/02/ws-therm-bon.htm

14   For a frank and revealing account of the CFR, see the official history: Peter Grosse, Continuing the Inquiry: The Council on Foreign Relations from 1921 to 1996, (New York: Council on Foreign Relations, 2006). The entire book can be read online at: Council on Foreign Relations: http://www.cfr.org/about/history/cfr/index.html

15   Jack Kemp, et al, Russia's Wrong Direction: What the United States Can and Should Do, Independent Task Force Report no. 57 (New York: Council on Foreign Relations, 2006) xi. The entire publication can be downloaded at: http://www.cfr.org/publication/9997/

16   Ibid., p. 7.

of atomic energy, which was seen by the Soviets to be a ruse for subordinating the USSR to the USA.[17] The result was the 'Cold War'.[18] For several decades the USA launched an intensive subversive campaign that has been called the "cultural cold war," via the CIA front, Congress for Cultural Freedom.[19] This, significantly, emerged from out of the pre-war Committee for Cultural Freedom founded by Professor Sydney Hook, 'life-long Menshevik' (and recipient of the Congressional Medal of Freedom from President Reagan), and his academic mentor Professor John Dewey. Both had led the campaign to exonerate Trotsky at the time of the Moscow Trials.

With the eclipse of the Congress for Cultural Freedom, the cause was taken up and conflated by a myriad of NGOs and 'civil society' organisation, with the backing of U.S. Congress and official U.S. agencies such as USAID and the State Department, precisely in the manner being undertaken presently in North Africa. In particular, the mantle of the anti-Soviet crusade was assumed by the National Endowment for Democracy, founded in 1983 by Tom Kahn of the AFL-CIO, an adherent of the post-Trotskyite Shachtmanite line, in keeping with the anti-Soviet, pro-U.S. party line followed by many Trotskyites, including the Old Man's widow Sedova, who supported the U.S. in the Korean War, and viewed the USSR rather than the USA as the prime obstacle to 'world revolution'.[20]

With Congressman George Agree, Kahn believed that the USA needed a means of supporting subversive movements against the USSR, aside from the CIA. Kahn was International Affairs Director of the AFL-CIO.[21] As the personal assistant to AFL-CIO president George Meany, Kahn was editor of *Free Trade Union News*, in which he continually attacked the Soviet Union. From 1977, in alliance with the League for Industrial Democracy,[22] Kahn built

---

17 *Andrei Gromyko, Memories* (London: Hutchinson, 1989).

18 K. R. Bolton, 'Origins of the Cold War', in *Stalin: The Enduring Legacy*, op. cit.

19 Frances Stonor Saunders, *The Cultural Cold War: The CIA and the World of Arts and Letters* (New York: the New Press, 2000).

20 Natalia Trotsky, 'In Defense of Trotskyism', Labour Action (June 17, 1951). Re-printed by: League for the Revolutionary Party (New York), Proletarian Revolution, No. 38 (Winter 1991). http://www.marxists.org/history/etol/newspape/socialistvoice/Back_Issues.html#pr38

21 Rachelle Horowitz, 'Tom Kahn and the Fight for Democracy: A Political Portrait and Personal Recollection', Dissent Magazine, pp. 238-239. http://www.dissentmagazine.org/democratiya/article_pdfs/d11Horowitz.pdf

22 Kahn had been an Executive Director of the LID until 1972. Horowitz, ibid., p. 224.

up an anti-Soviet network throughout the world in 'opposition to the *accommodationist* policies of détente'.[23] There was a particular focus on assisting *Solidarity* in Poland from 1980.[24]

President George W. Bush, speaking to the NED conference in 2003 on the war in Iraq being a continuation of the 'world democratic revolution' that started in the Soviet bloc, credited the USA with the destruction of the USSR and the Warsaw Pact: 'The revolution under former president Ronald Reagan freed the people of Soviet-dominated Europe, he declared, and is destined now to liberate the Middle East as well'.[25]

Apart from the prescience of Bush in his prophesying the 'spontaneous revolts' now taking place in the Middle East eight years before the tumult, the numerous scenes of Reagan and Gorbachev in moods of joviality take on more significant meaning: They were both having a good laugh at what was planned for the Soviet bloc.[26]

Gorbachev's 1988 U.N. Speech

In 1988, Gorbachev gave the green light for the break-up of the Soviet bloc by stating before the UNO that the USSR would no longer defend pro-Soviet regimes. Analysts of the US National Security Archive have stated of Gorbachev's speech:

> Late October 1988 brought a major break with past Soviet positions, when Gorbachev decided to offer deep reductions in Soviet forces in Europe as a unilateral initiative, and to deliver a major address at the United Nations. Gorbachev conceptualized this speech as an "anti-Fulton, Fulton in reverse" in its significance – comparing it with the historic Winston Churchill "Iron Curtain" speech of 1946 in Fulton, Missouri, at the beginning of the Cold War. Gorbachev wanted his speech to signify the end of the Cold War, offering deep Soviet reductions in conventional weapons as proof of his policy. These reductions would address the most important Western

---

23   Ibid., p. 234.

24   Ibid., p. 235.

25   Fred Barbash, 'Bush: Iraq Part of 'Global Democratic Revolution': Liberation of Middle East Portrayed as Continuation of Reagan's Policies', *Washington Post*, 6 November 6, 2003.

26   See for example Reagan, Vice President Bush and Gorabcehv: http://www.gwu.edu/~nsarchiv/NSAEBB/NSAEBB261/index.htm

concern about the threat of war in Europe, where the Soviets enjoyed significant conventional superiority. This move, in Gorbachev's mind, would build trust and open the way for a very fast progress with the new American administration. His meeting with President-elect Bush and President Reagan would take place immediately after the U.N. speech.[27]

Gorbachev's speech to the UNO reflected a palace coup that was taking place in the USSR, in opposition to the military, and involving only a small coterie:

> Gorbachev seemed well aware of the potential opposition to his initiative both in the Politburo and in the Armed Forces – a very sensitive issue to handle. The decision making on the U.N. speech involved a very narrow circle of advisers…[28]

The 'green light' for the 'velvet revolutions' assiduously prepared by NED and others was overtly declared by Gorbachev before the UNO, Savranskaya and Blanton stating of this:

> Gorbachev's U.N. speech on December 7 explicitly endorsed the "common interests of mankind" (no longer the class struggle) as the basis of Soviet foreign policy and, significantly for Eastern Europe, declared "the compelling necessity of the principle of freedom of choice" as "a universal principle to which there should be no exceptions." Gorbachev particularly surprised CIA and NATO officials with his announcement of unilateral cuts in Soviet forces totaling 500,000 soldiers, and the withdrawal from Eastern Europe of thousands of tanks and tens of thousands of troops.[29]

The intentions were unequivocal: Gorbachev and his coterie were globalists who were committed to bringing Russia into the 'new world order' by scuttling the Warsaw Pact, and adhering to globalist aims. The reaction of the globalist press was expressed by *The New York Times*, which described Gorbachev as a 'visionary'.[30] Senator Daniel

---

27 Dr. Svetlana Savranskaya and Thomas Blanton (ed.) 'Previously Secret Documents from Soviet and U.S. Files on the 1988 Summit in New York, 20 Years Later', National Security Archive Electronic Briefing Book No. 261, December 8, 2008.

28 Dr. Svetlana Savranskaya and Thomas Blanton, ibid.

29 ibid.

30 *The New York Times*, December 8, 1988, p. 34.

Moynihan called the speech 'the most astounding statement of surrender in the history of ideological struggle'.[31]

The record of the meeting Gorbachev had with his coterie of advisers regarding the U.N. speech is essential reading for those wanting to understand his motives, not only back then, but now. Gorbachev intended to use the UNO speech to declare before the world that he was a globalist committed to making the UNO pivotal in the creation of what Bush was to later call a "new world order" in explaining the role of the war in Iraq and the opportunities provided for such global governance via the UNO with the demise of the Soviet bloc:

> ...This is an historic moment. We have in this past year made great progress in ending the long era of conflict and cold war. We have before us the opportunity to forge for ourselves and for future generations a new world order – a world where the rule of law, not the law of the jungle, governs the conduct of nations. When we are successful – and we will be – we have a real chance at this new world order, an order in which a credible United Nations can use its peacekeeping role to fulfil the promise and vision of the U.N.'s founders...[32]

However, Gorbachev's U.N. speech pre-empted Bush's in expressing the same doctrine. Gorbachev stated of the UNO:

> This organization is called the United Nations for a reason. In this context it should have a universally accepted doctrine, which would reflect the rights of the peoples, their right of free choice, human rights. Show the U.N. role as an instrument of the new world.[33]

Perhaps beginning with U.S./NED support for Poland's *Solidarity* movement since 1980, as stated previously, oppositionist groups had been cultivated within the Soviet bloc by globalist and US interests, and Gorbachev's speech could only be interpreted positively by

---

31 T Blanton, "When did the Cold War End?", Cold War International History Project Bulletin, no. 10 (March 1998), p.184.

32 George W Bush, speech to US Congress, January 17, 1991

33 M Gorbachev, 'What are we going to take to the United Nations?', Conference with advisers, October 31, 1988, Attended: Shevardnadze, Yakovlev, Dobrynin, Falin, Chernyaev, Archive of the Gorbachev Foundation. Fond 2. Notes of A.S. Chernyaev. On file at the National Security Archive. Translated by Svetlana Savranskaya. http://www.gwu.edu/~nsarchiv/NSAEBB/NSAEBB261/sov03.pdf

anti-Soviet dissidents as a policy of "scuttle," no less so than Harold Macmillan's 'winds of change speech' had signalled the end of the British Empire. It was a stab in the back for those who had for decades stayed firm against the USA. The year after Gorbachev's U.N. speech the *Solidarity* movement overthrew the Soviet regime in Poland. Carl Gershman, the Shachtmanist president of NED, remarked that *Solidarity* set in motion the 'velvet revolutions' that would eventually collapse the Soviet bloc.[34] Gershman analysed the impact in classically Trotskyite ideological mode,[35] showing how comfortably Trotskyism synthesizes with globalism:

> The most notable contribution of *Solidarity*, aside from precipitating the unravelling of the Soviet Union and the Warsaw Pact, has been the introduction of a new concept of incremental democratic enlargement, based on the idea of building on the gains in one country to extend support and solidarity to democracy movements in contiguous countries and beyond. In the NED we call this cross-border work, and it had its origins, at least in our own thinking and programs, in a conference that was sponsored by the Polish-Czech-Slovak Solidarity Foundation in Wroclaw in early November of 1989.[36]

Gershman outlines the continuing role of these networks in the present-day undermining of Russia and those 'contiguous countries' which have, in CFR parlance, 'taken a wrong turn'.

And so cross-border work was born, and it has continued to expand ever since. The Polish-Czech-Slovak Solidarity Foundation went from providing support for desktop publishing in the Czech Republic and Slovakia to providing similar aid in Ukraine and Belarus, and today it works in Russia, Moldova, the Caucasus and Central Asia. Other Polish groups also engage in cross-border work, from the Foundation for Education for Democracy, an outgrowth of the Solidarity Teachers Union which provides training in civic education for teachers and NGO leaders throughout the former Soviet Union,

---

34   C. Gershman, 'Giving Solidarity to the world', Georgetown University, May 19, 2009, http://www.ned.org/about/board/meet-our-president/archived-remarks-and-presentations/051909

35   Trotsky and Lenin believed that communist revolution would spread to Central Europe, with Germany as a pivotal state, and that the Soviet Red Army must be ready to intervene. Robert Service, Trotsky: A biography (London, Pan book, 2010), 'World Revolution', 247-25.

36   Gershman, op. cit.

to the East European Democratic Center which supports local media in Ukraine and Central Asia.[37]

Gershman reminisced that the above-mentioned Polish-Czech-Slovak Solidarity Foundation was created in 1989 to spread the work of *Solidarity* to neighbouring states, and had the support of NED. After the NED-backed Festival of Independent Czechoslovak Culture at Wroclaw University, 'The Velvet Revolution began two weeks after the festival and Vaclav Havel had declared that the festival was its "prologue."'[38]Gershman stated that this 'festival' had been funded with $7,500 by NED, 'dollar for dollar, the best grant NED has ever made'.[39] But the NED backing of the anti-Soviet dissident groups goes back to their beginning, Gershman stating in 1999 that:

> For example, in its early years NED was able to assist the Polish *Solidarity* movement through its trade union institute, while at the same time providing help to independent publishing and citizen groups in Poland through its discretionary program. Discretionary grants were also made to support dissident publishing in Czechoslovakia and Hungary, often through European-based NGOs.[40]

There is much more that could be said about NED and many other NGOs and globalist foundations, such as those of George Soros, creating the anti-Soviet dissident movements, but the main point here is that the whole Soviet edifice had been destroyed within a short time of Gorbachev giving the go ahead with his U.N. speech. Like the present Arab revolts, there was nothing sudden or 'spontaneous' about the 'velvet revolutions'. They had been well-planned and funded, and Gorbachev gave the signal.

It is significant that among the "wrong directions" taken by Russia the most notable according to Gershman are the actions taken against the oligarchs. It a recent statement, Gershman considered that, 'As 2010 drew to a close, the backsliding accelerated with a flurry of new setbacks – notably the rigged re-sentencing of dissident entrepreneur

---

37   Ibid.

38   C. Gershman, 'Bridging time and Borders 1989-2009', December 2, 2009, http://www.ned.org/for-reporters/bridging-time-and-borders-1989-2009

39   Ibid.

40   C. Gershman, 'NED: Its History, Structure and Role in Promoting Democracy', July 8, 1999, http://www.ned.org/about/board/meet-our-president/archived-presentations-and-articles/the-national-endowment-for-democracy

Mikhail Khodorkovsky in Russia'.[41] Gershman stated just a few weeks prior to Gorbachev's warning about Putin's standing for presidential re-election, that:

> ...Putin may be in control in Russia, but he has lost the support of the political elite which fears that his return to the presidency will usher in a period of Brezhnev-like stagnation and continued economic and societal decline...

> International groups should be prepared to provide whatever assistance is needed and desired by local actors. Areas of support would include party development and election administration and monitoring, strengthening civil society and independent media, and making available the expertise of specialists in such fields as constitutionalism and electoral law as well as the experience of participants in earlier transitions.[42]

Gershman is outlining a program that has been played repeatedly throughout the ex-Soviet bloc and central Asia and currently in the Near and Middle East: wholesale organization by NED and a myriad of other bodies such as Freedom House, the Soros networks, The Solidarity Center, International Republican Institute, *ad nauseam*, right down to creating political parties and formulating their programs.[43]

Gorbachev Foundation

Gorbachev has created his own Foundation as befits a luminary in the globalist elite, operating in tandem with a gaggle of others.[44] His hopes for the UNO are precisely those that were rejected by Stalin when mooted by the USA. The full name of the Gorbachev flagship is the International Foundation for Socio-Economic and Political

---

41   C. Gershman, 'The Fourth Wave: Where the Middle East revolts fit in the history of democratization – and how we can support them', March 14, 2011, http://www.tnr.com/article/world/85143/middle-east-revolt-democratization

42   Ibid.

43   There are two regimes that are also mentioned in particular by Gershman here: those of Belarus and Venezuela. They also figure prominently in the conferences and statements of Movements.org and others, so they are certainly states to watch out for in the near future as being particularly marked out for "spontaneous people's revolts."

44   Bolton, 'The Globalist Web of Subversion', *Foreign Policy Journal*, February 7, 2011, https://www.foreignpolicyjournal.com/2011/02/07/the-globalist-web-of-subversion

Studies, established in 1991. This is how its doctrine is self-described:

>...The Foundation's conceptual framework is based on the belief that in the age of globalization Russia and the rest of the world need new thinking – a new interpretation of the ideas of progress and humanism and evolving principles for a more equitable world order...[45]

The ultimate goal is nothing less than a new civilization based on humanism: 'The keynote of the Foundation's activities is *Toward a New Civilization*'.[46]

The U.S. branch is the Gorbachev Foundation of North America (GFNA), founded in 1997. The aim of GFNA is stated as being: '...to contribute to the strengthening and spread of democracy and economic liberalization through a program of advocacy, research, and education...'[47] Note that democracy is predicated on commitment to 'economic liberalisation'. Another way of phrasing this is that the propagandizing about 'democracy' and concomitant slogans such as 'equality', 'human rights', and the 'open society' is as a façade for the plundering of a state by predatory international capital, as has been happening to the mineral wealth of Kosovo since its 'liberation' from Serbia via NATO bombs.

Gorbachev, like Soros, has created a network of organizations and 'spin-offs'. One of the first was the State of the World Forum (SWF), co-founded with James Garrison. Like the Bilderbergers and the Trilateralists, SWF brought together sundry luminaries to discuss how best to run the world. What was apparently pregnant with meaning for these world planners was that the inaugural gathering took place at 'the historic Fairmont Hotel in San Francisco where in 1945 the U.N. Charter was negotiated'.[48]

Convened by Mikhail Gorbachev and fellow Co-Chairs Oscar Arias, Ruud Lubbers, Thabo Mbeke, George Schultz, Rigoberta Menchu Tum, Maurice Strong and Ted Turner, more than 500 innovative

---

45   Gorbachev Foundation, 'About Us', http://www.gorby.ru/en/gorbi_fund/about/

46   Ibid.

47   'Mission', The Gorbachev Foundation of North America, http://www.gfna.net/staff. php

48   'State of the World Forum, The First Five Years 1995-1999', http://www.worldforum. org/conferences/1995_1999.htm

leaders from 50 nations came together.[49] James Garrison, who originally chaired the GFNA, and now heads the SWF, stated the aim of the globalists unequivocally:

> We are going to end up with world government. It's inevitable ... There's going to be conflict, coercion and consensus. That's all part of what will be required as we give birth to the first global civilization.[50]

Of other co-founders of the SWF, Maurice Strong was the Secretary General of the 1992 UN Conference on Environment and Development (Earth Summit) that issued *Agenda 21*. Such is his influence that Strong was described by the *New York Times* as 'the Custodian of the Planet', being a principal advocate of "global governance" to overcome environmental and population problems, like others such as Gorbachev and his colleague Ted Turner. Strong served as Senior Advisor to U.N. Secretary General Kofi Annan; Senior Advisor to World Bank President Wolfensohn; and as Chairman of the Earth Council; Chairman of the World Resources Institute; Co-Chairman of the Council of the World Economic Forum; and member of Toyota's International Advisory Board.[51] He served as an adviser to the Rockefeller Foundation, and on the Commission on Global Governance (CGG). He co-drafted the *Earth Charter* with Mikhail Gorbachev for presentation at the Earth Summit in Rio de Janeiro, which Strong chaired. After the Rio Earth Summit in 1992 the Commission on Global Governance was established at the suggestion of former German Chancellor Willy Brandt, head of the Socialist International.[52] As per the formula of Gorbachev and others, in 1991 Strong stated that the Earth Summit would have a significant role in "reforming and strengthening the United Nations as the centerpiece of the emerging system of democratic global governance." In 1995, the CGG stated in *Our Global Neighborhood*: 'It is our firm conclusion that the United Nations must continue to play a central role in global governance'.[53] The environment is an important means by which the

---

49   Ibid.

50   J. Garrison, The Daily Record, Dunn, North Carolina, p. 4, October 17, 1995.

51   Ronald Bailey, 'International Man of Mystery: Who is Maurice Strong?', The National Review, 1 September 1997. http://www.afn.org/~govern/strong.html (Accessed 14 February 2010).

52   Ibid.

53   Commission on Global Governance, Our Global Neighborhood, Chapter 1, 'A New World', http://www.gdrc.org/u-gov/global-neighbourhood/chap1.htm

globalists aim to scare the world into 'global governance' to give them enhanced power. Create the problem and offer the solution: a type of dialectics. Strong is one of nine directors of the privately owned Chicago Climate Exchange (CCX), the only such exchange in North America.[54] Carbon credits are the new form of international banking.

George Schultz, who has served as Secretary of Labor, Treasury and State under presidents Nixon and Reagan, and as an adviser to George W Bush, is the chairman of the J.P. Morgan Chase Bank's International Advisory Council Board of Advisors, the New Atlantic Initiative,[55] Committee for the Liberation of Iraq, and Committee on the Present Danger, and is a member of the Council on Foreign Relations. He is also a member of Soros' Drug Policy Board, as is Vaclav Havel, first president of the post-Soviet Czech Republic in the wake of the 'velvet revolution' orchestrated by Soros, et al.

In a scenario that has become familiar with globalist organizations, the SWF has engendered 'spin-off organisations'. These include the Ethical Globalization Initiative. This in turn includes as its "institutional partners," The Aspen Institute, Columbia University, Saatchi & Saatchi and others. Global Security Institute deals with the problem of nuclear weapons, and in turn has a number of affiliated groups. Others are The Coexistence Initiative, and the Emerging Leaders Network, the latter to focus on influencing youth. Then there's the Commission on Globalization. Each has their own programs and staff.[56]

Among the Foundations that fund SWF are: Ford Foundation, Rockefeller Foundation, Rockefeller Brothers Fund, The William and Flora Hewlett Foundation.[57] Corporate sponsors include: American Express, Time Magazine/Time Warner, Royal Bank of Canada, PriceWaterhouseCoopers, Rabobank, KRW International...[58]

---

54   Chicago Climate Exchange, CCX Directors, http://www.chicagoclimatex.com/content.jsf?id=67

55   New Atlantic Initiative is yet another globalist think tank of industrialists, bankers, politicians, journalists, etc. aiming to push the USA and Europe closer together and counter protectionist and nationalistic economic policies. Shultz is listed as a patron, along with former Secretary of State Henry Kissinger. http://www.jcpa.org/nai.htm

56   http://www.worldforum.org/history.htm

57   'About Us – Supporters', http://www.worldforum.org/supporters.htm

58   Ibid.

Gorbachev also founded the Club of Madrid, and Green Cross International. The Club of Madrid focuses on bringing together former heads of state, currently comprising 79 former presidents and prime ministers from 56 countries.[59] Green Cross International (GCI) was founded by Gorbachev in 1993.[60] Again, this has a series of programs advancing the globalist agenda on the pretext of environmental concerns.

The Gorbachev Foundation, like other NGOs, actively seeks to reformulate the political processes and ideology of Russia via affiliates. The Raisa Maximovna Club, founded by Raisa Gorbachev in 1997 focus on Russian women. The same types of programs are used by Soros and others to undermine the traditional foundations of societies, generally in the guise of promoting 'women's rights'. The 'Club' 'supports initiatives that advance civil society's influence in Russia and is an effort to actively involve women in this process'. This is done mostly in the guise of wanting to help children and mothers, but the politicization of women for the purposes of globalist agendas is evident:

> ...The Club has become a forum to regularly discuss achievements and problems of the new research area in the Russian social science, gender studies.

> ...On December 9-10, 2002, at the Gorbachev Foundation, the Club and the Women's Information Network held the conference "Contemporary Women's Movement of Russia Facing New Challenges". It was attended by activists of the women's movement coming from 20 regions of Russia. The conference discussed the need for a new strategy of women's organizations, consolidation of women's movement and its participation in the 2003 parliamentary elections.[61]

Among the 'partners of the Foundation', along with Green Cross, etc., is the New Policy Forum, founded in 2010 by Gorbachev as successor to the World Policy Forum. This has precisely the same intent as other globalist forums such as the Bilderberg Group, Trilateral Commission, and CFR: '...to bring together current political leaders, veterans of international politics, intellectuals and civil society representatives in

---

59   Club of Madrid, http://www.clubmadrid.org/en/estructura/board_of_directors

60   Green Cross, 'History', http://www.gci.ch/en/who-we-are/history

61   The Raisa Maximovna Club, 'Projects', http://www.gorby.ru/en/activity/projects/show_27843/

a common effort to develop new ideas and new policies for the XXI century'.

The main priority of the New Policy Forum at its initial stage is: Considering issues relating to global governance. Sovereignty issues and efforts to diminish the negative impact of decisions taken at the government level and having global repercussions. The role and the future of European development in the contemporary world.

The NPF was launched in Luxembourg in 2010, with the first meeting of its Academic Advisory Board, which includes 'prominent experts, scholars and mass media figures'.

Conclusion

Gorbachev's political future in Russia was dim, and he became an unpopular figure, to the extent that he was feted by Western politicians.[62] Although the reconstructed Communist Party under Zyuganov – which looks more to Stalin than to Lenin and champions Russian traditionalism, including the Orthodox Church[63] – emerged as the largest party in the Duma, Yeltsin won the presidency with the help of an abundance of funds from oligarchic supporters.[64] Gorbachev's future clearly rests not within the confines of Russia, but as a luminary on the world stage as an international statesman promoting a "new world," and as a zealot for the reanimated corpse of 19th Century "economic liberalization" that over the past several decades has become a fad with ex-socialists. Hence Gorbachev, like other globalist high-fliers, is not bound to any nation, let alone a political party, and has developed a worldwide network that appears to be just as extensive as that of George Soros, NED, Freedom House, and others, for the purpose of undermining the sovereignty of states, with a focus on Russia.

Gorbachev has delivered an ultimatum to Putin, several weeks after similar comments by NED's Gershman, not to stand for presidential re-election, or else there will be "social unrest." Russia's interregnum

---

62   Robert Service, Comrades: Communism: A World History (London: Pan Books 2008), 456.

63   Ibid., 463.

64   Robert Service says of this period that the December 1993 referendum that endorsed Yeltsin's constitutional reforms was 'fiddled'. In the 1996 presidential campaign Zyuganov was in the lead at the start, 'but lacked the resources available to Yeltsin, who enlisted the wealthiest businessmen on his side'. Service, ibid

along the globalist path under Gorbachev and Yeltsin was brief. As with the rise of Stalin, Russia again has shown herself to be untrustworthy in following the "right direction" according to the requirements of international capital.

II. VACLAV HAVEL

That the collapse of the Warsaw Pact was greeted with such acclaim and is remembered as 'inspirational' by the Right, from Nazis to conservatives is an indication of the banality of much of the 'Right'. There remains obliviousness to the Soviet bloc having been the only major force of conservatism in the world, and to the USA being the global harbinger of decay.[65] This American role was recognised approvingly by Trotskyites, many of whom became avid Cold Warriors,[66] and by neocon strategists such as Ralph Peters,[67] who glory in the USA's 'revolutionary mission' as a purveyor of contagions against tradition across every corner of the globe.

Given that the Warsaw Pact was the only geopolitical entity that constrained American global hegemony, Havel's contribution to its demise is lauded as a great victory for 'democracy' and 'freedom'. However, those are words that are used by many regimes and systems, no matter what their character, and have been euphemisms since the time of Woodrow Wilson's Fourteen Points for post-war international reconstruction in the image desired by the USA, for the subordination of all nations, peoples and cultures to everything that is conjured by the word 'America': Hollywood, MTV, Rap, McDonalds, Harvey Weinstein, market economics.

Havel is said to have been an idealistic opponent of the consumerist ethic, yet what is one to think of an individual who allowed himself to be mentored and patronised by the likes of George Soros, and flitted about among the luminaries of plutocracy? Solzhenitsyn did not allow himself to be used in such a manner by the forces of Culture decay nor did he succumb to their blandishments. Solzhenitsyn was a mystic,

---

65   K. R. Bolton, 'Origins of the Cold War' in *Stalin: The Enduring Legacy*, op. cit.

66   Bolton, 'America's 'World Revolution': Neo-Trotskyist Foundations of U.S. Foreign Policy'. *Foreign Policy Journal*, 3 May 2010, http://www.foreignpolicyjournal. com/2010/05/03/americas-world-revolution-neo-trotskyist-foundations-of-u-s-foreign-policy/

67   Ralph Peters, 'Constant Conflict', *Parameters*, Summer 1997, pp. 4–14. http://www. usamhi.army.mil/USAWC/Parameters/97summer/peters.htm.

Havel, as will be shown, a seedy Zionist purveyor of cultural syphilis. Havel's critique of 'The West', like Solzhenitsyn's was perceptive, stating:

> There is no need at all for different people, religions and cultures to adapt or conform to one another. ... I think we help one another best if we make no pretences, remain ourselves, and simply respect and honour one another, just as we are.[68]

Yet here was a cultural icon who obviously knew the processes of levelling that were taking place in the world, but who was nonetheless willing to let himself be used in their service, for the sake of nebulous sales pitches like 'human rights'. Like the much-lauded Gorbachev, Havel became an icon of manufactured dissent in the interests of international capital that pulls the strings behind the façade of 'democracy', and of the Culture-destroyers, the 'rootless cosmopolitans'; as those 'evil' Soviet Russians called them, who had long been fearful of the directions being taken by the descendants of the Black Hundreds, since Trotsky was unceremoniously ousted.

The 'velvet revolutions' that were instigated, funded and planned by the Soros network, National Endowment for Democracy, Freedom House, and dozens of others, were a prelude to the same types of revolt that continue to be inflicted upon the former Soviet bloc states and that took place under the mantle of the 'Arab Spring'.[69]

'Rootless Cosmopolitanism'

The collapse of Czechoslovakia as part of the implosion of the Soviet bloc provides a special example of the role of Culture subversion. The Soviet leadership following the ousting of Trotsky and the Old Bolsheviks, were fully aware of the destructive nature of cultural nihilism. Ironically, the Soviet bloc stood as the only significant bulwark against what Hitler had termed 'cultural bolshevism'.

Kulturkampf – the Culture War – is a major part of the world offensives of both plutocracy and Zionism to the extent that at the

---

68   Philip K. Howard, 'Vaclav Havel's Critique of the West', The Atlantic, December 20, 2011, http://www.theatlantic.com/international/archive/2011/12/vaclav-havels-critique-of-the-west/250277/

69   K. R. Bolton, 'Egypt and Tunisia: Plutocracy Won', *Foreign Policy Journal*, June 28, 2011, http://www.foreignpolicyjournal.com/2011/06/28/egypt-and-tunisia-plutocracy-won/0/

very beginnings of the Cold War, as shown previously, the CIA recruited sundry disaffected anti-Soviet socialists, and in particular Trotskyites, into the Congress for Cultural Freedom to try and subvert the Soviet bloc and impose 'American' values over the world in the name of 'freedom of artistic expression'.

The program of *kulturkampf* against the Soviet bloc can be traced to Trotsky, always a very handy tool for international finance. In 1938 André Breton[70], Mexican communist muralist Diego Rivera[71] and Leon Trotsky issued a manifesto entitled: *Towards a Free Revolutionary Art*[72]. The Manifesto was published in the autumn 1938 issue of *The Partisan Review*, a magazine that was of significance in the Cold War-Trotskyite offensive. Trotsky, according to Bretton, had actually written the Manifesto, which states:

> Insofar as it originates with an individual, insofar as it brings into play subjective talents to create something which brings about an objective enriching of culture, any philosophical, sociological, scientific or artistic discovery seems to be the fruit of a precious *chance*, that is to say, the manifestation, more or less spontaneous, of *necessity*... Specifically, we cannot remain indifferent to the intellectual conditions under which creative activity takes place, nor should we fail to pay all respect to those particular laws that govern intellectual creation.

> In the contemporary world we must recognize the ever more widespread destruction of those conditions under which intellectual creation is possible... The regime of Hitler, now that it has rid Germany of all those artists whose work expressed the slightest sympathy for liberty, however superficial, has reduced those who still consent to take up pen or brush to the status of domestic servants of the regime... If reports may be believed, it is the same in the Soviet Union... True art, which is not content to play variations on ready-made models but rather insists on

---

70 Breton was the founding father of Surrealism. Joining the Communist Party in 1927 he was expelled in 1933 because of his association with Trotsky. Breton wrote of Surrealism in 1952: 'It was in the black mirror of anarchism that surrealism first recognised itself'.

71 In Mexico Trotsky lived with Diego Rivera and then with Diego's wife, the artist Frida Kahlo, having reached Mexico in 1937, where he had his brain splattered by a Stalinist assassin in 1940.

72 Leon Trotsky, André Breton, Diego Rivera, Towards a Free Revolutionary Art, July 25, 1938.

expressing the inner needs of man and of mankind in its time - true art is unable *not* to be revolutionary, *not* to aspire to a complete and radical reconstruction of society... We recognize that only the social revolution can sweep clean the path for a new culture. If, however, we reject all solidarity with the bureaucracy now in control of the Soviet Union it is precisely because, in our eyes, it represents, not communism, but its most treacherous and dangerous enemy...

The criterion for art given here by Trotsky seems more of the nature of the anarchism of Breton and of the future New Left than of the collectivist nature of Marxism. F Chernov, from a Stalinist viewpoint, was to refer to such art as 'nihilism'. Given that the manifesto was published in *The Partisan Review*, which was later to receive subsidies from the CIA and the Tax-exempt Foundations as party to what became the 'Cultural Cold War', this Trotskyist art manifesto served as the basis for the art policy that was adopted after World War II by the CIA and the globalists as part of the Cold War offensive.[73] Trotsky wrote *Towards a Free Revolutionary Art* as a call for mobilization by artists throughout the world, to oppose on the cultural front Fascism and Stalinism, which to many Leftists and communists were synonymous:

We know very well that thousands on thousands of isolated thinkers and artists are today scattered throughout the world, their voices drowned out by the loud choruses of well-disciplined liars. Hundreds of small local magazines are trying to gather youthful forces about them, seeking new paths and not subsidies. Every progressive tendency in art is destroyed by fascism as "degenerate." Every free creation is called "fascist" by the Stalinists. Independent revolutionary art must now gather its forces for the struggle against reactionary persecution.[74]

The Stalinists responded with a vigorous call not only to 'Soviet patriotism' but also to the cultural legacy of the Russian people. If one were looking for a Marxist articulation of cultural theory, it would

---

73   The Cold War was precipitated by Stalin's rejection of the UNO as the basis for a world government. Stalin insisted that authority be vested in the Security Council with members' power to veto, rather than the American proposal of authority being with the General Assembly where the Soviets would always be outvoted. Secondly, the Soviets perceived that the Baruch Plan for the 'internationalization of atomic energy', would mean US control. Bolton, 'Origins of the Cold War', in Stalin, op. cit.

74   Leon Trotsky, Breton, Rivera, 1938, op. cit.

more likely be found coming from the official and semi-official agencies of the USA, rather than those of the Soviet bloc. In 1949 a major article in the organ of the Central Committee of the Bolshevik party, F. Chernov condemned the infiltration of cosmopolitanism in Soviet arts, sciences and history.[75] The article, cited above, stands as a counter-manifesto not only to the Trotskyites and the "cultural cold war" of the time, but also as an enduring repudiation of modernism and rootless cosmopolitanism as it continues to manifest in the present age of chaos.

The Role of Culture Distortion in Czechoslovakia: Charter 77, Plastic People of the Universe

This globalist *kulturkampf* was directed with effect against the Soviet bloc. As can be seen from the seminal article by Chernov, the Soviet authorities knew precisely how this was being undertaken, and they remained conscious of it until overwhelmed by these forces. While the intelligentsia, the media and their wire-pullers voiced their indignation and derision against the philistinism of the Soviet authorities, and their regressive character, and, like the Fascist aesthetic, the supposed "banality" of "socialist realism," an examination of both the American sponsorship of cultural nihilism and the Soviet understanding of this, shows that the Soviets were correct in their suspicions.

The Czechoslovak Soviet authorities were regarded as ridiculous throwbacks for their actually rather lame efforts to keep their youth from the supposedly wonderful freedoms of their counterparts in the West. This globalist *kulturkampf* in its *present-day* form, has been described by neocon military strategist Ralph Peters, who worked at the Office of the Deputy Chief of Staff for Intelligence, and elsewhere, stating that, 'We are entering a new American century, in which we will become still wealthier, culturally more lethal, and increasingly powerful'. Peters outlined a strategy for subverting nations and peoples reticent about entering the 'new American century', by way of Hollywood, pop icons, and the dazzle of technology,[76] imposing a type of soft servitude over the world of the type described in Huxley's *Brave New World*.[77] As Peters and Huxley have perceived, youth in particular are unable to resist the temptation of the 'soft' option, of ego-

---

75 F. Chernov, "Bourgeois Cosmopolitanism and its reactionary role," Bolshevik: Theoretical and Political Magazine of the Central Committee of the All-Union Communist Party (Bolsheviks) ACP(B), Issue #5, 15 March 1949, 30-41.

76 Ralph Peters, op. cit.

77 K. R. Bolton, *Revolution from Above*, op. cit., 48-54.

driven nihilism and what amounts to 'freedom' from responsibility, in comparison to the Spartan regimentation of the Soviet bloc.

The 'rootless cosmopolitanism' or *kulturkampf* directed against Czechoslovakia centred around 'pop' music. The Charter 77 manifesto was drafted and a movement formed after the imprisonment of fans of the rock band, 'Plastic People of the Universe'. It is significant that this was catalyst for what became the 'velvet revolution'.

The rot that was eating away within the Warsaw Pact was organisationally focused on groups such as Charter 77 in Czechoslovakia and Solidarity in Poland. These groups were instigated and funded by the network of currency speculator George Soros and an array of subversive, largely U.S.-based and Government connected NGOs. When Charter 77 was co-founded by Havel in 1977, its manifesto was published by the Western media by pre-arrangement, in the *Frankfurter Allgemeine Zeitung*, *Corriere della Sera*, *The Times* of London, and *Le Monde*.[78]

Just how significant this *kulturkampf* in the service of globalisation is, and not merely as a matter of 'free expression', and individualistic 'personal choice' or 'taste', etc., can be seen in the role the band Plastic People of the Universe (PPU) played in serving as a catalyst for the 'velvet revolution'. The band is acknowledged as musically 'unremarkable', yet its backers ensured that it became politically remarkable. Their origins go back to the Zionist-orchestrated revolt in Czechoslovakia in 1968.[79] The band obtained the assistance of Canadian music teacher Paul Wilson, then resident in Czechoslovakia. They became the 'fathers of the Czech musical underground'.[80]

One commentator states that 'an entire community of Czech dissidents sprung up around the band'. According to bassist and founding member Milan Hlavsa:

> The Plastic People emerged just as dozens and hundreds of other bands - we just loved rock'n'roll and wanted to be famous. We were too young to have a clear artistic ambition. All we did was pure intuition: no political notions or ambitions at all.[81]

---

78 'Charter 77 After 30 Years', The National Security Archive, The George Washington University, http://www.gwu.edu/~nsarchiv/NSAEBB/NSAEBB213/index.htm

79 http://www.progarchives.com/artist.asp?id=2800

80 Ibid.

81 R. Unterberger, 'The Plastic People of the Universe', http://www.richieunterberger.com/ppu.html

Despite the expressions of naiveté by Hlavsa it was precisely the type of youthful nihilism that the CIA and plutocrats had been promoting in the West in the form of the 'New Left' as a means of manipulating pseudo-dissent. It followed the formulae that had been prescribed by the Congress for Cultural Freedom, and which is still utilised.

Although the band's professional license was revoked by the Government in 1970 they hedged around the regulations, and their music was released in the West. Lyrics for the 'non-political' PPU were written by 'Czech dissident poet Egon Bondy'.[82] What emerged around PPU was a so-called 'Second Culture' or 'Other Culture' which played at Music Festivals. There were arrests, but apart from a few, due to 'international protests most were released. Canadian Paul Wilson was expelled. The official indictment accused the bands of 'extreme vulgarity with an anti-socialist and an anti-social impact, most of them extolling nihilism, decadence and clericalism'.[83]

It was in support of this cultural nihilism that Charter 77 emerged as a movement, with Havel as the figurehead, Havel stating that PPU were defending 'life's intrinsic desire to express itself freely, in its own authentic and sovereign way'.[84] Havel began selecting lyrics for PPU. This supposedly 'non-political', innocent, artistic free expression has since been described by *The New York Times* as being 'wild, angry and incendiary', and 'darkly subversive'. *The NY Times* enthused that PPU 'helped change the future direction of a nation', stating:

> Vaclav Havel, the music-loving former Czech president and dissident who championed the band's cause when several members were imprisoned in 1976 for disturbing the peace, credits it with inspiring Charter 77, the manifesto demanding human rights that laid the groundwork for the 1989 revolution. 'The case against a group of young people who simply wanted to live in their own way', he recalled, 'was an attack by the totalitarian system on life itself, on the very essence of human freedom'.[85]

---

82 Ibid.

83 Ibid.

84 Ibid.

85 D. Bilefsky, 'Czech's Velvet Revolution Paved by Plastic People', The NY Times, November 15, 2009, http://www.nytimes.com/2009/11/16/world/europe/16iht-czech.html

It was, stated Bilefsky, 'the ultimate rock 'n' roll rebellion'.[86]

Paul Wilson reminisced that it was through music that the puerile ideals of manipulated Western youth were introduced to their Czechoslovak counterparts:

> One of the things that was very marked in the 1960s was that although intellectuals found it very hard to get a hold of books it was very easy for kids to be right on top of things because records were brought in and the music was broadcast over Voice of America and other radio stations. So, there was a very current music scene here, with a lot of knock-off bands and a lot of fans of different groups just the way you'd find them in the West. The other thing, too, is that the Prague music scene, very early, attracted the attention of the western press, because for them the existence of rock bands in a communist country was a sign of change.[87]

Note that the Voice of America and other U.S. agencies were promoting this movement.

Charter 77 & Soros

It was against this background that the Charter 77 Foundation was established in Stockholm. Soros relates that he had funded this since 1981. The movement 'sprung into operation inside Czechoslovakia armed like Pallas Athena', in 1989. Soros hastened to the country, and with Charter founder F. Janouch, set up committees in Prague, Brno and Bratislava, and 'I put $1 million at their disposal'. He then began paying the staff of the Civic Forum party and the newspaper *Lidove Noviny* by currency speculation. Soros states that together with Prince Kari Schwarzenberg, a supporter of the Charter 77 Foundation, and acting President Marian Calfa, 'we all agreed that it was imperative to have Vaclav Havel elected president by the current rubber-stamp parliament'.[88]

---

86   Ibid.

87   J. Velinger, 'The Impact of the Plastic People on a Communist Universe', Radio Praha, May 31, 2005, http://www.radio.cz/en/section/one-on-one/paul-wilson-the-impact-of-the-plastic-people-on-a-communist-universe

88   George Soros, Underwriting Democracy: Encouraging Free Enterprise & Democratic Reform Among the Soviets & in Eastern Europe (Jackson, TN: Public Affairs, 2004), 26-27.

Havel, like Gorbachev, was duly recognised for services rendered. An exhibition in his honour was established at Columbia University in 2006, with support from luminaries such as Soros, George H. W. Bush, Bill Clinton, [89] Richard Holbrooke, et al.[90] Havel served on the Board of Directors of Soros' Drug Policy Alliance, lobbying for liberalised laws on narcotics, which might be viewed as part of the Soros agenda for undermining the stability of societies that are targeted for globalisation, as part of a 'liberal' and 'progressive' agenda. One is here again reminded of the use of a narcotic, 'Soma,' to keep the citizens docile in Huxley's dystopian novel *Brave New World*; another cause that can moreover be portrayed as 'radical' and 'anti-Establishment', while serving the 'Establishment'. Among members on the 'U.S. Honorary Board' are such 'progressives' and 'humanitarians' as Former Secretary of State George P. Schultz, and former Reserve Bank Chairman Paul Volcker. The 'International Honorary Board' includes, apart from Havel, Richard Branson, Sting, and others.[91]

Havel became a member of the globalist elite, in attendance at their international conclaves for reshaping the post-Soviet world. One of these is the Club of Madrid,[92] one of many globalist think tanks that are designed to arrive at consensus on global governance among the self-chosen rulers. The Club of Madrid is a grant-making foundation set up in 2004 to raise funds for causes that promote the plutocratic version of 'democracy'.[93] As one would expect, the omnipresent Soros is among the Club 'President's Circle of Donors'.[94] Havel was also an 'Honorary Chair' of Freedom Now, a globalist organisation with a cross-over of membership with the Council on Foreign Relations.[95]

National Endowment for Democracy

Of particular interest is Havel's association with the Congressionally-funded National Endowment for Democracy (NED), established in 1983 by Act of Congress. Havel is esteemed by NED, an organisation

---

89   'Havel at Columbia', http://havel.columbia.edu/about.html

90   http://havel.columbia.edu/hostcommittee.html

91   Drug Policy Alliance, http://www.drugpolicy.org/about-us/leadership/board-directors

92   Club of Madrid, Members, http://www.clubmadrid.org/en/estructura/members_1/letra:h

93   http://www.clubmadrid.org/en/about

94   'Partners & Collaborators' http://www.clubmadrid.org/en/partners_collaborators

95   Freedom Now, 'Honorary Co-Chairs', http://www.clubmadrid.org/en/partners_collaborators

intended to take over the role of the CIA in sponsoring 'regime change'. NED was conceived by veteran Trotskyites whose hatred of the USSR turned many into rabid Cold Warriors, and from there into the present clique of neocons. NED was the brainchild of Tom Kahn, International Affairs Director of the AFL-CIO. He was a veteran of the Shachtmanite faction of U.S. Trotskyism. He had joined the Young Socialist League, the youth wing of Max Shachtman's Independent Socialist League,[96] and the Young People's Socialist League, which he continued to support until his death in 1992. Kahn was impressed by the Shachtmanite opposition to the USSR, which Trotskyites regarded as the primary obstacle to world socialism.[97] At the outset of the Cold War Max Shachtman set his course, declaring: 'In spite of all the differences that still exist among them, the capitalist world under American imperialist leadership and drive is developing an increasingly solid front against Russian imperialism'.[98]

In 2004 Havel received the American Friends of the Czech Republic (AFCR) 'Civil Society Vision Award', and was on the occasion eulogised by NED's founding President, veteran Social Democrat Carl Gershman. AFCR appears close to globalism. Its Officers include former U.S. Government functionaries such as Thomas Dine, of Radio Free Europe. The Treasurer and co-Director, Hana Callaghan, is a former advisor to Goldman Sachs.[99] Zbigniew Brzezinski, the rabidly anti-Soviet and Russophobic former U.S National Security adviser, presently with the Center for Strategic and International Studies, is an AFCR 'adviser', as is fellow Russophobe, former U.S. Secretary of State Henry Kissinger. Another is Michal Novack of the neocon American Enterprise Institute.[100] Havel is listed as a sponsor of AFCR, along with George W. Bush; former U.S. Secretary of State Madeleine K. Albright; James D. Wolfensohn, of the World Bank; Colin L. Powell, former U.S. Secretary of State. On the AFCR 'Wall of Honor', along with Havel are many corporates, including American International Group; Goldman, Sachs & Co.; Citigroup; J.P. Morgan Chase & Co.; David Rockefeller, et al.[101]

---

96   Rachelle Horowitz, 'Tom Kahn and the Fight for Democracy: A Political Portrait and Personal Recollection', Dissent Magazine, pp. 238-239. http://www.dissentmagazine. org/democratiya/article_pdfs/d11Horowitz.pdf

97   Ibid. p 211.

98   Max Shachtman, 'Stalinism on the Decline: Tito *versus* Stalin, The Beginning of the End of the Russian Empire', *New International*, Vol. XIV No.6, August 1948, 172-178.

99   AFCR, 'Officers', http://www.afocr.org/afocr-officers.html

100   AFCR 'Advisers', http://www.afocr.org/afocr-advisors.html

101   http://www.afocr.org/afocr-wall-of-honor.html

How the Soviet Bloc was Pushed from Within

In 2007 Havel received NED's "Democracy Service Medal." [102] NED, like Soros, had been a major factor in the 'velvet revolutions' throughout the Warsaw Pact states. This is termed by NED as 'cross-border work' and had its origins 'in a conference that was sponsored by the Polish-Czech-Slovak Solidarity Foundation in Wroclaw in early November of 1989'. According to Gershman:

> That conference was the culmination of collaborative meetings and joint activities of Solidarity and the Workers' Defense Committee in Poland and the Charter 77 dissidents in Czechoslovakia that began in October 1981, shortly before the declaration of Martial Law, and continued throughout the 1980s with gatherings on the "green border" of Poland and Czechoslovakia in the Karkonosze Mountains. The purpose of the Wroclaw conference was to support from the base of the new Polish democracy the dissident movement in Czechoslovakia in the hope that a similar breakthrough could be achieved there. Vaclav Havel was later to credit the conference and the cultural festival that accompanied it with helping to inspire the Velvet Revolution that occurred less than two weeks later.[103]

Gershman alludes to NED's role in sponsoring the subversion that spread from Poland to Czechoslovakia:

> It became clear to me from the many discussions I had with Polish activists in the aftermath of 1989 that they had a very firm and clearly thought through determination to support democracy in Poland's immediate neighborhood and in the larger geopolitical sphere that once constituted the Soviet Bloc. This determination was partly based on moral considerations, since these activists had received support in their struggle from the NED, the AFL-CIO and others in the U.S. and Europe and felt an obligation to extend similar support to those still striving for democracy.[104]

Gershman states that this 'cross border work' continues, and reaches today throughout the former Soviet Union in providing training.

---

102 http://www.ned.org/about/board/meet-our-president/archived-remarks-and-presentations/061704

103 C. Gershman, 'Giving Solidarity to the World, at the symposium "Solidarity and the Future of Democratization" Georgetown University - Washington, D.C.,' May 19, 2009, http://www.ned.org/about/board/meet-our-president/archived-remarks-and-presentations/051909

104 Ibid.

The Zionist Factor

The offensive against the Soviet bloc was multi-faceted, and the fantasies of many 'Rightists' to the contrary, the Soviet bloc was not only a bulwark against American hegemony, but also against the international ramifications of Zionism. The USSR became the principal enemy of American hegemonic interests with Stalin's repudiation of the United National World Government and of the 'Baruch Plan' for the internationalisation of nuclear energy under U.N. (that is, U.S.) control. This repudiation was the catalyst of the Cold War. However, the message was clear to Zionism with the purging of Zionists and Jews in 1952, that the Soviet bloc, which had armed Israel at an early stage as part of a geopolitical plan for the Middle East, considered Zionism a primary enemy. The battle lines were drawn in Prague, when Jewish leaders of the Communist party were accused of Zionism, which was deemed treason, and hanged. The Zionists went frenetic from this point, while the Soviet bloc established Governmental departments to examine Zionism and some of the best material on the subject came from the Soviet presses. Moscow became what Lendvai termed the 'center and exporter of anti-Semitism',[105] a Zionist euphemism for anyone who resists Zionism.

Hence, in 1968 Zionists were a major factor in the first strike against the Soviet regime in Czechoslovakia. Zionists acknowledge this. The 1967 Arab-Israeli war 'became the catalytic agent' for the disruption of the Czechoslovak regime. The regime had launched an anti-Zionist campaign during the war and was the first Soviet state after the USSR to sever diplomatic relations with Israel in 1967, and the first to send high-level military delegations to Egypt and Syria.[106] As with the revolt led by Havel, the liberal-infected intelligentsia were behind the effort to establish 'socialism with a human face'. Letters and articles by disaffected elements protested against the regime's anti-Zionist campaign, and these were read at the Czechoslovak Writers' Congress of June 26-29, 1967. Ladislav Mnacko, the country's most successful playwright, defiantly visited Israel, and condemned the Czechoslovak regime for its opposition to Zionism, with allusions to the 1952 purge.

A familiar theme emerged: supposedly 'spontaneous' student protests, held on May Day, where youth carried Israeli flags and banners reading 'Let Israel Live'. Students and faculty at Prague's Charles University issued a petition calling for diplomatic relations with Israel to be resumed. This was followed by an appeal in the youth paper,

---

105 P. Lendvai, Anti-Semitism in Eastern Europe (London: Macdonald & Co., 1971), 10.

106 Ibid., 260-261.

Student, which announced the formation of a 'Union of the Friends of Israel'. Student riots occurred in Warsaw, Poland, and the Communist party in Yugoslavia also condemned the anti-Zionist position of the Czechoslovaks.[107] It is unlikely that this Zionist agitation arose 'spontaneously', any more than the 'velvet revolutions' today occur 'spontaneously', despite the same claims. TASS reported, 'Israel and international Zionism had watched developments in Czechoslovakia closely since January 1968... Israel as well as Zionist organizations in the United States and the West European counties have allocated huge sums to finance internal opposition in Czechoslovakia'.[108] The pattern follows the same as that of the actions of Soros, NED, et al in Poland, Czechoslovakia and elsewhere. The attempt by Dubcek and others to install 'socialism with a human face' was aborted by the Soviet military. The reconstructed regime was more avidly opposed to Zionism than ever. The Slovak Minister of the Interior, Gen. Pepich, referred to 'thirty-two foreign centres organizing subversive activities against Czechoslovakia', including Zionist organisations operating from Austria.[109] Lendvai states that the Soviet invasion and its aftermath put an end to hopes by the Jews that the celebration of the Jewish millennium would be held in Prague. Few Jews were left, and only one rabbi.[110]

The subversion of Czechoslovakia had been long in the making. In 1951, shortly before the 'treason trial', William Oatis, Associated Press correspondent, was sentenced to 10 years imprisonment for espionage. In September 1968, *Newsweek* mentioned that he had had extremely wide connections in Czechoslovakia among Zionists. In 1957, a Secretary at the Israeli Embassy, Moshe Katz, was expelled from the country.[111] While Zionist apologists such as Lendvai insist that the pro-Zionist activism in Czechoslovakia that prompted the Russian invasion in 1968 was a spontaneous opposition to anti-Semitism, even he admits broadly the allegations of the Soviet press and regime. Soviet author Yuri Ivanov, in his book on World Zionism, writes:

A leading role in the Zionist activities was to be played by the inconspicuous 'Main Documentary Centre' tucked away in

---

107 Ibid., 260-269.

108 Ibid., 290-291.

109 Ibid., 294.

110 Ibid., 296.

111 Y. Ivanov, Caution: Zionism, Chapter 5, http://home.alphalink.com.au/~radnat/zionism/chapfive.html

Vienna. On the eve of the events in Czechoslovakia the Centre created a 'daughter enterprise', the Committee for Czechoslovak Refugees. It is significant that almost simultaneously a Centre for the Co-ordination of Fighters for the Freedom of Czechoslovakia was set up in Israel (which must have seemed a rather strange move, surely, to the ordinary Israeli, for whom the main thing in 1968 was the Israeli-Arab conflict).[112]

The Tel Aviv Zionist newspaper *Maariv* revealed the nature of the Centre's activities in a routine report of October 6, 1968:

> Yesterday the Co-ordination Centre sent a group of young Czech intellectuals resident in Israel to various European countries. The group's task is to establish contact with Czechoslovak citizens outside the country. They are also to investigate the possibility of establishing contact with various groups inside Czechoslovakia. Part of the group is to go to Prague.

> The Co-ordination Centre in Israel, the paper went on to say, is becoming a world centre of fighters for the freedom of Czechoslovakia… Those who meet material difficulties and have insufficient means for activities in or outside Czechoslovakia are given material support… The Co-ordination Centre has prepared a programme for organising the publication of *Literarni Listy*, a paper which is the voice of democracy in Czechoslovakia. Contributions for this purpose may be sent to: Discount Bank, account No. 450055, Tel Aviv.[113]

Zionist apologists do not explain the Soviet documentation on Zionism but broadly refer to Soviet contentions as being without merit and lacking credible evidence.

Havel Feted by Zionists

Hence, given the history of relations between Zionism and the Soviet bloc, and in particular Czechoslovakia, Havel readily endeared himself to the Zionists, as did Gorbachev. As can be seen by comparing the *modus operandi* between the 'velvet revolutions' in the Warsaw Pact states and the machinations of Zionism in Czechoslovakia in 1967-1968, there are many parallels.

---

112 Ibid.

113 Ibid.

Eulogies quickly appeared for Havel throughout the world Zionist press. *Jewish World* reported that the European Jewish Congress, in 'mourning the death' of Havel issued a statement that, 'Havel was known as a great friend of the Jews and did much to confront anti-Semitism and teach the lessons of the dark chapter of the Holocaust during his two terms in office'.

> EJC President Dr. Moshe Kantor, who was a colleague of Havel's on the European Council on Tolerance and Reconciliation, said that he would be sadly missed. 'He was a figure for a new and modern Europe to emulate. President Havel lived through communism and led the Czech Republic to a new era helping move his countrymen through a troubled past to a more open, free and tolerant future. 'President Havel was a true and steadfast friend of the Jewish people and will be missed by European Jewry'.[114]

Israeli President Shimon Peres described Havel's death as 'a loss for the entire world'. 'Peres said that Havel was both his personal friend and a friend of Israel'.[115] The Jewish newspaper *Forward* relates the occasion that Havel attended the 1990 Salzburg Music Festival where he delivered a speech pointedly aimed at former U.N. Secretary General Kurt Waldheim (albeit without naming him) who was being pilloried for having fought with Germany during World War II, like most Austrians. As related by *Forward*, World Jewry found Havel's moralising humbuggery as the finest of sentiments, Havel ending with 'confession liberates'. It is perhaps indicative of how low Havel would stoop to curry favour with those of wealth and power, and one might ask how much moral fortitude it takes to merely join the clamour of a global lynch party? *Forward* comments: 'It was a quintessentially Havel-esque performance: deeply moral and slightly mischievous at the same time'.[116] Kirchick in the *Forward* article

---

114   'EJC mourns death of Havel', Jewish World, ynetnews.com, December 19, 2011, http://www.ynetnews.com/articles/0,7340,L-4163744,00.html

115   N. Mozgovaya, 'Israel President: Vaclav Havels' death loss for entire world', Haaretz. com, December 18, 2011, http://www.haaretz.com/news/international/israel-president-vaclav-havel-s-death-a-loss-for-the-entire-world-1.402157

116   J. Kirchick, 'Havel was friend of Israel and Jews: Czech Playwright-Turned-President Led Region to Right Path', The Jewish Daily Forward, December 20, 2011, http://www.forward.com/articles/148247/
Kirchick, is a Fellow with the Foundation for Defense of Democracies, yet another neocon Cold War II think tank founded after 9/11, to help ensure that 'the new American century' comes to fruition. Funded by the likes of the Bronfmans, its 'leadership council' includes neocon identities such as former CIA director James

alludes to Czechoslovakia's special role in opposing World Zionism, and Havel's having pledged on New Year's Day 1990 to re-establish diplomatic relations with Israel, which was done the following month. Kirchick continues:

> In April of that year, Havel became the first leader of a free former Soviet bloc country to visit Israel. It was his second foreign trip as president of Czechoslovakia... As president, Havel opposed the sale of weapons to regimes hostile to Israel, like Syria, a controversial move considering that communist-era Czechoslovakia (and Slovakia in particular) was a major exporter of arms to Soviet clients. Today, according to Israeli Ambassador Yaakov Levy, 'the Czech Republic is considered by Israel to be its best friend in Europe and the European Union'.[117]

In the early years of Czecho/Slovak independence, when many in the West worried about a resurgence of nationalism across the newly independent nations of the Eastern Bloc, Havel spoke out forcefully against anti-Semitism. Because of this, he became an enduring enemy of the nationalist right. In 1993, following the 'Velvet Divorce' from Slovakia, a far-right party tried to block Havel's election as president of the Czech Republic with a parliamentary filibuster, accusing Havel of being paid off in 'shekels' by outside forces.

Havel continued to speak out for Israel well after his retirement in 2003. He co-founded the Friends of Israel Initiative, aimed at combating the delegitimisation of Israel in the realm of international institutions. He criticised a Czech education ministry official revealed as having links with 'far right' organisations. When the man's defenders said that his views should not have any bearing on his ability to hold a government job, Havel replied that he was 'struck... that quasi-fascist or quasi-anti-Semitic or similar opinions should be expressed in one's spare time, or during vacation, but not at the office. Yes, that's it exactly: After all, a certain house painter also founded his party in a pub in Munich, not at the workplace'. This indicates how far Havel believed in 'freedom'.

Like all such 'liberals' his liberality only extended to those who agree

---

Woolsey, Steve Forbes of *Forbes Magazine*, Bill Kristol of *The Weekly Standard*, Sen. Joseph Lieberman, et al. Its advisers include such familiar names as Charles Krauthammer and Richard Perle. A founding Chair was Jean Kirkpatrick, veteran post-Trot neocon.

117 Ibid.

with liberal views. Havel was apparently happy to see a Government official purged from his job on the basis that he did not share Havel's sycophantic attitude towards Zionism and plutocracy.

According to Foundation for Defense of Democracies 'Freedom Scholar', neocon strategist Michael Ledeen,[118] he can't watch a video of Havel's funeral without 'tearing up'. One might wonder whether he has the same reaction to footage of Palestinian children being shot-up by Israeli soldiers, of wars of destruction meted out by the USA on the civilians of Serbia, Iraq, Libya, and Syria? Tellingly Ledeen brings us back to a major theme, writing of Havel:

> Did I mention that he loved music? Both rock and jazz, because he recognized their subversive power. He loved Frank Zappa, and made him the Czech 'cultural ambassador'. When Bill Clinton visited Prague in the mid-nineties, Havel took him to a seedy nightclub, where the American president played sax with the locals (and his wife, Dagmar, visited the club on a walking tour of the city shortly after Havel's death)… Havel loved to write 'absurdist' plays and poems. He was a true heir to Kafka. Like Kafka, he had an uncanny grasp of the dynamics and resulting horrors of bureaucracy. And, like Kafka, he was a Zionist.[119]

III. KULTURKAMPF

Vaclav Havel and his globalist sponsors were continuing an important programme of culture-war against the Soviet bloc that was formally organised by the CIA immediately after World War II, although drawing from Trotskyites and other Marxists who opposed the triumph of 'National Bolshevism' over international Marxism. When Stalin dislodged the Trotskyite and other alien Marxist cabals from the body *politick* of the USSR he inaugurated not only a Russianised direction for the economy, as we have seen, stymying Western economic colonisation, but recognised the importance of maintaining Russia's cultural identity. The importance of this continues to be recognised under the Putin regime.

---

118 Former consultant to the National Security Department, Defense Dept., and State Dept., media pundit.

119 M. Ledeen, 'Havel, Kafka and Us', FDD, December 21, 2011, http://www. defenddemocracy.org/media-hit/havel-kafka-and-us/

Lines of Culture-War Drawn

The lines of the culture-war were drawn in what is now known as the 'Cultural Cold War'.[120] Cultural subversion became the USA's means of undermining nations and this remains the case.[121] The USSR since the time of Stalin defined the role of 'Soviet culture', vis-à-vis the 'rootless cosmopolitanism' that was being sponsored around the world by the USA via the CIA and plutocratic interests.

While 'socialist realism' was formulated in 1932 by Maxim Gorky of the Union of Russian Writers,[122] the position of a new Soviet culture founded upon tradition, was developed and publicly declared in 1946 by A. Zhdanov.[123] Classical composers from the Czarist era, such as Tchaikovsky, Glinka, and Borodin, were revived after being sidelined in the early years of Bolshevism, as were great non-Russian composers such as Beethoven, Brahms, and Schubert.[124]Modernists who had been fêted in the early days of Bolshevism were relegated to irrelevance by the 1930s.[125] Jazz and the associated types of dancing were condemned as bourgeoisie degeneracy.[126] Soviet culture was to be folkish and heroic.[127]

In 1948, Zhdanov's speech to the Central Committee of the Communist Party of the Soviet Union (Bolshevik) intended primarily to lay the foundations of Soviet music, represents one of the most cogent attempts to define culture.[128]The Zhdanov speech also helped set the foundation for the campaign against 'rootless cosmopolitanism' that was launched several years later.[129]

---

120 Frances Stonor Saunders, The Cultural Cold War: the CIA and the world of arts and letters (New York: The New Press, 1999).

121 Ralph Peters, 'Constant Conflict', Parameters, Summer 1997, 4-14. http://www. usamhi.army.mil/USAWC/Parameters/97summer/peters.htm

122 Richard Overy, The Dictators: Hitler's Germany and Stalin's Russia (London: Allen Lane, 2004), 352-353.

123 Ibid., p. 361.

124 Ibid., 366-367.

125 Ibid., 371.

126 Ibid., 376.

127 K.R. Bolton, Stalin, op. cit., pp. 21-27.

128 A. Zhandov, Speech, Central Committee of the Communist Party SU (Bolshevik), February 1948. p. 6.

129 Bolton, Stalin, op. cit., p. 22.

It is notable that these definitive statements on Soviet culture were being made at the very beginning of the 'Cold War', when the USSR rejected U.S. offers to be a junior partner in a post-War 'new world order', under the auspices of the United Nations Organisation. It is also notable that the USSR was launching its campaign against 'rootless cosmopolitanism' at the same time that the USA was launching its campaign to spread 'modernism' throughout the world, primarily via 'abstract expressionism', the preferred artistic mode of the Rockefellers, CIA, et al, and their Left-wing lackeys such as Jackson Pollock.

In 1949 F. Chernov wrote a seminal article declaring war against 'rootless cosmopolitanism'.[130] He described the 'rootless cosmopolitans' that had entered both the Soviet arts and the sciences as 'nihilistic' and 'anti-national'. Speaking for the Soviet state, Chernov even repudiated any notion of a 'united world science', seeing this as part of an attempt to create a 'world philosophy' devoid of 'national distinctions and features', stating:

> The forms in which bourgeois-cosmopolitan petty ideas are dragged into the area of ideology are multifarious: from concealment of better products of socialist culture to direct denigration of it; from denial of the world-historical significance of Great Russian culture and elimination of respect for its traditions to the frank propagation of servility before decadent bourgeois culture; from the spreading of national nihilism and negation of the significance of the question of priority in science to the slogan about 'international solidarity' with bourgeois science and so forth and so on. But the essence of all these forms is this antipatriotism, this propaganda of bourgeois-cosmopolitan ideology setting its goal of spiritual disarmament of the Soviet people in the face of aggressive bourgeois ideology, the revival of remnants of capitalism in peoples' consciousness.[131]

As we have seen in a previous chapter, Russian Bolshevism quickly assumed the traditional and messianic characteristics of a Great Russian revival. Chernov in his definition of Soviet culture shows just how Russianified it had become with his reference to 'the world-historical significance of Great Russian culture', and his repudiation of any notion of a 'cosmopolitan' or 'international culture', even in

---

130 F. Chernov, 'Bourgeois Cosmopolitanism and its reactionary role', Bolshevik: Theoretical and Political Magazine of the Central Committee of the All-Union Communist Party (Bolsheviks) ACP(B), Issue #5, March 15 1949, pp. 30-41.

131 Ibid.

the sciences. Chernov identified 'rootless cosmopolitism' as part of a specific foreign agenda, which was certainly formalized that year – 1949 – with the founding of the Congress for Cultural Freedom:

> In the calculation of our foreign enemies they should divert Soviet literature and culture and Soviet science from the service of the Socialist cause. They try to infect Soviet literature, science, and art with all kinds of putrid influences, to weaken in such a way these powerful linchpins of the political training of the people, the education of the Soviet people in the spirit of active service to the socialist fatherland, to communist construction.[132]

Explaining the meaning of cosmopolitanism, Chernov stated:

> Cosmopolitanism is the negation of patriotism, its opposite. It advocates absolute apathy towards the fate of the Motherland. Cosmopolitanism denies the existence of any moral or civil obligations of people to their nation and Motherland.[133]

Chernov then outlined the manner by which cosmopolitanism serves global capital:

> The bourgeoisie preaches the principle that money does not have a homeland, and that, wherever one can 'make money', wherever one may 'have a profitable business', there is his homeland. Here is the villainy that bourgeois cosmopolitanism is called on to conceal, to disguise, 'to ennoble' the antipatriotic ideology of the rootless bourgeois-businessman, the huckster and the traveling salesman.[134]

Chernov's cultural manifesto could certainly serve as a manifesto of the conservative-Right to the present day: there is nothing Marxian in its character, other than some references to 'socialism', while the definitions are ever-more apt for this era of globalisation. No wonder Trotskyites and other Marxists remain outraged. Chernov identified precisely who was behind this global *kulturkampf*:

> In the guise of cosmopolitan phraseology, in false slogans about the struggle against 'nationalist selfishness', hides the brutal face of the inciters of a new war, trying to bring about

---

132 Chernov, ibid.

133 Ibid.

134 Ibid.

the fantastic notion of American rule over the world. From the imperialist circles of the USA today issues propaganda of 'world citizenship' and 'universal government'.[135]

At the time the CIA was launching its front, the Congress for Cultural Freedom, with the assistance of Trotsky-apologist Professor Sidney Hook, and other Leftists. Its cultural ideology can at least in part be traced to the manifesto on the arts written by Trotsky along with *avant garde* André Breton and Diego Rivera in 1938, entitled *Towards a Free Revolutionary Art*.[136] This was published in the Autumn 1938 issue of the Marxist magazine *Partisan Review*, which was to play a significant role in the 'Cultural Cold War' and was to receive CIA funding.

One of the first projects launched upon the world was an exhibition of 'abstract expressionism' in 1952 via the International Program of the Rockefeller-founded, funded and run Museum of Modern Art (MoMA). This received a five-year annual grant of $125,000 from the Rockefeller Brothers Fund, under the direction of Porter McCray, who had also worked with Nelson Rockefeller's Latin American Department at the U.S. State Department, and in 1950 as an attaché of the cultural section of the U.S. Foreign Service.[137] Russell Lynes, writing of this period stated that MoMA now had the entire world to 'proselytise' with what he called 'the exportable religion' of Abstract Expressionism.[138]

'Pussy Riot'

Although the Congress for Cultural Freedom, after numerous exposés, was wound up, and the CIA publicly acknowledges its role,[139] the National Endowment for Democracy largely took over its role, and there has been an ever-growing plethora of NGOs and think tanks

---

135 Ibid.

136 Leon Trotsky, André Breton, Diego Rivera, Towards a Free Revolutionary Art, 25 July 1938.

137 Saunders, op. cit., p. 267.

138 Russell Lynes, Good Old Modern Art: An Intimidate Portrait of the Museum of Modern Art (New York: Atheneum, 1973), cited by Saunders, ibid.., 267.

139 'Cultural Cold War: Origins of the Congress for Cultural Freedom, 1949-50', Central Intelligence Agency, https://www.cia.gov/library/center-for-the-study-of-intelligence/kent-csi/docs/v38i5a10p.htm#rft1

throughout the world to continue the globalist web of subversion, with Russia remaining the primary target. As shown above with the example of Havel, the culture front remains important. Today, following the same scenario as the manner by which culture-junk was used in Soviet Czechoslovakia, there has been great tumult fermented by the punk-Left group 'Pussy Riot'.

Overnight this banality became a *cause celebre* of well-organised mass demonstrations of the type that are always termed 'spontaneous', and quickly garnered a clamorous chorus of pontificating Russophobes. Some even referred to this inanity as a 'global revolution'. What was tantamount to a Black Mass in an Orthodox Cathedral became a banner for 'free speech' and a battering ram against Russia. If similar antics were tried in a synagogue in Israel, what would be the reactions of the Israeli Government, and 'world opinion', including that of U.S. officialdom? One young enthusiast, Madeline Carey, whom we might pick as typical of a generation (like those of the 'Hip Generation'), easily swayed into thinking that nonsense is 'revolutionary', gushed:

> After they blessed themselves with the sign of the cross and bowed toward the altar, the members of the band, clad in vibrantly coloured masks called *balaclavas* that cover most of the face except for the eyes, performed a 'punk prayer' for a camera and a few straggling worshippers in the cathedral.[140]

Ms. Carey further enthused that the cause has been taken up by others as if this is surprising, considering the legions of the naïve that can be mobilised in short-order by Machiavellian interests in the name of the most inane 'issues', so long as slogans such as 'human rights' and 'democracy' are sufficiently bandied about:

> After igniting this flame of protest, it has been estimated that *Pussy Riot has become one of most influential artists of our generation*. Moreover, many politicians and artists, including Paul McCartney, Madonna and Pete Townshend have publicly stood behind the band. Citizens of New York City—as well as those in Bulgaria, Scotland, Germany and Russia—have taken notice and united under the cause....[141]

---

140 Madeline Carey, 'Defend the Riot: Pussy Riot's Global Revolution', November 20, 2012, Huff Post, http://www.huffingtonpost.com/madeline-carey/pussy-riot-free-speech_b_2109754.html

141 Ibid.

Ms. Carey, then a sophomore, was like many others eager to re-create the entire world in the image of American 'democracy'. She and the multitude of others are in influential company, which one would think would give them pause for reconsideration as to whose agenda they are following,[142] had the education system and mass entertainment media not atrophied their critical faculties. However, youth are easily incited by clichés as they were in the 1960s and 1970s and as they have been during the 'Arab Spring' and the multitude of other 'colour revolutions' sweeping the world in the name of 'human rights' and in the interests of global capital.

With the jailing of several of the activists of 'Pussy Riot' for 'hooliganism' as the result of their antics at the Orthodox Church, in which a 'prayer' to Mary for the overthrow of Putin was the theme, condemnation of the verdicts also came from Freedom House. Like the National Endowment for Democracy, Freedom House receives U.S. government funding through USAID and the State Department. Board members have included Russophobic neocons such as Paul Wolfowitz, Donald Rumsfeld, Jean Kirkpatrick, and Zbigniew Brzezinski. In 2013, amidst the contrived international furore, the National Endowment for Democracy sponsored a symposium on the arts as a method of dissent in Russia, entitled 'Enemies of the State: Pussy Riot and the New Russian Protest Rock'.[143]

At the time the Pussy Riot support campaign was co-ordinated in Finland by Oksana Chelysheva, 'a member of the board of the Finnish-Russian Civic Forum, a member of the Steering Committee of the Soros-funded EU-Russia Civil Society Forum,[144] and Deputy Executive Director of the Helsinki-based Russian-Chechen Friendship Society, which was banned in Russia under the country's draconious "anti-extremism" legislation'.[145]

142　See: Tony Cartalucci, 'Russia's 'Pussy Riot' Supported by U.S. State Department', Global Research, August 18 2012, http://www.globalresearch.ca/russias-pussy-riot-stunt-supported-by-us-state-department/32395

143　National Endowment for Democracy, February 19, 2013; https://www.ned.org/events/enemies-of-the-state-pussy-riot-and-the-new-russian-protest-rock/

144　Founded in 2011 with sponsorship of the Open Society Institute, Prague, a part of the Soros global network. See: http://eu-russia-csf.org/home/general-assemblies/032011-prague/

145　'Art and Politics in Russia Today', Finrosfourm, https://finrosforum.wordpress.com/2012/03/26/art-and-politics-in-russia-today/

The LGBT Offensive

The subversion of traditional morality, custom and religion in targeted societies has been an integral part of the globalist agenda, indicated by the grant-making trends of organisations such as the Open Society Foundations. In particular, gender issues, including the promotion of feminism and liberalised abortion laws (called 'reproductive rights') has been significant. In 2012 international outrage was invoked against Russia because a law was passed prohibiting 'propaganda of homosexuality to minors'. That prohibiting the attempted induction of children by those with a 'gay agenda' should be regarded as an outrage against 'human rights' itself says something about the decay of the West. The Open Society Foundations predictably started funding activities designed to challenge the Russian states laws. Primary among these is a ten-day 'Side-by-Side LGBT Film Festival', started in 2008, which is 'a long-time grantee of the Open Society Foundations'.[146]

In 2017 the European Court on Human Rights stated that the Russian law is discriminatory after 'gay rights activists' were fined[147] – not for homosexuality, which is legal – but for promoting homosexuality among minors. Vitaly Milonov, a member of the *Duma* for Putin's ruling United Russia party, who introduced the bill, responded that the court's decision 'is absolutely harmful, and those who set up this decision are enemies of Europe'. That the 'activists' were *prosecuted for demonstrating outside a secondary school and a children's library,*[148] seems to be a matter of no consequence to the Russophobes.

Among the most vociferous has been Human Rights Watch,[149] which postures as an independent monitoring group, but which has among its primary 'partners' Soros' omnipresent Open Society Foundations, along with the Ford Foundation, and other globalist entities.[150]

146 'another side of the Struggle for LGBT Rights in Russia, Open Society Foundations, February 13, 2014; https://www.opensocietyfoundations.org/voices/another-side-struggle-lgbt-rights-russia

147 There is no prison sentence.

148 'European court blasts Russia 'gay propaganda law', BBC News, June 20, 2017; http://www.bbc.com/news/world-europe-40338637

149 'The Olympics have left Sochi but don't forget LGBT Russian', February 8, 2018; https://www.hrw.org/about/partners

150 Human Rights Watch, 'Partners', https://www.hrw.org/about/partners

How the Soviet Bloc was Pushed from Within

The Russian 'LGBT Network', founded in 2006, is 'partnered' with Freedom House. Freedom House was a significant factor in the Cold War, stating that among its activities were the establishment of a propaganda outlet for the Afghan 'freedom fighters' (who became today's *Jihadists*) fighting the Russians, and being among the first to support the Solidarity movement in Poland.[151] Freedom House states that it assisted the former Soviet bloc states 'in the establishment of independent media, independent think tanks, and the core institutions of electoral politics'. That is to say, Freedom House, like a multitude of others, sought to re-make these states in the decaying image of the Late West, and is now part of a global offensive in this region because many of those Eurasian, Magyar and Slavic peoples, other than Russia, have rejected the West's liberal rot and predatory economics. Democracy did not deliver what the globalists expected. Given that the Freedom House board of directors largely comprises heads of global corporations, and that the present chairman, D. Jeffrey Hirschberg, has a background in organising U.S. investments in Russia in partnership with the U.S. Government,[152] one might ask whether the ideal of 'freedom' is a euphemism for the freedom of predatory international capital?

---

151   Freedom House, 'History', https://freedomhouse.org/content/our-history

152   U.S. Russia Center for Entrepreneurship, and U.S.-Russia Investment Fund Freedom House. Hirschberg, https://freedomhouse.org/content/d-jeffrey-hirschberg

Behind the Ukraine Crisis

The situation in the Ukraine follows the same scenario as sundry other states that have been brought into the globalist fold. The riots on the streets of Kiev and elsewhere amounted to a 'colour revolution' of the type that went, like a dose of salts, through the states of the former USSR, and recently through North Africa in the so-called 'Arab Spring'.[1] Interestingly, at the time there were also globalist sponsored revolts in Venezuela,[2] and Syria.[3]

Ukraine: Target of Globalists

The 'Cold War' against Russia only had a brief respite during the Gorbachev and Yeltsin years. Hence the present crisis over the Ukraine does not represent a 'return to the Cold War', as foreign policy pundits have been claiming; the 'Cold War' hardly stopped. The U.S. policy makers have stated plainly that post-Yeltsin Russia remains an enemy and that anyone who aims to reassert Russia as a world power – as Putin has – is a legitimate target of the USA.[4]

As we might expect, the Ukraine has been one of the states that is of much interest to the National Endowment for Democracy. One might see from NED's financial program that here again NED was sponsoring young cadres in various sectors of society, including 'educating' electorates on how to vote in the October 2012 elections. This was flagrant interference in the political processes. The 2012 NED financial report listed the NGO's in the Ukraine that received $3,380,834 during that year.[5] The amount represented the upper

---

1   K. R. Bolton, 'Tunisian revolt, another Soros/NED jackup', *Foreign Policy Journal*, January 18, 2011, http://www.foreignpolicyjournal.com/2011/01/18/tunisian-revolt-another-sorosned-jack-up/

2   See for example, National Endowment for Democracy, 'Venezuela', 2012 annual report, http://www.ned.org/where-we-work/latin-america-and-caribbean/venezuela

3   K. R. Bolton, 'Attack on Syria planned nearly two decades ago', *Foreign Policy Journal*, September 16, 2013, http://www.foreignpolicyjournal.com/2013/09/16/attack-on-syria-planned-nearly-two-decades-ago/

4   K. R. Bolton, *Stalin*, op. cit., 137-139.

5   National Endowment for Democracy, NED 2012 Annual report, http://www.ned.org/

end of funds sent by NED throughout the world. The 2017 NED report on the Ukraine shows the ongoing preoccupation with the region.[6] Donbas is particularly targeted for interference, to the extent of directing the creation and development of political parties, via the National Democratic Institute for International Affairs.[7] NDI is sponsored by the U.S. Government, via USAID and the State Department.[8] Other sponsors include the Open Society Foundations, and corporates such as Coca Cola, Google, and Chevron.[9] How typically hypocritical that the USA feigns outrage that Russia allegedly 'interfered' with the presidential elections, when the U.S. has for decades expended vast amounts on not only interfering but on *creating* the political machinery of targeted states.

Ukraine was among the states targeted for a 'colour revolution' in 2004; the 'Orange Revolution'. A symposium on the Ukraine held by the NED-linked International Forum for Democratic Studies lamented that 'following its failure to consolidate the democratic gains of the much-celebrated 2004 "Orange Revolution", Ukraine under the rule of authoritarian President Viktor Yanukovych has suffered numerous setbacks in its struggle to achieve a more democratic system'.[10]

Veteran globalist foreign policy adviser Zbigniew Brzezinski, when interviewed by *Ukrainian Pravda*, a journal connected with NED, lauded the rioting youth that, as with other 'colour revolutions', precipitated the collapse in the Ukraine. He praised their sense of 'nationhood', as 'an optimistic sign'.[11] Brzezinski speaks of 'independent nationhood'. This praise of Ukrainian nationalism by Brzezinski is odd coming from someone who has spent most of his

where-we-work/eurasia/ukraine

6 'Ukraine 2017', NED, https://www.ned.org/region/central-and-eastern-europe/ukraine-2017/

7 The NDI's chairman of the board is Madeleine Albright, Secretary of State under Clinton.

8 'Our Supporters', NDI, https://www.ndi.org/partners

9 Ibid.

10 'Ukraine's Lessons Learned: From the Orange Revolution to the Euromaidan', National Endowment for Democracy, February 12, 2014, http://www.ned.org/events/ukraine-lessons-learned-from-the-orange-revolution-to-the-euromaidan

11 Segei Leshchenko, 'Zbigniew Brzezinski: Yanukovych understand that has no chance of fair elections. So went under the umbrella of Putin', Ukrainian Pravda, January 15, 2014, http://www.pravda.com.ua/articles/2014/01/15/7009577/ Note that Leshchenko, who conducted the Brzezinski interview, is a NED Fellow.

life, since his days as a young academic, condemning nationalism and asserting that international capitalism, founded upon a globalist elite that transcends territorial borders, is the next phase of historical evolution in a dialectical process. Brzezinski does not even believe in 'independent nationhood'. He believes that it is passé.[12] However it is the line followed by all the other mouthpieces of globalisation, including the USA and the E.U., and all the pontificators at the United Nations, who in condemning Russia suddenly became zealots for nationalism. None, of course, are champions of nationalism, which they regard as anathema. 'Nationalism' is only used as a dialectical strategy as part of a globalist agenda.

Brzezinski alluded to what is the real bugbear of the globalists: the fear that Russia will lead a Eurasian bloc which, we might add, would also find allies across the world, from India, to Venezuela to Syria;[13] hence the simultaneous actions against the latter two states, fomented by the same forces that were backing chaos in the Ukraine. Brzezinski, as a principal spokesman for the globalists, talks of an 'expansion of Europe'. Brzezinski openly states that the globalists want the Ukraine to be part of the E.U. as the start of a process that will integrate Russia also. He states that this is the wave of the future, and that a Russia-led 'Eurasian union' will fail. However, if the E.U. represented a truly independent third force, it would have been targeted as avidly by the globalists as Russia and the previous Soviet bloc. Unfortunately, the E.U. has not emerged as a third force, but as an appendage of U.S. foreign policy, and its position on the Ukraine situation was another example of this.

From Brzezinski's statements, we can see why the globalists were so eager to oust the Yanukovych regime, with the prospect of the Ukraine coming closer to Russia rather than opting for the E.U. Brzezinski referred to Russia increasingly interfering in Ukrainian affairs, yet the interference of NED, funded by U.S. Congress, and other such agencies, is long and pervasive. As indicated by their 2017 report on the Ukraine, NED is reshaping the Ukraine according to globalist requirements.

NED funding helped instigate another 'Orange Revolution'. Their sponsorship included the rather obvious organisation named *Aplesin*

---

12   Zbigniew Brzezinski, Between Two Ages: America's role in the technotronic era (New York: The Viking Press, 1970), 29.

13   K. R. Bolton, Geopolitics of the Indo-Pacific: emerging conflicts, new alliances (London: Black House Publishing, 2013), 174-180.

(meaning 'Orange'), more formally entitled 'Center of Progressive Young People', founded in 2001. *Aplesin* listed its 'international financial partners' as the U.S. Embassy; NED; Freedom House; Polish-Ukrainian Cooperation Foundation[14]; International Relief and Development, another U.S.-based globalist front;[15] Princes Foundation Benefactors Ostrozki Ruslan Kraplych, a Ukrainian based organisation receiving funding from Microsoft Ukraine and USAID; among others.[16] The Soros network of globalist subverters operates in the Ukraine through the International Renaissance Foundation.[17] The Foundation was active in assisting rioters injured in fighting with authorities. The foundation includes a special tribute to its founder.[18] The Foundation states its 'mission is to foster an open, participatory, pluralist society based on democratic values in Ukraine. It is part of the Open Society Foundations network established by investor and philanthropist George Soros'.[19] One of its primary aims is to integrate the Ukraine into the E.U.: 'We promote European integration of Ukraine through the support of civil society initiatives, aimed at strengthening the influence of civil society on EU-Ukraine relations'. [20]

Oligarchs Given Fiefdoms

One of the first actions of the regime that ousted Yanukovych was to give Ukraine oligarchs their own fiefdoms. Suddenly, oligarchs became 'nationalists'. Rinat Akhmetov, the wealthiest of the oligarchs, head of the SCM group employing 300,000 people and spanning the entirety of the Ukraine, pledged to defend his homeland – although he had lived at One Hyde Park, London - in the event of a Russian

---

14   In December 2013, the Foundation was calling on the USA and E.U. to freeze the bank accounts of the 'Yanukovych regime'. The sponsors of the Foundation include the Charles Stewart Mott Foundation, E.U., and NED, among others. The stated purpose of the Foundation, founded in 1999, is to make the Ukraine into a 'market economy', 'to integrate the Ukraine into Euro-Atlantic structures', based on the experiences of Poland, and to involve the Ukraine in fomenting regime change in Russia and former Soviet bloc states.

15   http://www.ird.org/our-work/by-region/europe/ukraine

16   See links at http://www.cpmapelsin.com.ua/partners?lang=en

17   Open Society Foundations, http://www.opensocietyfoundations.org/about/offices-foundations/international-renaissance-foundation

18   International Renaissance Foundation, 'George Soros', http://www.irf.ua/en/about/soros/

19   International Renaissance Foundation, http://www.irf.ua/en/about/irf/

20   Ibid.

invasion. The previous day two other oligarchs, Igor Kolomoisky and Serhiy Taruta, accepted governorships over two regions and responsibility for preparing defense against a Russian invasion. Kolomoisky, 'a prominent member and supporter of the country's Jewish community', was given the governorship of Dnipropetrovsk in eastern Ukraine. After his time as a Ukrainian nationalist, funding militias, he left to live in the USA and Switzerland, but in 2016 was elected as a leader of the political party UKROP. Taruta was governor of Donetsk, in the far east of the Ukraine, and is now a member of the Ukraine parliament.

As for Akhmetov, he is said to have had influence over a bloc of forty members of the Ukraine parliament,[21] and one might wonder if it was this influence that was instrumental in the ousting of Yanukovych?

Petro Poroshenko, billionaire confectionery and automobile manufacturer, TV channel owner, and former Minister of Foreign Affairs and of Trade and Economic Development, also headed Ukraine's National Bank (2007-2012). He was a major supporter of the 2004 'Orange Revolution,', and chief campaign manager for Viktor Yushchenko's Our Ukraine Bloc. *Forbe's* profile states of Poroshenko that he 'was a major supporter of anti-government protestors in the Ukraine'. His business focus is on external markets, particularly in E.U. states, having been excluded from Russia.[22] Perhaps this explains his enthusiasm for Ukraine's entry into the European market? Poroshenko is now president of the Ukraine. He advocates Ukraine's membership of NATO.

Victor Pinchuk is second wealthiest oligarch in the Ukraine, behind Akhmetov, and has impeccable globalist credentials. He is founder of EastOne LLC investment, London, a media magnate, and a proponent of Ukraine's entry into the E.U. His international links include being an adviser for the Brookings Institution, and a friend of former U.S. president Bill Clinton, former British Prime Minister Tony Blair, and George Soros. He founded the Yalta European Strategy (YES) to promote Ukrainian entry into the E.U.[23] His Victor

---

21   Edward Malnick, 'The Ukrainian oligarchs living it large in London', *The Telegraph*, London, February 23, 2014, http://www.telegraph.co.uk/news/worldnews/europe/ukraine/10655081/The-Ukrainian-oligarchs-living-it-large-in-London.html

22   'Petro Poroshenko', Forbes, March 2014, http://www.forbes.com/profile/petro-poroshenko/

23   See 'About Victor Pinchuk', Victor Pinchuck Foundation, http://pinchukfund.org/en/about_pinchuk/biography/

Pinchuk Foundation is partnered with the usual globalists, including Clinton Global Initiative, Brookings Institute, Aspen Institute, Open Society Foundations, et al.[24] The stated aim of YES is to integrate the Ukraine into 'key international systems'.[25] The Pinchuk Foundation is associated with the Open Ukraine Foundation, which focuses on youth leaders.

Open Ukraine was founded by Arseny Yatsenyuk, Minister of Economics (2005-2006), Minister of Foreign Affairs (2007), and chairman of the Supreme Council (2007-2008), and Prime Minister (2014-2016). He headed the Front for Change party (2009-2012), and during the last half of 2012 headed the 'United Opposition', also known as the All-Ukrainian Union Fatherland. Open Ukraine is partnered with some major globalist players: Soros' International Renaissance Center; Chatham House; NATO Information and Documentation Center; Democracy Promotion Foundation, Press Education and Culture Department, U.S. Embassy in the Ukraine; NED; Horizon Capital, which arranges foreign investments in the Ukraine. An article in *Forbes* by Arseny Yatsenyuk, when he was Prime Minister, and 'Washington's man'. Correspondent Kenneth Rapoza alluded to a leaked phone call where Victoria Nuland, U.S. Assistant Secretary of State for European Affairs, told the Ukrainian ambassador that the USA wants 'Yats' in. 'Yats' was elected by the Ukraine parliament, with just one dissenting vote, despite previously being behind other opposition leaders as choice of prime minister, because he 'had friends in high places and while he does not have strong support of the electorate, and would have no chance of winning an election, he is pro-IMF austerity and apparently the bulk of parliament is as well'.[26] When Horizon Capital sold its shares in Ciklum I.T. corporation to Soros' Ukrainian Redevelopment Fund LP in 2015, Michael Vachon, spokesman for Soros' fund issued a statement that:

> Private investment, especially from Europe and North America, helps consolidate the gains that Ukraine's reformers have made in the past year. We are pleased to partner with Ciklum and contribute to the growth of what George Soros calls 'the New Ukraine'.[27]

---

24   Victor Pinchuk Foundation, https://pinchukfund.org/en/about_fund/partners/

25   Yalta European Strategy, http://pinchukfund.org/en/about_pinchuk/biography/

26   Kenneth Rapoza, "Washington's Man Yatsenyuk setting Ukraine up for ruin," Forbes, February 27, 2014, http://www.forbes.com/sites/kenrapoza/2014/02/27/washingtons-man-yatsenyuk-setting-ukraine-up-for-ruin/

27   'George Soros's Ukrainian Redevelopment Fund LP Will Acquire Stake in Ciklum

Vachon's statement cogently explains what globalisation, including 'colour revolutions', and the brouhaha on 'democracy' and 'human rights' is ultimately about: 'private investment'.

Co-founder of Open Ukraine was Dzhymala Zbigniew, director of the financial and industrial group Inter-Groclin.[28] Pinchuk is a member of the governing body of Open Ukraine. Other Open Ukraine luminaries include corporate board director Roman Shpek, CEO of JSC Alfa-Bank.[29] The current Chair is Teresa Yatsenyuk, Arseny's wife.

Holding Limited', Horizon Capital, November 18, 2015; http://horizoncapital.com.ua/news/george-soros-s-ukrainian-redevelopment-fund-lp-will-acquire-stake-in-ciklum-holding-limited-2/

28   Open Ukraine, 'Founders', http://openukraine.org/ua/about/founders

29   Open Ukraine, 'Governing bodies', http://openukraine.org/ua/about/management

Psycho-War

Dr. Igor Panarin, dean of the Russian Foreign Ministry's school for future diplomats, is a geopolitical analyst, scholar and media commentator, who has significant influence on Russian thinking. An examination of his ideas is therefore of important in discerning the outlook of Russia's leading academic and political circles, as well as considering what influences are helping to shape a Russian national consciousness. He is a former officer of the KGB. In 1991 he reached the rank of colonel in the Russian intelligence and security service, the Federal Agency of Government Communications and Information.

Panarin considers the two eras of U.S. psycho-war against Russia; that of the Cold War, and that directed against the Putin epoch. Psychological warfare is his specialty, about which he wrote his doctoral thesis. As a strategist his methodology is based on five stages of response: Forecasting and planning, Organization and stimulation, Feedback, Operation adjustment, Performance control. In response to U.S. belligerence Panarin proposes a centrally controlled information warfare campaign using propaganda, intelligence, analysis, secret agents, and the news media, in defence of Russian sovereignty and identity.

Russia's destiny he sees as being with a Eurasian bloc. He has proposed a Eurasian Union, which has become an official policy for Putin, and what Panarin calls 'Eurasia-Rus'.

USA: Centre of Trotskyite World Revolution

Present-day advocates of 'Eurasia' see eternal Russia even under what was called 'Bolshevism'. Panarin explained this dichotomy as a struggle between the world-outlooks of international Marxism and 'National Bolshevism', in terms that we have considered previously:

> On 3 July 1941 when Stalin addressed the Soviet people as 'Brothers and sisters', this doctrine became the dominating geopolitical idea of the USSR-Rus and replaced the Lenin-Trotsky's idea of world revolution that was an external (imported) geopolitical project. The Pan-Eurasian nationalism

of Trubetzkoy, joined with the 'Moscow – a Third Rome' idea realised in the conditions of the Soviet order yielded a result – the USSR won a victory in the global skirmish with Fascism. And the Trotskyist ideas won at the end of the 20th century in the USA and brightly manifested themselves in the ideology of the liberal globalism of a part of the contemporary American political elite (globalists).[1]

Panarin's comment shows a depth of political understanding that one cannot readily find among the West's political and scholarly circles. Particularly notable is that Panarin sees the USA as the custodian of Trotskyite 'world revolution'. This will be perplexing to superficial observers, especially the banal academics of the West who understand little of history. What are called 'neocons' or 'neoconservatives', again an example of the fundamental ignorance of Western academics and journalists in thinking of such ideas as any form of 'conservativism', even if called 'new'; are Trotskyites and the heirs of Trotskyites who took over U.S. foreign policy. Such was their hatred of Stalinism that the Trotskyites became the vanguard of the USA's Cold War.

The 'colour revolutions' including the 'Arab Spring', and those in the former Soviet bloc states, are recognised by Panarin as having been fostered by the USA. Panarin has called Mikhail Gorbachev 'the Antihero of Russia' for his pivotal role in the destruction of the Soviet bloc, on the 20th anniversary of Gorbachev's assumption to power (11 March 1985). Panarin initiated a 'Public Tribunal Against Gorbachev for the downfall of the USSR and crimes against its peoples', via the web portal *KM.ru*, from 2 to 22 December 2005.

'Velvet Revolution' and the 'Information War'

Panarin is acutely aware of the methods used by the USA to bring down reticent nation-states that do not fit into globalist visions. Among them are the 'colour' or 'velvet revolutions'.

It is ironic or, better said, hypocritical, that the U.S. ruling coteries have been vociferous in their allegations against Russia having supposedly 'interfered' in the U.S. presidential election, although evidence seems elusive. The USA has been interfering in the political processes of nations for generations. When subversion and political manipulation do not work, mass bombing as in Yugoslavia or Iran is the final resort.

---

1   Ivor Panarin, 'From United Russia to Eurasian Rus', Cyril and Methodius, 12 January 2006.

Paranin's perception of the USA as the leader of a neo-Trotskyist world revolution makes him one of the most astute political observers in the world. He has defined precisely the character of a world struggle between two antithetical outlooks, both messianic, both having their own world-missions. Hence, Panarin, sees the 'velvet revolution' in Czechoslovakia (1989), and the 'colour revolutions' in other former Soviet-bloc states and the 'Arab Spring' as manifestations of American geopolitical strategy. A primary element of this subversion is the 'information war', on which Panarin is a specialist. Panarin sees the phases of this as being:

> 'Social control'; 'social manoeuvring', based on 'influencing society' to achieve 'intentional control of the public aimed at gaining certain benefits'; 'Disinformation'; 'fabrication of information', and 'information manipulation' all these phases being based on the manipulation of incorrect information.[2]

These tactics have been clearly seen in operation against Russia, including the propaganda offensive against Russia's role in the Ukraine and Syria.

Panarin Targeted

It is surely because the Kremlin does have advisers who are head and shoulders in intellect above anything at the disposal of the globalists, that he is targeted by the organs of plutocracy. Bret Perry in his well-researched but antagonistic article towards Russia, states of Panarin: 'Although not officially confirmed, it is believed that the Russian government worked with Panarin to set up an office managed by a presidential special adviser "to oversee an international network of NGOs, information agencies and training institutions" for coordinating Russia's whole-of-government information operation'.[3]

An article by Matthew Sussex (National Security College, Crawford School of Public Policy, College of Asia and the Pacific, Australian National University) for the Lowy Institute, focuses on the measures

---

2   Jolanta Darczewska, 'The Anatomy of Russian Information Warfare: The Crimean Operation, A Case Study' (Warsaw, Poland: Ośrodek Studiów Wschodnich im. Marka Karpia, Centre for Eastern Studies, May, 2014)15; quoted by Bret Perry, 'Non-Linear Warfare in the Ukraine: The Critical Role of Information Operations and Special Operations', Small Wars Journal, 14 August 2015, http://smallwarsjournal.com/jrnl/art/non-linear-warfare-in-ukraine-the-critical-role-of-information-operations-and-special-opera#_edn44

3   Bret Perry, op. cit.

of ideological counter-insurgency that Russia is allegedly taking under the direction of Panarin, and almost laughingly comments that, 'The West is understandably reluctant to openly engage in similar behaviour. One of the main constraints of deliberately manipulating information is that it is deceitful and dishonest'.[4] The source of this odd opinion is the Lowy Institute for International Policy, founded as an Australian globalist think tank by shopping mall magnate Frank Lowy, a veteran Zionist. To claim such moral rectitude for the 'West' enters the realm of tragi-comedy.

It would be naïve to assume that Russia would not respond to the information war against her, although it is difficult to discern that Russia has anything approaching the 'network of NGOs, information agencies and training institutions', operated by the globalist Russophobes and their dupes around the world, with vast funding from the National Endowment for Democracy, the George Soros network and a multiplicity of others. One should readily see Putin's expulsion of this NGO network from Russia as an obvious requirement in the interests of Russia, despite the squeals about 'democracy' from the Machiavellian subversives who were given the boot.

Panarin's view is that Russia needs to respond to the information war for her 'protection'. Russophobia has been escalating over several years, especially after Russia acted to defend her interests in the Ukraine, where U.S. interference was blatant. In a 2015 interview Panarin explained in regard to the creation of a 'Russian internet' that "it is not censorship and regulation, but 'protection'". Again, this is condemned as an encroachment on 'freedom', but the USA has long used such 'freedom' to propagandise and agitate. Panarin's concern is that 'colour revolution' is being planned for Russia. It was social media that played a pivotal role, with sponsorship from globalist interests, in the fomenting of 'colour revolutions' in the former Soviet bloc states and across North Africa. Russian paranoia? Not at all.

In 2008 social media and other globalist corporations founded an organisation specifically to utilise social media to agitate youth. The Alliance of Youth Movements or Movement.org.[5] was co-founded by Jason Liebman of Howcast. Movements.org has worked with the

---

4   Matthew Sussex, 'Trump, Putin and Information Warfare', The Interpreter, Lowy Institute, 27 July 2016, https://www.lowyinstitute.org/the-interpreter/trump-putin-and-information-warfare

5   Tony Cartalucci, 'Google's Revolution Factory – Alliance of Youth Movements: Color Revolution 2.0', Global Research, 23 February 2011, http://www.globalresearch.ca/

U.S. State Department, and the U.S. Defense Department. Among the corporate sponsors have been: Howcast, Edelman, Google, Music TV, Meetup, Pepsi, CBS News, Mobile Accord, Youtube, Facebook, MSN/NBC, National Geographic, Omnicom Group, Access 360 Media, and Gen Next. The 'public partnerships' were Columbia Law School and U.S. State Department. Now the partners include the National Endowment for Democracy and 'Free Russia Foundation'. Here is how 'Free Russia' is described:

> The Free Russia Foundation is a nonprofit, nonpartisan, nongovernmental U.S.-based organization, led by Russians abroad that seeks to be a voice for those who can't speak under the repression of the current Russian leadership. Free Russia represents and coordinates the Russian diaspora and is focused on developing a strategic vision of a free and democratic Russia and a concrete program for the transition period.[6]

The Washington-based SAIS Center for Transatlantic Relations is another 'partner', acting as a nexus between the U.S. government, NGOs and corporations, which 'engages international scholars and students directly with government officials, journalists, business executives, and other opinion leaders from both sides of the Atlantic on issues facing Europe and North America. The goal of the Center is to strengthen and reorient transatlantic relations to the dynamics of the globalizing world'.[7]

The Free Russian Foundation states that, 'We are focused on developing a strategic vision of Russia "After Putin" and "Without Putinism" and concrete programs for the transition period'. The administrators include those who have worked with the International Republican Institute, Chattham House, U.S. Defense Department, Council on Foreign Relations and Pentagon.[8] The FRF sponsors so-called 'civil society';[9] so-called 'activists' trying to destabilise Russia.

Regardless of what one thinks of Putin, the fact remains that Panarin and others are accurate in stating that there is a vast network directed

---

index.php?context=va&aid=23283
Movements.org: https://www.movements.org/

6   Movements.org: 'partners': https://www.movements.org/en/movements/our-partners/

7   Ibid.

8   'About Free Russia': http://www.4freerussia.org/about/

9   'Programs': http://www.4freerussia.org/about/

from outside Russia, with sponsorship by the U.S. Government, actively trying to change Russia. What type of Russia is sought 'after Putin' can be discerned from the FRF being partnered with the Committee for Russian Economic Freedom, an organisation comprised of lawyers, founded in 2009 to promote the 'free market' ideology.[10] The chairman and founder of CREF, Pavel Ivlev, was 'long time legal counsel for YUKOS', the oil company that Putin nationalised, and for its CEO Mikhail Khodorkovsky,[11] whom it might be recalled is one of the primary oligarchs whom Putin purged from Russia's economic life. Another CREF 'expert' is Bruce Misamore, who was another YUKOS CEO. Perhaps now we understand the actual aims behind the rhetoric about 'democracy' and 'human rights' in Russia?

It was through social media manipulation that the 'Arab Spring' was fomented by Movements.org. On the role of social media and Movment.org in agitating the 'Arab Spring' Ariel Schwartz writing for the Fast Company, stated: 'We have existed for three years as a support network for grassroots activists using digital tools, and today we come out of alpha launch to make our platform and resources available to everyone. In other words, the revolution is now centralized'.[12]

But according to America's apologists the 'West' would not consider such nefarious activities by interfering in the internal politics of a country. Rather, we are told, it is unscrupulous Russians such as Panarin who have the audacity to advocate counter-measures that intrude on such 'democracy', including the freedom of oligarchs to pillage Russia. Panarin responded that the Russian state needs to address its lack of social media for countering the Russophobic offensive: 'In general, we underestimate the work in social networks. First of all, we do not have a public Internet holding company, which could deal with and work on the internal and external field in social networks... Our defeat in the German information field is evident when in 2008 (armed conflict in the Caucasus), the ratio of positive to negative news about Russia was 1:4, and was 1:70 in the Ukrainian crisis. This compels me to try to figure out what happened, who affects German public opinion... and how it works'.[13]

---

10   'About CREF', http://russianeconomicfreedom.org/about/

11   'Experts', http://russianeconomicfreedom.org/experts/

12   A. Schwartz, 'More Tech Tools for Egypt's Protesters: Movements.org, an Online Hub for Grassroots Activists', Fast Company, 3 February 2011, http://www.fastcompany.com/1723468/movementsorg-an-online-hub-for-grassroots-activists

13   Panarin interview, August 2015, https://toinformistoinfluence.com/2015/04/25/igor-panarin-its-time-to-draw-conclusions-from-the-defeat-in-the-information-war-

Balkanisation of USA

In 2010 Panarin predicted that the USA would balkanise, amidst ethnic conflict, and split into separate ethnic states. Certainly the proposition of a 'United States' based on constitutionalism rests on weak foundations and has nothing of an organic character about it. There is no defining feature of an 'Amercian ethnos', and no basis for a positive symbiotic relationship enduring between the sundry ethnicities. Panarin stated that the USA is on course to balkanise due to the stressors of its huge debts, deficits and social protests.[14] So far from being a fantastical scenario, the U.S. Military have recently addressed the same problems emerging from rapid urbanisation in 'megacities'.

The U.S. Military regards 'megacities' (populations of 10,000,000 or more) as an approaching problem of world instability, with the finite capacity of resources, and the cosmopolitan, multi-ethnic character of megacities that will cause conflict. The U.S. Army comments that megacities are a unique environment that they do not fully understand.[15] The report gives a picture of proliferating criminal networks and underground economies, natural disasters and the inability of decaying infrastructures to withstand the stressors. A feature is predicted to be the breakdown of civic order through ethnic and religious conflict among groups that are forced increasingly together to share diminishing resources and utilities.

> As resources become constrained, illicit networks could potentially fill the gap left by over-extended and undercapitalized governments. The risk of natural disasters compounded by geography, climate change, unregulated growth and substandard infrastructure will magnify the challenges of humanitarian relief. As inequality between rich and poor increases, historically antagonistic religions and ethnicities will be brought into close proximity in cities. Stagnation will coexist with unprecedented development, as slums and shanty towns rapidly expand alongside modern high-rises. This is the urban future.[16]

---

and-go-to-system-actions/

14   Panarin, 'U.S. Break-up: Myth or Reality?, Russia Times, 27 October 2011; https://www.rt.com/politics/panarin-usa-collapse-economy-905/

15   Colonel Marc Harris, et al., Megacities and the United States Army: Preparing for a Complex and Uncertain Future, Chief of Staff of the Army, U.S. Army Strategic studies Group, June 2014, 4; https://www.army.mil/e2/c/downloads/351235.pdf

16   Ibid.

The report comments on the increasingly heterogeneous populations inherent in a megacity as potentially 'explosive'. 'One of the hallmarks of megacities is rapid hetero and homogeneous population growth that outstrips city governance capability. Many emerging megacities are ill-prepared to accommodate the kind of explosive growth they are experiencing'.[17] 'Radical income disparity, and racial, ethnic and sub cultural separation are major drivers of instability in megacities. As these divisions become more pronounced they create delicate tensions, which if allowed to fester, may build over time, mobilize segments of the population, and erupt as triggers of instability'.[18] The U.S. Army analysis accords with the 2010 analysis of Panarin.

---

17   Ibid.

18   Ibid.

What is Really Behind the Campaign Against Putin?

When the war-drums start beating from Washington and the mass media are against a state or statesman, one is entitled to wonder what transgression might have been made against the 'new world order'. Over the past few decades we have seen one nation after another succumb to either financial blandishments, or when those fail long-planned, well-funded 'spontaneous' colour revolutions, and as a last resort bombs. The states of the ex-Soviet bloc largely succumbed to 'colour revolutions' orchestrated by the Soros network, aligned with the National Endowment for Democracy, USAID and a host of other funds and NGOs.

Gaddafi's Libya, Saddam's Iraq and Milosevic's Serbia, were bombed into submission; with ground support for *jihadists* such as the Kosovo Liberation Army (once listed by the U.S. State Department as 'terrorists'), and for their counterparts currently in Syria.

The globalists have no objection to *jihadists* when they serve to keep the world in a state of "constant conflict," in accordance with globalist aims. That particular ball got rolling when the USA, supported by China and sundry Muslim states (but not Iran), backed the *Mujahidin* against the USSR in Afghanistan with $2 billion over eight years.[1] As in Chechnya, the USA will use 'Islamists' where they can, both as dupes and as bogeymen.[2]

There is one major spanner in the world; Russia – again. Putin has been vilified relentlessly from the start of his leadership of Russia. A

---

1   Robert Pear, "Arming Afghan Guerrillas: A Huge Effort Led by U.S.," *The New York Times*, 18 April 1988, http://www.nytimes.com/1988/04/18/world/arming-afghan-guerrillas-a-huge-effort-led-by-us.html
     Note that a U.S. official commented that China worked "hand in glove" with the U.S. on this.

2   Wayne Madsen, "Washington's Civil Society' and CIA Financing of Chechen and other Caucasus Regional Terrorists," Strategic Culture Foundation, 29 April 2013, http://www.strategic-culture.org/pview/2013/04/29/washington-civil-society-cia-financing-chechen-other-regional-terrorists.html

second 'Cold War' followed so soon in the aftermath of the first, that the two can be regarded as one.

'Wrong Direction'

Things seemed to be going well for the globalists. Russia had at last been deconstructed, and was ready for bringing into the 'new world order'. Gorbachev gave the green light for the dismantling of the Eastern bloc, and paved the way for idiot democracies of the Westminster style. Appropriately a drunken buffoon, Boris Yeltsin, who started his climb to power under Gorbachev in 1985 as a member of the Politburo, Mayor of Moscow and other positions, was offered up to usher in the new democratic Russia that could take her place in the world as another colony of finance-capitalism. He had earned his credentials as a liberal when criticising the lack of haste in reform in 1987. The first democratically elected president of Russia, he lasted through 1991-1999. Under Yeltsin Russian assets were sold off at knock down prices to oligarchs in the name of economic liberalisation. From the start of his presidency Yeltsin brought in advisers from the IMF, World Bank and U.S. Treasury. His 1996 presidential campaign was funded by the oligarchy and promoted by their controlled media. Boris Berezovsky was described by a Council on Foreign Relations analyst, Daniel Treisman (who served in a 1997 U.S. team in Russia on tax reform), as the 'godfather of godfathers', the oligarch who sat at the top of the dung-heap.[3]

Having devastated Russia Yeltsin resigned, begging Russians for forgiveness for the ruin he had brought. The presidency was assumed by vice president Putin in December 1999. It was assumed that Putin would continue to allow Russia to be vampirised, but he took what the globalists have ever since been calling a "wrong direction," the title of a Council on Foreign Relation (CFR) position paper being 'Russia's wrong direction'. Written in 2006, the CFR paper recommended increased funding for the *Freedom Support Act*, in this instance referring specifically to the 2007-2008 presidential elections. Authors of the CFR report included Jack Kemp, Republican Party politico and libertarian; Mark F. Brzezinski, who served on the National Security Council as an adviser on Russian and Eurasian affairs under President Clinton, as his father Zbigniew had served in the Carter Administration; Antonia W. Bouis, founding executive director

---

3   Daniel Treisman, 'Blaming Russia First', Foreign Affairs, Council on Foreign Relations, November/December 2000, http://www.foreignaffairs.com/articles/56649/daniel-treisman/blaming-russia-first

of the Soros Foundations; James A. Harmon, senior advisor to the Rothschild Group, et al.[1]

While Putin has been criticised for been associated with a coterie of oligarchs of his own, they have been incorporated into the strengthening of the Russian state; not its undermining for globalist interests. Those who have acted otherwise have been purged, and are celebrated as 'dissidents' and champions of 'human rights' by anti-Russia interests. These include the 'godfather of oligarchy', Berezovosky, who was living in exile in England where he was found hanging;[2] and Mikhail Khodorkovsky (hailed as a hero in the West), onetime owner of Yukos, jailed for ten years, while his oil empire was taken back for Russia. His son Pavel heads the Institute of Modern Russia to continue the work of his father's Open Russia Foundation[3] to promote 'Russia's integration into the community of democracies',[4] which is to say, Russia's subordination to international finance. The Institute is based in New York.

In particular Putin has challenged the notion of 'the New American Century' as one prominent think tank optimistically termed the 21st century. Putin has moved to limit the influence of the same subversive networks that undermined the Eastern bloc via 'velvet revolutions' by obliging employees of NGOs to register as 'foreign agents', and the state started an investigation of these subversives in March 2013. In that year NED provided $8,226,487 to NGOs, programmes and seminars in Russia for the undermining the state in the name of 'human rights'.[5] In 2012 Putin expelled USAID, a governmental agency, stating that it was undermining Russia's sovereignty. Pavel Khodorkovsky found Putin's action objectionable.

Geopolitically, the globalists aim to encircle Russia. The alliances

---

1   Jack Kemp, et al, *Russia's Wrong Direction: What the United States Can and Should Do*, Independent Task Force Report no. 57 (New York: Council on Foreign Relations, 2006) xi. The entire publication can be downloaded at: http://www.cfr.org/publication/9997/

2   Ian Cobain, 'Boris Berezovsky inquest returns open verdict on death,' The Guardian, 27 March 2014, http://www.theguardian.com/world/2014/mar/27/boris-berezovsky-inquest-open-verdict-death

3   Institute of Modern Russia, https://imrussia.org/en/authors/pavel-khodorkovskiy

4   'Russia : A Postmodern Dictatorship?', NED forum, 2013, http://www.ned.org/events/russia-a-postmodern-dictatorship

5   'Russia', 2013 NED Annual Report, http://www.ned.org/where-we-work/eurasia/russia

created by Putin with central Asia and further afield have meant that this has not entirely succeeded, with the Shanghai Cooperation Organisation including Kazakhstan, Kyrgyzstan, Tajikistan and Uzbekistan; and with India, Iran, Mongolia and Pakistan having observer status. Belarus and Sri Lanka are dialogue partners, and Turkmenistan has guest attendance.

America's Hypocrisy

The outgoing Obama administration in expelling 35 Russian diplomats from the USA[6] indicated the Russophobic regime that would have been maintained had the plutocrats' choice, Hillary Clinton, won the presidency. More likely, the situation with Russia would have escalated in a rather psychotic manner. Russophobia was a feature of the electoral campaign. Obama stated of alleged Russian cyber activity during the campaign:

> I have issued an executive order that provides additional authority for responding to certain cyber activity that seeks to interfere with or undermine our election processes and institutions, or those of our allies or partners'.[7]

Homeland Security 'disclaims' its own report

'Certain cyber activity', interfering with the elections of Russia and her allies has long been a featured part of the attack on Russia sponsored by the US Congress and State Department. The accusations that Russia had interfered in the elections by the release of information against Clinton was a smear designed to depict Trump as somehow being manipulated by Russia. Evidence was not forthcoming, but Obama used the smears as a parting shot. Obama said that the evidence is supposedly so secret that not much of it – if any – will be released.

In November, seven Democrats on the Security Intelligence Committee urged the White House and CIA to declassify evidence on the alleged hacking of Democratic Party campaign and Clinton emails, but nothing was forthcoming. The House Intelligence Committee asked for a briefing, but were rebuffed. Obama's bizarre reply is that

---

6   'Obama expels 35 Russian diplomats as part of sanctions for US election hacking', The Guardian, 29 December 2016; https://www.theguardian.com/us-news/2016/dec/29/barack-obama-sanctions-russia-election-hack

7   Ibid.

the Amercian public 'know all they need to know',[8] which is to say, nothing. The report that was issued by the Department of Homeland Security (DHS) and the FBI on 29 December, is five pages long, plus seven on recommendations. Like a sick joke, the report comes with a 'disclaimer' from the DHS, stating that it does not provide 'warranties of any kind' for the information the report contains.[9]

The US Administration maintains that the move was the response to harassment of American diplomats in Russia and of Russian state interference in the US election in favour of Trump and against Clinton. Yet the US has maintained an antagonistic attitude towards Russia because the Russian electorate has not chosen a government compliant to US/globalist interest; hence, the Cold War only had a brief respite when the drunken buffoon Boris Yeltsin held office. Therefore, the Russian electorate has to be 're-educated' so that it votes according to the will of Washington and New York.

The allegations of harassment of American diplomats seem to have been first floated in June by *The Washington Post*. The Russian foreign office repudiated the allegations, and contended that it was a matter of the US projecting its own behaviour onto Russia, stating of unacceptable practices, that:

> There even had been cases when such actions were carried out in the presence of pregnant wives of our diplomats. Instead of receiving our signal, identifying the problem and creating conditions to improve our relations, they (the US) flip everything upside down.[10]

The Washington Post allegations came a month after Congress had passed a bill to subject the travel plans of Russian diplomats in the USA to FBI scrutiny.

8   Tyler Durden, 'Obama Under "Intense Pressure" To Release Evidence Proving Russians Hacked The Election', 29 December 2016; http://www.zerohedge.com/news/2016-12-29/obama-under-intense-pressure-release-evidence-proving-russians-hacked-election

9   G. Washington, 'What the Russian Hacking report DOESN'T say', 29 December 2016; http://www.zerohedge.com/news/2016-12-29/what-russian-hacking-report-doesnt-say

10   'Russian diplomats harassed by US, not other way around – Moscow on Wash Post article', *Russian Today*, 29 June 2016; https://www.rt.com/news/348793-russian-diplomats-harassed-us/

Russia Expels Subversives

Russia is one of the few states that has fully recognised the subversive character of the sundry 'civic society' organisations that have mushroomed, under US/NED/Soros sponsorship, within Russia and bordering states. Putin gave these organisations, headed up by NED, their marching orders, being described by the Russian prosecutor general's office as posing 'a threat to the constitutional order of the Russian Federation and the defensive capability and security of the government'.[11] Russia charged NED with interference in internal politics:

> Using Russian commercial and noncommercial organisations under its control, the National Endowment for Democracy participated in work to declare the results of election campaigns illegitimate, organise political actions intended to influence decisions made by the authorities, and discredit service in Russia's armed forces.[12]

The state news agency RIA Novosti commented on the Ukrainian example:

> Ukrainian democracy - it is expensive, but the Ukrainians do not pay for it. Money is given to radicals and insurgents from where suspicious individuals usually get it – Washington. As it turned out ... the National Endowment for Democracy. ... Under their supervision there are constant revolutions and military coups. Paid here, bribed there... For them, a change of government in any country - is just another line in the financial statements.[13]

Referring to a NED statement, the report cites NED giving $14,000,000 during 2011 to 2014 to get the government they wanted in Ukraine. It should be recalled that US assistant secretary of state Victoria Nuland was right on scene among the useful idiots of NED et al. when they undertook their 'colour revolution'. She is married to U.S. neocon luminary Robert Kagan, a cofounder in 1998 of the

---

11 Alec Luhn, National Endowment for Democracy is first 'undesirable' NGO banned in Russia', *The Guardian*, 28 July 2015, https://www.theguardian.com/world/2015/jul/28/national-endowment-for-democracy-banned-russia

12 Ibid.

13 A. Solovyev, 'NED invested nearly $14 million', 15 July 2015; https://ria.ru/radio_brief/20150715/1129708824.html

Project for a New American Century which drafted the blueprint for US-created chaos in the Middle East, which was followed by Bush and Obama administrations. The duo would have held greater influence under a Clinton government.[14]

Carl Gershman, president of NED, stated that the Washington/NED strategy is to topple Putin by working on the Russian peripheries, isolating and surrounding Russia. Of particular worry is the Eurasian Customs Union, which is stymying U.S. plans to use the E.U. to control states, which Gershman calls 'Russian bullying', and he described Ukraine 'the biggest prize'. In detaching sundry states from alignment with Russia Gershman stated that 'Russian democracy also can benefit from this process. Ukraine's choice to join Europe will accelerate the demise of the ideology of Russian imperialism that Putin represents… Russians, too, face a choice, and Putin may find himself on the losing end not just in the near abroad but within Russia itself'.[15]

Interference in Russian Political Process

NED is open about its role, because all is justified by the magic word 'democracy'. NED states that it uses 'activists' and others in undermining those states that are targeted. It is able to do so more effectively as a 'nongovernmental' organisation. NED states that it is 'Funded largely by the U.S. Congress', and was 'created jointly by Republicans and Democrats'.[16] NED was established by U.S. Congress via the National Endowment for Democracy Act in 1983. During 2006 to 2014, $US 963,000,000 was given in grants to NED by the U.S. State Department.[17]

On the periphery of Russia, NED boasts of its initiatives in installing regimes compliant to the USA, and integrated into the EU:

As Europe celebrated 25 years since the 'Fall of the Wall,' the countries in which NED grantees are active exhibited two

---

14 Philip Giraldi, 'Clinton's Haw-in-Waiting', The Amercian Conservative, 19 May 2016; http://www.theamericanconservative.com/articles/clintons-hawk-in-waiting/

15 Carl Gershman, 'Former Soviet states stand up to Russia. Will the U.S.?', The *Washington Post*, 26 September 2013; https://www.washingtonpost.com/opinions/former-soviet-states-stand-up-to-russia-will-the-us/2013/09/26/b5ad2be4-246a-11e3-b75d-5…

16 'About NED', http://www.ned.org/about/

17 Office of Inspector General, US State Dept., 'Management assistance report: oversight of grants to NED', June 2015; https://oig.state.gov/system/files/aud-si-15-34.pdf

trajectories. Some, like Ukraine, Moldova and Albania, made important strides in reinvigorating their democratic transitions and moving closer to the West. These historic steps towards EU integration committed their governments to further democratization. The Endowment assisted civil society in supporting these countries' European choice, pushing for greater reforms, and holding officials responsible for the obligations they have taken on. Other countries, such as Belarus, Bosnia and Herzegovina, and Macedonia, made no democratic progress or actually regressed. In response, NED supported civil society groups opposing backsliding, assisting democrats at risk, and expanding space for alternative views and voices.[18]

However one dresses it up with references to democracy against repression, NED states that it sponsors those who are committed to destroying the legitimate governments of sundry states, to bring the targeted states 'closer to the West', which is to say, to Washington and New York. NED states that it intervened in the elections in the Ukraine, which it calls 'election monitoring'; and other euphemisms. NED states that it assists 'activists' in Belarus against the state, and supported alternative media that undermined the government. In Moldova NED 'grantees' were active in the elections. Regardless of whether one accepts the ideological agenda of NED, this Congressionally-funded institution interferes in the elections of many states throughout the world, in order to bring them 'closer to the West'. That is their *raison d'etre*.

NED describes Russia as trying to extend its 'authoritarianism' (sic) throughout Eurasia. For NED Putin's 'record high approval ratings' are regarded as a 'challenge'. Despite the Russian government having identified 'civil society organizations' such as NED as 'foreign agents', NED states that it continues to work with the anti-Putin opposition in Russia. Again, whatever one thinks of Putin, this is still Congressionally-funded interference in Russia's politics.[19]

American interference in Russian elections has included the funding of the Movement for Defence of Voters' Rights ('Golos') via NED and USAID. Golos has undertaken a series of manoeuvres to avoid being registered as 'foreign agents' by the Russian state, being used as a propaganda outlet against the government. In a 2011

---

18   NED Central and Eastern Europe, http://www.ned.org/region/central-and-eastern-europe/

19   NED Eurasia, http://www.ned.org/region/eurasia/

report Ellen Barry wrote: 'Golos receives financing from Western governments, including the United States, and some Russian officials have suggested that the organization's real aim is to incite an Arab Spring-type revolution in Russia'. Putin alleged that 'so-called grant recipients' were interfering with elections on behalf of foreign governments. Duma members from three parties asked state prosecutors to investigate Golos. Prosecutors alleged that 'one of Golos's most popular features — an online "map of violations" where people can post reports — violates a Russian law against publishing data, especially polling results, during the five days before voting. ...' Prosecutors also accused Golos of 'dissemination of rumors under the guise of trustworthy reports, with the goal of defaming a party as well as its individual members. ... Golos's critics in the Russian government say its work is tainted by the money it receives from two American agencies, the National Endowment for Democracy and the United States Agency for International Development.'[20] Flyers found at a raid on a Golos office in the Russian Far East urged voters to invalidate the voting papers. Golos was prosecuted and was fined $1,000. The Obama administration condemned the prosecution as 'harassment'.[21] Presently Golos is appealing a July 2016 court ruling for liquidation for 'serious irremediable breaches of law'.[22]

USAID projected a budget $54.2 million for Russia for 2013 funding groups such as Golos, when it was told by the authorities in 2012 to cease its activities there. *The Moscow Times* reported:

> USAID, which has a mandate to support U.S. foreign policy and has spent more than $2.6 billion over the past 20 years in Russia, says on its website that it has been "a proud supporter of Russia's oldest human rights organizations" and supported civic watchdog groups that have "provided non-partisan oversight over electoral processes."[23]

USAID founded during the Cold War (1961) by President John F.

---

20   Ellen Barry, 'Russian Authorities Pressure Elections Watchdog', *New York Times*, 1 December 2011; http://www.nytimes.com/2011/12/02/world/europe/russia-puts-pressure-on-elections-monitor-golos.html

21   Ibid.

22   'Ban on Golos NGO appealed in Moscow court', Russian Legal Information Agency, 29 August 2016; http://rapsinews.com/judicial_news/20160829/276741401.html

23   'USAID Exit to Hit Small Organizations Hard', Moscow Times, 20 September 2012; https://themoscowtimes.com/news/usaid-exit-to-hit-small-organizations-hard-17960 xxiii USAID, 'Who we are', https://www.usaid.gov/who-we-are

Kennedy, states of its objectives:

> U.S. foreign assistance has always had the twofold purpose
> of furthering America's interests while improving lives in the
> developing world. USAID carries out U.S. foreign policy by
> promoting broad-scale human progress at the same time it
> expands stable, free societies, creates markets and trade partners
> for the United States, and fosters good will abroad.[24]

Russia and Predatory Capital

USAID are to be congratulated in their openness: they are overt in
stating that their purpose is to further U.S. foreign policy behind the
façade of humanitarian work. Part of their agenda is to transform
states into 'market economies', which enables predatory international
capital to exploit resources. It might be recalled that the peace
agreement imposed by NATO with mass bombs on Serbia was to
ensure that mineral rich Kosovo would be a market economy, whose
resources would be opened to 'privatisation', especially the Trepca
mining region, albeit the economy of the region remains in chaos. The
Kosovan government was obliged to establish a Privatization Agency
of Kosovo, and the Government Privatization Committee.[25] President
Woodrow Wilson's 'Fourteen Points' for the restructuring of the world
after World War I were based on international free trade. President
Roosevelt's 'Atlantic Charter' for the post-1945 world had the same
foundation.

Presently, a major bug-bear of the same internationalists is the trading
bloc being promoted by Russia, the Eurasian Customs Union. In
each of these wars, and conflicts, including the present confrontation
with Russia, 'democracy' and 'human rights' has served as a façade
for the aims of predatory international capital. Of Russia, following a
list of USAID programmes relative to health and welfare in Russia,
the actual purposes are listed, such as: Supporting 'civic watchdog
groups in Russia' 'that have provided non-partisan oversight over
electoral processes including through innovative uses of technology',
as part of a 'world-wide movement for open government'; supporting
'civil society organizations whose number and influence has grown
from 40 registered organizations in 1987 to approximately 300,000
today, not including state-funded public organizations'; supporting

---

24   Ministry of Economic Development, Republic of Kosovo, http://mzhe-ks.net/en/
     government-privatization-committee-gpc#.WGYN4f196M8

25   USAID in Russia, https://www.usaid.gov/news-information/fact-sheets/usaid-russia

the development of professional relationships between Russian and American journalists, publishers, electronic media managers, designers, content developers, advertising specialists and new media practitioners'; facilitating the funding of 'the U.S. Russia Investment Fund ' with '$329 million to promote 'the development of a free market economy in Russia'.[26] These multilevel outreach programmes sound all very charitable but are designed to achieve the last named 'development of a free market economy', for the purpose of opening Russia up to oligarchical exploitation. This generosity, when not achieved by grants to 'civil society organisations' is discarded in favour of fomenting 'colour revolutions', and ultimately of war as per Serbia and Iraq, or revolution and war in tandem, as in Libya.

Trump Problematic

The Trump victory is seen as a significant reversal of globalist interests, although one already might look in askance at his appointment of executives from Goldman Sachs in the primary finance posts. It seems vindictive that Obama used his closing days in the White House to leave with a Russophobic gesture of the type one might expect from a psychotic. Trump and Lt. Gen. Mike Flynn, national security adviser, and others in the new administration indicated they wanted rapprochement with Russia. As will be seen in the concluding chapter, further appointments soon became problematic for such a new course.

---

26   Bolton, 'Trump victory an epochal event?', Katehon, 10 November 2016; http://katehon.com/article/trump-victory-epochal-event

Russia 'Bigger Threat' than ISIS to Globalist Hegemony

U.S. Senator John McCain has stated clearly in an ABC News (Australia) interview that Russia is a 'bigger threat', or 'greater challenge' than the Islamic State organisation.[1] The only surprise about this statement is that McCain made it in such an open and unequivocal manner. *Jihadism* was a creation of the U.S.A. originally to hit at Russia in Afghanistan, in a long running war that was intended to weaken Russia. This played a part in the implosion of the USSR. Islamism was then used to destroy Milosevic and fracture Yugoslavia for the purpose of gaining the mineral wealth of Kosovo. Gadaffi was another inconvenience who was removed by U.S.-based Islamic extremists.

ISL has been a convenient factor in trying to destroy Assad's Syria as one of the primary remaining bugbears of the neocons and their Zionist allies. In practice, whether by coincidence or design, ISL is a handy instrument to have dumped on any 'rogue state' to create the chaos that justifies U.S. military intervention.

Islamic Chechen separatists are also backed by the U.S.A. as a catspaw against Russia. Indeed, McCain is one of the more vocal supporters of Chechnya's separatism. Chechnya, Ukraine... is there a pattern here? The USA gives asylum to Ilyas Akhmadov, who is wanted by Russia as a leading Chechen terrorist leader, has been funded by the National Endowment for Democracy.[2] In 2008 McCain called for the recognition of a Chechen state.[3]

---

1   'Vladimir Putin a bigger threat than Islamic State, McCain said', ABC News 29 May 2017; http://www.abc.net.au/news/2017-05-29/putin-a-bigger-threat-than-islamic-state-mccain-says/8570158

2   Aaron Klein, 'US gave asylum to accused Chechen terrorist leader', http://www.wnd.com/2013/04/u-s-gave-asylum-to-accused-chechen-terror-leader/

3   A. Smirnov, 'McCain's call to recognise Chechnya has inspired Chechens', 5 September 2008; https://jamestown.org/program/mccains-call-to-recognize-chechen-independence-has-inspired-chechens/

U.S. Created *Jihadism* to Undermine Russia

The CIA describes its role in founding *Jihadism* with the sponsoring of the *Mujahidin* against Russia:

> After the Soviet Union invaded Afghanistan in December 1979, President Carter directed the CIA to assist the Afghan Mujahidin. The CIA came to see that the indigenous Afghan opposition to the Soviets was less an organized movement than widespread opposition by villages and tribes. Through Pakistan, the CIA provided the Mujahidin with money, weapons, medical supplies, and communications equipment. Initially the goal was to drain Soviet resources by keeping their forces bogged down. In 1985, CIA shifted from a plan of attrition to one that would help the rebels win. One of the pivotal moments came in September 1986, when the Mujahidin used CIA-provided Stinger missiles to shoot down three Soviet Mi-24D helicopter gunships. As part of this escalation of financial and material support, President Reagan issued new guidance that put the CIA into more direct contact with rebel commanders, beginning an era of CIA interaction with tribal and local leaders that continues through the post-9/11 era.[4]

The CIA then supported the Northern Alliance against the Taliban government. The CIA also claims that it supported the Northern Alliance against Al Qaeda and bin Laden when they moved into Afghanistan from the Sudan. However, an NBC report states of CIA support for bin Laden:

> As his unclassified CIA biography states, bin Laden left Saudi Arabia to fight the Soviet army in Afghanistan after Moscow's invasion in 1979. By 1984, he was running a front organization known as Maktab al-Khidamar – the MAK – which funnelled money, arms and fighters from the outside world into the Afghan war.

> What the CIA bio conveniently fails to specify (in its unclassified form, at least) is that the MAK was nurtured by Pakistan's state security services, the Inter-Services Intelligence Agency, or ISI, the CIA's primary conduit for conducting the covert war against Moscow's occupation.

---

4   'Afghanistan', Central Intelligence Agency, https://www.cia.gov/library/publications/
     additional-publications/devotion-to-duty/afghanistan.html

The CIA, concerned about the factionalism of Afghanistan ... found that Arab zealots who flocked to aid the Afghans were easier to 'read' than the rivalry-ridden natives. While the Arab volunteers might well prove troublesome later, the agency reasoned, they at least were one-dimensionally anti-Soviet for now. So bin Laden, along with a small group of Islamic militants from Egypt, Pakistan, Lebanon, Syria and Palestinian refugee camps all over the Middle East, became the 'reliable' partners of the CIA in its war against Moscow.[5]

These Afghan veterans became the nucleus for Jihadists further afield.[6]

Islamists have likewise proven useful within the Russian Federation. The primary pro-Chechnya lobby in the USA was the Freedom House-founded American Committee for Peace in Chechnya. This included some of the most notable neocons and Zionists: Richard Perle; Elliott Abrams; former U.S. Ambassador to the U.N., Kenneth Adelman; Midge Decter of the Heritage Foundation; Frank Gaffney of the Center for Security Policy; Bruce Jackson of the U.S. Committee on NATO; Michael Ledeen of the American Enterprise Institute, and former CIA director R. James Woolsey.[7] It is strange that of these enthusiasts for the rights of Muslims in Russia, all but Abrams and Ledeen were members of the arch-Zionist Project for a New American Century, founded in 1997. A sub-branch was the Study Group on a New Israeli Strategy Toward 2000 headed by Perle, which prepared a blueprint for the reorganisation of the Middle East, that calls in particular for 'regime change' in Syria and Iran.[8]

While the American Committee for Peace in Chechnya changed its name to American Committee for Peace in the Caucasus, with a broader subversive agenda against Russia, it seems to have become largely defunct since 2013. That is the year of the Chechen bombing in Boston. Wayne Madsen, writing for the Strategic Culture Foundation, commented:

---

5   Michael Moran, 'Bin Laden Comes Home to Roost', NBCNews.com, August 24, 1998, http://www.nbcnews.com/id/3340101/#.VD9w2TY5QqR

6   Ibid.

7   'American Committee for Peace in Chechnya', Right Web, http://rightweb.irc-online. org/profile/American_Committee_for_Peace_in_Chechnya

8   Study Group on a New Israeli Strategy Toward 2000, *A Clean Break: A New Strategy for Securing the Realm*, 1996.

After revelations that an entity called the Caucasus Fund was used by the CIA-linked Jamestown Foundation of Washington, DC to sponsor seminars on the North Caucasus in Tbilisi from January to July 2012, Georgian authorities moved to shut down the fund. The reason given by Georgia was that the organization had 'fulfilled its stated mission'. Caucasus Fund and Jamestown Foundation events were attended by accused Boston Marathon bomber Tamerlan Tsarnaev, a citizen of Kyrgyzstan born to parents from Dagestan. Jamestown had previously held a seminar in Tbilisi on 'Hidden Nations' in the Caucasus, which, among other issues, promoted a 'Greater Circassia' in the Caucasus.[9]

Madsen remarked of the general strategy:

U.S. 'humanitarian' and 'civil society' assistance to radical Islamist groups has, for the past three decades, filtered into the coffers of terrorist groups celebrated as 'freedom fighters' in Washington. This was the case with U.S. support for the Afghan Mujahidin through such groups as the Committee for a Free Afghanistan during the Islamist insurgency against the People's Democratic Republic of Afghanistan in the 1980s and the Bosnia Defense Fund in the 1990s. In the case of Afghanistan, U.S. and Saudi money ended up in the hands of insurgents who would later form 'Al Qaeda' and in Bosnia U.S. funds were used by Al Qaeda elements fighting against Yugoslavia and the Bosnian Serb Republic and, later, Al Qaeda elements supporting the Kosovo Liberation Army (KLA) in its war against Serbia.[10]

The McCain Institute

As seems to be the habit, McCain has his own NGO, the McCain Institute for International Leadership, at Arizona State University. Among the trustees are Lynn Forester de Rothschild of the famous banking dynasty; investment banker and Kissinger colleague John F. Lehman; former Senator and Zionist notable Joseph Lieberman, et al.[11]

---

9   Wayne Madsen, 'Washington's 'Civil Society': CIA Financing of Chechen and Caucasus Regional Terrorists', Global Research, May 6, 2013, http://www.globalresearch.ca/washingtons-civil-society-and-cia-financing-of-chechen-and-other-caucasus-regional-terrorists/5333359

10 Ibid.

11 Trustees, https://www.mccaininstitute.org/staff/?filter=board-of-trustees

McCain alleged that Russia intervened with the internal affairs of other nations, stating:

> I think ISIS can do terrible things. But it's the Russians who tried to destroy the fundamental of democracy and that is to change the outcome of an American election. I've seen no evidence they succeeded, but they tried and they are still trying to change elections. They just tried to affect the outcome of the French election. So I view Vladimir Putin—who has dismembered Ukraine, a sovereign nation, who is putting pressure on the Baltics—I view the Russians as the far greatest challenge that we have.[12]

Yet the McCain Institute was created to change the character of the world—no less—in the image of the U.S.A. according to the McCain family's ethos; which is to say the globalist ideology. The McCain Institute states that it is committed to 'sustaining America's global leadership'. If this does not involve interfering in the internal affairs of other states, in the name of 'democracy and human rights', then what? The Institute states that it serves to 'identify, develop and train the next generation of American and international leaders'.[13] That is to say, the Institute selects likely dupes, cultivates them and tries to foist them on to other states, so that they will serve as U.S. lackeys in upholding America's 'global leadership'.

Among what the McCain Institute calls the 'next generation leaders' who they train up and direct, Venezuelan journalist Leon Hernandez, writing of his observations of the Institute's Sedona conference in 2017 commented that he 'felt a particular empathy for those speakers who voiced opposition to regimes in Russia and Syria'.[14] This is significant given the present riots in Venezuela, one of those states whose existence is inconvenient to America's 'global leadership'. The McCain Institute states it 'selects target countries and sectors that are specific to each program year'. 'A Leadership Action Plan (LAP) is a detailed plan of character-driven action for implementation that creates change in your home environment that impacts the public, private or social sector. NGLs [Next Generation Leaders] are expected to implement their LAP upon the conclusion of the initial program year'.[15] One

---

12 ABC News op. cit.

13 'About', https://www.mccaininstitute.org/about/

14 'We chose to fight', https://www.mccaininstitute.org/blog/we-chose-to-fight/

15 FAQ, https://www.mccaininstitute.org/faq/

might wonder whether the selection of individuals to be trained at Arizona university, in Washington D.C. and New York to implement an 'action plan' that 'changes' the 'target' country in 'public, private or social sectors' is interference in the affairs of another state? The word subversion comes to mind. NGL's are sponsored by 'placement organisations' that might be public or private; that is to say, an NGL might be sponsored by the U.S. State Department for example. Once these NGL's are trained and sent back to their homelands they are expected to be part of a global network and report on what they are achieving: 'NGLs are called on to be active members in the NGL Global Network and to inform the Institute on a bi-annual basis of the status of their LAPs and their impact in their home environments'.[16]

U.S. Interference

If subversion and colour revolutions do not work, just try war. McCain spent New Year's Eve 2016 fraternising with frontline Ukrainian troops, tweeting: 'We stand w/them in their fight against #Putin's aggression'.[17] Has Putin or any other Russian official or politician ever done anything remotely near as provocative and war-mongering against the USA? McCain's actions were a flagrant endorsement for military confrontation against Russia and against those Russians who have broken with the Ukraine to defend their 'human rights'. However, 'human rights' like 'democracy' since the days of President Woodrow Wilson is nothing but a sham slogan used by the USA to justify any action to serve its world-conquering interests, or 'the American way of life' as McCain and sundry others put it. Ukrainians are serving as proxy troops against Russia, as did the Mujahedeen in Afghanistan.

McCain is pushing for economic sanctions against Russia, with the allegation of election interference as the pretext:

> We have done nothing since the election last November to respond to Vladimir Putin's attempt to change the outcome of our elections. So, way to go Vladimir. We haven't responded at all,' he said. 'Hopefully when we get back from recess the Senate will enact sanctions on Russia.[18]

---

16   Ibid.

17   'McCain visits frontline Ukraine troops in anti-Putin gesture', *USA Today*, 31 January 2016; https://www.usatoday.com/story/news/2016/12/31/mccain-visits-frontline-ukraine-troops-anti-putin-gesture/96036782/

18   ABC News, op. cit.

However, in 2014 the U.S.A. was very active in 'regime change' in the Ukraine, pouring in money. Russian senior adviser Sergei Glazyev said at the time that the U.S.A. was spending $20m (£12.3m; 14.8m euros) a week on Ukrainian opposition groups, supplying 'rebels' with arms, among other things. At the time, intercepted conversations between the State Department's Victoria Nuland and US Ambassador Geoffrey Pyatt revealed them discussing the merits of three opposition leaders. Glazyez accused the U.S.A. of 'interfering flagrantly and unilaterally in the internal affairs of Ukraine. There is information that within the grounds of the American embassy, there is training for fighters, that they're arming them'. The U.S. remained mute on the allegations.[19]

NED and IRI

Both the National Endowment for Democracy (NED) and the International Republican Institute (IRI) are among the organisations shut down in Russia for their interference in internal affairs. Nonetheless, in 2015 NED expended $US 18,555,967[20] on trying to destroy Russia, funding anti-state propaganda euphemistically called 'journalism' and 'freedom of information', and backing agitators euphemistically called 'supporting civil society'. While there are many other NGOs that are also pouring in funds, NED is subsidised by the U.S. State Department and was formed by Congressional mandate in 1983, reports to Congress and consults with the State Department, in accordance with the terms of its founding.

The International Republic Institute is chaired by McCain. IRI is yet another NGO committed to 'freedom' as defined by the globalist elite. IRI states that it works 'Throughout Eurasia' 'with political parties, citizens and public officials' to create what IRI deems is a suitable political system. IRI 'supports multi-party structures', and aims to 'expand voter outreach'. Another aim is more blatantly stated: 'Applying methodologically-sound public opinion research to develop issue-based political party platforms and campaign strategies that address voter concerns'; and 'building skills for candidates'. That is, IRI trains budding politicians, creates parties, and formulates what the issues are.[21] Again, there is a relationship between this NGO and the U.S. Government. Funders include USAID.

---

19 'Ukraine crisis, Putin adviser accuses US of meddling', BBC News, 6 February 2014; http://www.bbc.com/news/world-europe-26068994

20 Russia 2015 NED Annual Report, http://www.ned.org/region/eurasia/russia-2015/

21 'What we do', http://www.iri.org/country/eurasia/details

Russia 'Bigger Threat' than ISIS to Globalist Hegemony

Given the expenditure of money and the many other ways the U.S.A. and its plutocracy works against Russia one can be sure that the present state is the only real hindrance left to 'American triumphalism'. McCain is a leading spokesman for a globalist coterie, and he has declared 'Putin's Russia' to be the main enemy.

Trump and Putin met for a prolonged discussion on 7 July. The day previously Trump had spoken in Poland using all the blatantly Russophobic rhetoric of the Cold War era, while NATO troops prepared to engage in the largest 'Saber Guardian' exercises, across Bulgaria, Hungary and Romania. The Trump administration within weeks of the presidential inauguration, was purged of perceived pro-Russia elements such as General Flynn, in favour of Russophobes such as Lt. General McMaster.

Trump & the Russophobes

With the initial diversity of advisers and cabinet appointees in the Trump Administration matters were not going to be straight-forward. Because Trump does not have any ideological background he is cast adrift with some broad ideas of a populist nature, which are identified with the traditional Right, or *palaeoconservativism*, while he chose his Cabinet from among many who are antithetical to 'America First' and trade protectionism, on the assumption that he was getting conservatives of one type or another that stood for such issues. Hence the presence of Goldman Sachs eminences at the Cabinet's top finance jobs, and 'Israel Firsters' who cannot or will not make a distinction between U.S. interests and those of Israel.

Flynn Axed

Despite some worrying aspects of General Mike Flynn as Trump's initial choice for National Security adviser, such as his adherence to a messianic U.S. 'world mission', he was unacceptable to both liberal and neocon Russophobes because of his not being on board with their common fear of a resurgent Russia. While the global oligarchy and its NGOs indulge regularly in private diplomacy, to the extent of overthrowing governments, the Russophobes seized on General Flynn's inconsequential comments to a Russian diplomat in regard to Trump's attitude towards Obama's sanctions against Russia. Reiterating what was publicly known provided a pretext for the Russophobe axis, and their whores in the mass media, to bray for Flynn's resignation. The alternative was for the Russophobes to be told to collectively 'get stuffed', and Trump should have done so.

General McMasters

So with the purging of Flynn in short order Trump appointed Lt. General H. R. McMaster. He seems an excellent choice in many ways. What creates suspicion is the praise he receives from the mass media and other obsessive complainers against every move made by Trump. One should ask, then, why in the opinion of these, has Trump made a good choice in McMaster?

Forbes columnist John Baldoni opines that McMaster could keep Trump in line. In patronising tones towards Trump, Baldoni writes of McMaster: 'He must find ways to connect his orthodoxy with Trump's unorthodoxy in ways that are understandable to the commander in chief'. In particular, it is hoped that McMaster can diminish the influence of Stephen Bannon, the number one bugaboo of the oligarchs and their whores on the Left.[1]

So why does McMaster provide such hope for the oligarchic-left-liberal axis? Unlike Flynn, he is noted for his antagonism towards a resurgent Russia. *Politico Magazine* columnist Brian Bender wrote of McMaster at the Pentagon in April 2016 as having a new 'target': 'Moscow'. Following Russia's response to the U.S./oligarchic-sponsored mobs in the Ukraine, McMasters oversaw a 'high level' study on the USA's options in responding to Russia:

> McMaster's response is the *Russia New Generation Warfare Study*, whose government participants have already made several unpublicized trips to the front lines in Ukraine. The high-level but low-profile effort is intended to ignite a wholesale rethinking—and possibly even a redesign—of the Army in the event it has to confront the Russians in Eastern Europe'.[2]

Wargame Simulation run by U.S. NGO

Hence, McMaster's attitude towards Russia is confrontational, in contrast to that of Flynn's. 'Russia's new generation warfare' is the term of the Russophobic axis to whatever action Russia takes among a long list of possibilities, when defending its own interests, including responses to U.S./NATO provocations on Russia's borders. The think tank, The Potomac Foundation, lists these Russian 'new generation warfare' tactics, all of which apply to actions that have long been undertaken by the USA, especially in those states on Russia's borders.[3] The Potomac staff and fellows include General Wesley C. Clark and others associated with U.S. Defense, NATO, and states bordering

1   John Baldoni, 'How General H. R. McMasters can Lead the President', Forbes, 20 February 2017, http://www.forbes.com/sites/johnbaldoni/2017/02/20/how-general-h-r-mcmaster-can-lead-the-president/#663022da5fcd

2   Bryan Bender, 'The Secret U.S. Army Study that Targets Moscow', Politico Magazine, 14 April 2016, http://www.politico.com/magazine/story/2016/04/moscow-pentagon-us-secret-study-213811

3   'Russia's new generation warfare', The Potomac Foundation, 13 May 2016, http://www.thepotomacfoundation.org/russias-new-generation-warfare-2/

Russia. Here is something of Potomac's latest activities:

> The Potomac Foundation and the **Casimir Pulaski Foundation** hosted their first joint Baltic Security Scenario Simulation in Warsaw, Poland on January 23-26, 2017. The purpose of this wargaming initiative is to assist the Polish national security decision-makers in the development of a regional and NATO accepted understanding of the nature of the Russian military threat to the Baltic States and Poland... Wargame participants included defense experts and government representatives from Poland, the United States, Baltic and Nordic countries.[4]

Is it not worrying that an NGO in conjunction with sundry government and military officials from the USA, Poland and elsewhere, can undertake joint programme's that simulate war against Russia? Such belligerence against Russia is described in a nonchalant manner, indicating the collective sociopathy among the Russophobes, when any defensive measure by Russia is termed 'aggressive', yet war strategies against Russia are routine normality.

Not surprisingly, the **Casimir Pulaski Foundation**, a wide-ranging Polish-based NGO, is associated with Soros through the Batory Foundation, at least. Sponsoring transnational corporations include mainly those of the weapons industry: Lockheed Martin, MBDA Missile Systems, MEADS (Medium Extended Air Defense System), Raytheon, Saab Technologies, WB Electronics, Defence 24. The European Academy of Diplomacy, a Pulaski Foundation sponsor, recently featured as its guest of honour Mikhail Khodorkovsy at the inauguration of the Academy of Young Diplomats.[5] Among its advisers is Zbigniew Brzezinski. This alliance of plutocrats, largely including weapons manufacturers in this case, with left-liberal NGOs posturing behind the slogans of 'democracy' and 'human rights', is common.

General Mattis

General Jim Mattis, Secretary of Defense, does not concede that the USA can co-operate with Russia on any level. He stated at a

---

4   'Baltic Security Scenario simulation in Poland', 19 January 2017, http://www. thepotomacfoundation.org/baltic-security-scenario-simulation-in-poland/#more-917

5   https://diplomats.pl/mikhail-khodorkovsky-guest-honor-inauguration-academy-young-diplomats/

conference of the Heritage Foundation that Russia's defence of Donbas and Crimea should have been regarded as 'much more serious' by the Obama Administration.[6] Described by Trump as the 'nearest we have to General George Patton', Mattis rejected Trump's conciliatory attitude towards Russia from the start. William Kristol, Israel First neocon eminence, even sought to have Mattis run for the presidency, and he was also sought as a campaign speaker by Hillary Clinton.[7] ABC News reported:

> The Trump administration signaled Thursday there will be no change soon in U.S.-Russian relations, putting the onus on Moscow to prove itself if it wants closer cooperation with Washington. Russia's support for Ukrainian separatists was underscored as a test case of its willingness to change behavior.
>
> At a NATO meeting in Brussels, U.S. Defense Secretary Jim Mattis made clear the United States isn't ready to collaborate militarily with its former Cold War foe against the Islamic State or other threats, a long-standing goal of the Kremlin's which new U.S. President Donald Trump says he wants, too. After meeting with Russia's top diplomat in Germany, U.S. Secretary of State Rex Tillerson said Moscow first must help stop violence in Ukraine.[8]

Tillerson Succumbed?

While Mattis stated that Russia would have to 'prove' herself, that is, acquiesce to the 'world order', Secretary Tillerson, who was widely assumed to favour rapport with Russia, having been awarded a friendship medal, has indicated that the Russophobes have nothing to worry about from him either. In the wake of Flynn's departure, the ABC report states, there was no discussion on the lifting of U.S. sanctions against Russia. The belligerence remains, and is perhaps worsening:

6　'General stating Russian aggression in Ukraine "much more severe" than U.S. treats it may become Defense Secretary', 19 November 2016, https://www.unian.info/world/1632767-general-stating-russian-aggression-in-ukraine-much-more-severe-than-ustreats-it-may-become-defense-secretary.html).

7　'James Mattis, Outspoken Retired Marine, Is Trump's Choice as Defense Secretary', *New York Times*, 1 December 2016, https://www.nytimes.com/2016/12/01/us/politics/james-mattis-secrtary-of-defense-trump.html?_r=0).

8　'Top Trump envoys signal no quick changes to US-Russia ties', ABC News, 16 February 2017, http://abcnews.go.com/International/wireStory/mattis-us-ready-collaborate-militarily-russia-45531272

But tensions clearly remained. A remark by Mattis at the NATO meeting about negotiating with Russia 'from a position of strength' prompted a sharp response from Russian Defense Minister Sergei Shoigu, who said such a strategy was 'futile.' Asked about Shoigu's reaction, Mattis said: 'I have no need to respond to the Russian statement at all'.[9]

It seems that with Flynn pushed out, and Tillerson towing the party line, the Russophobes have taken over the Trump Administration in prompt manner and without much, if any, difficulty. The extent to which Trump has been cornered, and whether he can break out, or whether he even wants to, remains to be seen.

John Bolton

An ominous sign for the future is that John Bolton, who had been a primary contender for the position of National Security adviser, is said by Trump to have been selected to serve his Administration in another capacity. The mind boggles at the prospect. He is another Russophobe who was quick to accept the Russian hacking myth and regarded Obama's response as insufficient. An Amercian *hegemonist* of the most fanatical variety, he made it clear that Russia should be pushed out of any role in world affairs as a hindrance to Amercian supremacy:

> Every extension of Russian influence in the Middle East is negative for American national interests, up to and including their new airbase at Latakia. And I think finding ways to limit and eventually remove Russian influence in the region, which is already trouble enough for all kinds of reasons, should be the highest priority.[10]

With these Russophobes, along with Vice President Pence, one might now begin to ask what will become of President Trump's goodwill towards Russia and Putin for which he, during the presidential campaign, received such pillorying from the globalist Establishment? The further down this path he goes the deeper the quagmire. [11]

---

9   Ibid.

10   'John Bolton splits with Trump on retaliation for Russian hacking', The Blaze, 30 December 2016, ww.theblaze.com/news/2016/12/30/john-bolton-splits-with-trump-on-retaliation-for-russian-hacking/

11   Since this was written, there has been the U.S. bombing of Syria on the pretext of destroying alleged chemical weapons plants in a direct challenge to Russia, and at

the same time that Trump appointed John Bolton as National Security adviser. The possibilities that Trump might have had the stamina of rejecting the Russophobia that was manically represented by Hilary Clinton seem to be rapidly diminishing.

Conclusion

Through centuries of attempts to impose on Russia alien doctrines, from Peter the Great to Trotsky to Gorbachev and Yeltsin, there has endured the archetypal 'eternal Russia': 'Russia the Third Rome' that, even under the name of 'Bolshevism', saw its place in the world as one of redeeming mankind and of suffering martyrdom in the process. Bolshevism was part of this martyrdom. Through Sovietism Russians and other Slavs, emerged as among the few not to have succumbed to the world-wide contagion of moral, spiritual and cultural syphilis spread by the USA as the leader of a 'West' that long ago entered an epoch of decay to the extent that it seems a travesty to use a term that should evoke images of Gothic Cathedrals, Crusader Knights, Shakespeare, Mozart, Charles Martel, Dante, Lindbergh... not the 'Golden Arches', Tupac Shukar, Sumner Redstone, Harvey Weinstein, Bernie Madoff...

All the players of today for the place of pre-eminence as leaders of the next cultural era of several millennia have their own diametrically opposing sense of world-mission – *messianism*. 'American exceptionalism' demands the world be a universal shopping mall; Israel expects all knees to bend towards Jerusalem, after the demolition of the Al-Asqa Mosque, the rebuilding of the Temple of Solomon on its ruins, and the consequent coming of the Messiah; China, still sees itself as the 'celestial kingdom', assuming the mantle of globalisation; and Russia, as always the *Katechon*, trying to hold back the forces of darkness. Islam strives to maintain its traditions but is tossed to-and-fro on the world stage, ironically a lethal adversary being the *Jihadism* that has been sponsored by the USA and Israel as a dialectical tactic for destabilising targeted states. Europe stands at a cross-roads: to continue to follow the USA into the abyss in the name of universal democracy and export capitalism, or to re-build on its own foundations. The only ally among these antagonists for such a revival is Russia, because Russia is the only people-nation-state capable of consciously rejecting the forces of decay.